LAURENCE BAIRD

Resilience Redeployed: A Veteran's Road from Exile to Humanitarian Frontlines

How Trauma Became My Compass in Service to the World

Photo Credits

First edition

ISBN (paperback): 979-8-2-9713756-1
ISBN (hardcover): 978-1-0697102-1-5

This book was professionally typeset on Reedsy.
Find out more at reedsy.com

To the humanitarian workers who carry invisible wounds from serving humanity's most vulnerable, those haunted by faces they couldn't save, whose hypervigilance learned in war zones makes peace feel foreign, and who traded pieces of their mental health for the privilege of first response. Your PTSD is not a weakness but a testament to having cared so deeply that others' pain became your own. You are not broken; you are beautifully, bravely human. You are not alone.

"The most beautiful people I've known are those who have known trials, have known struggles, have known loss, and have found their way out of the depths. These persons have an appreciation, a sensitivity, and an understanding of life that fills them with compassion, gentleness, and a deep loving concern. Beautiful people do not just happen."

- Dr. Elisabeth Kübler-Ross

Contents

Foreword

Stepping Into the Fire

In the winter of 2008, life found me standing in quiet hallways, clad in the blue uniform of the Canadian Corps of Commissionaires, my security badge reflecting the fluorescent lights inside the Department of National Defence headquarters in Ottawa. I was a security guard among dozens, a role that offered routine and order but left my mind wrestling with the unrelenting shadows of complex trauma. Diagnosed with PTSD and dissociative disorders, I was, in my psychiatrist's cautious words, a man teetering on the edge, not an ideal candidate for more chaos.

And yet, when the offer came to deploy as a security specialist to Khartoum, Sudan, to guard the Canadian Embassy during a period of acute crisis, I felt a mix of dread and undeniable purpose. Deep down, I knew this was a crossroads: continue to exist in the suspended animation of safety, or test myself in the world's unforgiving crucible once more. My psychiatrist voiced doubts, urging caution. But I was desperate for momentum, for the possibility that facing my demons head-on in Africa might chart a path forward, or at the very least stop my world from shrinking any further.

Within days, I was en route to Sudan. At the embassy in Khartoum, I was introduced simply as a guard. But the Senior Consulate Officer quickly recognized the breadth of my military training and the urgency of the mission, formally designating me "Mission Security Manager," responsible for every aspect of the mission's safety during an unfolding emergency. The job was far more than manning a post: it meant building trust with local staff, mapping evacuation routes, negotiating the ever-shifting perils outside the compound walls, and, perhaps more daunting, managing the sanctuary for an individual who had sought protection at the Canadian Mission, his own existence at risk.

Every decision in Sudan, from defending the embassy perimeter to gauging the true intent behind a soldier's glance at a checkpoint, was filtered through the fractured lens of my trauma. The flashbacks, the pounding heart, the constant threat-calculation, these symptoms of my military sexual trauma and CPTSD were no longer merely burdens; in those moments, they became survival skills. Hypervigilance, cynicism, and an unshakable memory for minor details, once signs of a mind under siege, now became tools I wielded to keep myself and others alive.

From an external perspective, my posting appeared as just another Canadian deployment to a high-risk area. But on my side of the embassy's fortified glass, it was something different: the first field test of whether a life shattered by institutional betrayal could be reforged through service on foreign ground. The familiar ache of nightmares and addiction, the urge to run or numb, and the need to protect, these companions came with me, uninvited but unrelenting.

I would not, could not, predict what would follow: the years of serial deployments, each one in lands wracked by human upheaval, Haiti's broken streets, Kenya's drought regions, and the battered corners of Syria, South Sudan, and beyond. Each mission would demand more from me than the last, but each would also offer something back: the realization that my wounds, though deep and unhealed, lent me empathy and strength that "normal" could never teach.

This memoir is the story of that journey: from an Ottawa office haunted by the past of military sexual trauma, where the work of guarding others gradually became a way of safeguarding myself. It is a reckoning with military trauma and addiction, a search for meaning in the world's broken places, and a testament to the hope that, sometimes, healing does not begin with comfort or control but with a single, defiant step into the fire.

This book is for every survivor who has ever doubted that the path out of darkness might begin with the courage to serve again, and for every helper who carries their own silent wounds as they answer the world's urgent call for protection.

Preface

There are journeys in life that begin not with a conscious choice, but with a collision, when trauma shatters the world as it was and leaves its survivors searching for a path forward amid the debris. Laurence Baird's journey is such a story: from the halls of Canadian military training bases, where innocence and dreams gave way to betrayal and lasting wounds, to the front lines of humanitarian crises, where service in the world's most volatile corners became both a refuge and a new kind of trial.

When I first learned of Laurence's work, it was not just the details of military sexual trauma (MST) or the shadow it cast that captured my attention, but the remarkable persistence of his drive to serve, after violence, after addiction, after an institution abandoned its own. Few people speak so honestly of both the devastation of institutional betrayal and the complexity of rebuilding oneself in its aftermath. Fewer still remake their brokenness into the very tools with which they try to heal others.

This book traces a singular odyssey: from the chilly corridors of DND headquarters in Ottawa, where a security position offered routine but little comfort, to the embattled embassy gates in Khartoum, Sudan, when professional purpose and personal risk collided. It is the story of a man whose psychiatrist doubted the wisdom of deployment but who saw, in the gamble of service, a chance to confront his demons head-on, perhaps a chance for something like redemption.

Laurence's work is not a simple narrative of suffering transformed into heroism. It is a nuanced testament to how trauma, especially complex PTSD born of repeated assault and institutional silence, never truly leaves a person; it is carried into each relationship, each deployment to the Horn of Africa, Syria, Haiti, South Sudan, Nepal, and beyond. Yet in those places of crisis, new meaning grew. Protecting others, families torn by conflict, and children lost amid chaos became a paradoxical way to safeguard what was left unguarded in himself. Hypervigilance, suspicion of authority, and a relentless attention to hidden dangers, once only symptoms, became assets in the world of humanitarian security.

But this journey is never tidy. There is pain in choosing duty abroad while parenting from afar; there is constant reckoning with the cost to family, self, and the relationships that fracture under the strain of ceaseless movement between worlds. There is also hope in witnessing the power of trauma-informed practice, in teaching others the skills that once meant survival, and in discovering, slowly, sometimes painfully, that recovery is not about returning to who you once were, but building anew with what remains.

This story is for those who have been betrayed by the very institutions they trusted most and for those who wonder if the fragments of a broken life can be refashioned into a force for good in the world. It is for survivors who fear that their wounds will forever separate them from purpose and for those who serve others while privately tending to their own invisible scars.

Laurence doesn't offer false certainty or neat closure. He instead urges readers to grapple with the meaning of service after being wronged and healing after trauma. His journey, from military darkness through humanitarian fire and into advocacy, lights a way forward: not just for himself, but for all who seek to transform pain into purpose and silence into voice.

Read on, then, with both courage and compassion. This is not only a chronicle of survival but also a powerful call to action for military, humanitarian, and survivor communities alike, a call to listen, to believe, and to build institutions worthy of our deepest trust.

Chronological Timeline: A Life of Service

Military Service & Trauma (1983-1989)

- 1984: Joins Canadian Armed Forces
- 1985-1989: Multiple sexual assaults during basic and trade training
- April 1989: Administrative discharge from CAF
- 1989-1992: Served US Marine Corps

Civilian Transition & Rebuilding (1993-2007)

- 1993: Discovers biological father, changes name to Baird
- 1994-1999: Marriage, children, custody battles
- 1996, 2002: Rejected for military re-enlistment
- 2006-2009: Volunteers with the Navy League of Canada
- 2007: Joins Canadian Corps of Commissionaires

Humanitarian Career Launch (2008-2010)

- 2008: First deployment - Mission Security Manager, Khartoum, Sudan
- 2009: Returns to Sudan with CARE International
- 2010: Haiti earthquake response with CARE US

- 2010: Joins World Vision Global Rapid Response Team

Global Security Specialist (2011-2016)

- 2011: Kenya famine response coordination
- 2013: Syria cross-border operations (30+ border crossings)
- 2014: South Sudan conflict zones (Malakal, Nyal)
- 2014: Central African Republic (Bangui under siege)
- 2015: Nepal earthquake/blockade response
- 2016: Harvard Humanitarian Response Intensive Course
- 2016: Terminated from World Vision due to addiction relapse

New Organizations & Growth (2016-2019)

- 2016: IRC deployment to Nigeria (Boko Haram response)
- 2017-2018: Multiple CARE Syria deployments
- 2019: World Council of Churches, West Bank security assessment

Current Role & Advocacy (2019-Present)

- 2019: Joins World University Service of Canada (WUSC)
- 2021: First Canadian INGO back to field post-COVID (Mali)
- 2024: Recent deployments include Guyana, South Sudan
- Ongoing: Restorative Engagement with Canadian Armed Forces

How to use this Book

This book is organized as a journey through trauma, resilience, and service, blending personal narrative with professional insights. To get the most out of **Resilience Redeployed**, follow these guidelines:

Begin with the Chapters That Speak to You Most

- If you seek practical security lessons, start with the operational chapters (Chapters 4–14).
- If you need guidance on managing trauma and transitioning to civilian life, jump to the reflective chapters (Chapters 1–3, 22–24).
- For institutional advocacy and policy ideas, focus on the analytical chapters (Chapters 27–30).

Read with Dual Awareness

Each chapter contains:

- Personal narrative of key moments in the author's journey.
- Professional takeaways based on firsthand experience and best practices.

As you read, note both the emotional lessons and the actionable strategies.

Use the Training Insights Practically

Chapters 31–34 detail how trauma-informed principles translate into security training and capacity-building. Keep a notebook to:

- Record scenarios and techniques that resonate.
- Develop your own "threat assessment" and "stress management" plans for your context.
- Adapt the provided frameworks to your organization or personal safety planning.

Reflect on Institutional Lessons

Chapters 27–29 analyze patterns of institutional betrayal and propose reforms. As you read:

- Compare these insights to your own organizational experiences.
- Identify one or two policies you can advocate revising.
- Use the "Prescription for Change" checklists to draft concrete proposals.

Engage with the "Restorative Engagement" Approach

Chapter 25 recounts a model for dialogue between survivors and institutions. Consider:

- How might you implement survivor-centred conversations in your workplace?
- What preparatory steps would ensure psychological safety and genuine accountability?

Integrate Personal and Professional Growth

The final chapters emphasize the lifelong journey of healing and service. Use them to:

- Develop a balanced self-care plan that honours both your need for calm and your desire to serve.
- Identify peer-support or mentorship opportunities in your network.
- Draft a personal "legacy statement" articulating how you intend to transform challenges into contributions.

Return as Needed

This book is not meant to be read only once. Return to specific chapters whenever you:

- Face a new security challenge and need practical guidance.
- Encounter personal or organizational setbacks and seek renewed perspective.
- Mentor others and want to share proven frameworks for resilience.

By combining the author's lived experience with tested methodologies, **Resilience Redeployed** offers both a roadmap and a toolkit. Whether you are a survivor, a humanitarian professional, or an institutional leader, use this book to turn wounds into wisdom, challenges into change, and isolation into impact.

A note on language and approach

This book has been written with deep intention and care, recognizing that trauma is not a rare experience but affects the majority of people in some way. As writers, we have a responsibility to attend to the emotional impact of our language and writing. When I share my experiences of military sexual trauma, I do so with the understanding that you, as the reader, bring your own experiences and vulnerabilities to these pages.

Trauma-informed writing involves both a process and a product that tends to the nervous system of both writer and reader so that all parties are more likely to stay present for the experience of the written work. This approach comes with the lens that reminds us that trauma is very prevalent and that people broadly have experienced all kinds of adversity. It could be little "t" trauma or big "T" trauma, and I want to come to these pages thinking about how I can best serve people who may be going through something hard or who haven't yet resolved something hard.

Content Awareness

Content Notice: This book contains detailed accounts of military sexual trauma, institutional betrayal, substance abuse, suicidal ideation, and other potentially distressing content. While recent research suggests that content warnings may not reduce distress and might even increase anticipatory anxiety, I believe in your right to make informed choices about when and how you engage with this material.

Rather than simply providing a warning, I want to offer you agency in how you approach this content. The experiences I describe are real and sometimes graphic, but they are shared with purpose: to break silence, foster understanding, and provide hope for healing. Violence is pervasive in our society, and regardless of your background, descriptions of abuse and violence can be triggering, meaning they bring up uncomfortable or frightening feelings or memories from the past.

Your Reading Experience

Reading at Your Own Pace: This book is not meant to be consumed in one sitting. Each chapter addresses different aspects of trauma and recovery, and you may find some resonate more deeply than others. Give yourself permission to:

- Take breaks when needed.
- Skip sections that feel overwhelming and return to them later.

- Read with a trusted friend or support person nearby.
- Have your own support resources readily available.

Staying Present: If you find yourself becoming overwhelmed while reading, grounding techniques can help you return to the present moment. Here are some immediate strategies:

- 5-4-3-2-1 Technique: Name 5 things you can see, 4 things you can touch, 3 things you can hear, 2 things you can smell, and 1 thing you can taste
- Physical Grounding: Place your feet firmly on the ground, take slow, deep breaths, and remind yourself that you are safe in this moment.
- Present Moment Awareness: State the current date and time and describe your immediate surroundings.

Self-Care Strategies for Readers

Reading about trauma can be emotionally demanding work. Self-care is not self-indulgent; it is an act of survival. Here are trauma-informed self-care strategies to support you through this reading experience:

Physical Self-Care

- Movement: Gentle exercise, walking, or stretching can help process emotions and reduce physical tension.
- Breathing: Deep, intentional breathing helps regulate your nervous system.
- Rest: Give yourself permission to rest when needed; trauma recovery requires energy.

Emotional Self-Care

- Acknowledge Your Feelings: It's important to recognize and accept your emotions without judgment. You might feel sad, angry, or triggered; all these responses are valid.
- Journaling: Writing about your reactions can help process emotions and reduce rumination.
- Connect with Support: Reach out to trusted friends, family, or professionals when you need to process what you're reading.

Cognitive Self-Care

- Limit Exposure: You don't need to read everything at once. Honour your capacity and emotional bandwidth.
- Remind Yourself: "That was then; this is now. It did happen, but it will not happen anymore."
- Seek Professional Support: If reading this book brings up unresolved trauma, consider connecting with a trauma-informed therapist.

Language Choices

Throughout this book, I have made deliberate choices about language to honour both my experience and yours:

Person-First Language: I use terms like "survivor" rather than "victim" when possible, though I recognize that different people prefer different language at different stages of their healing journey.

Avoiding Judgment: This book avoids language that implies judgment about responses to trauma. There is no "right" way to survive or heal.

Clarity Over Euphemism: While I aim to be respectful, I also believe in the power of clear, direct language to break through shame and silence. Sometimes healing requires naming things as they are.

Why This Approach Matters

Creating a trauma-informed reading experience is about more than just being considerate; it's about creating conditions where healing can occur. When we acknowledge that trauma is widespread and that reading about traumatic experiences can be activating, we create space for readers to engage with the material in ways that serve their healing rather than harm it.

This approach recognizes that you are not a passive consumer of this story but an active participant in your own healing journey. By providing you with tools and awareness, I hope to support you in staying present with both the pain and the hope contained in these pages.

The Therapeutic Power of Narrative

Stories have the power to heal, both in the telling and in the witnessing. The telling of stories is how we make sense of our lives, and with trauma, our understandings of our stories are dramatically altered and somewhat reduced. By sharing my story, I hope to offer you not just information but connection, hope, and perhaps a sense that your own story matters.

This book is an invitation to witness one person's journey from silence to voice, from victim to survivor to advocate. It is also an invitation to consider your own story and the ways that sharing our experiences can transform not just ourselves but the world around us.

Remember: You are not alone in whatever you have experienced. Your story matters. Your healing matters. And you have the right to engage with this material in whatever way serves your well-being.

Resources for Support

If you find that you need additional support while reading this book, please consider reaching out to the following resources:

- Crisis Text Line: Text CONNECT to 688868
- National Suicide Prevention Lifeline: 988
- Military Crisis Line: 1-800-268-7708
- Veterans Affairs Sexual Trauma Services: 1-844-750-1648
- Local trauma-informed therapists and support groups

Your healing journey is unique, and you deserve support that honours both your experience and your capacity for resilience.

This approach to trauma-informed writing and reader care is based on current research in trauma psychology, neuroscience, and narrative therapy. While I am not a mental health professional, I am writing from lived experience and extensive research into trauma-informed practices.

I

From Breakdown to Breakthrough (1992–2010)

Discharged in 1989 after military sexual trauma, I spent three decades rebuilding through dead-end jobs, failed relationships, custody battles, and relentless hypervigilance. Employment with the Canadian Corps of Commissionaires in 2007 gave purpose. Deployments as Mission Security Manager in Sudan (2008), re-establishing CARE in post-expulsion Sudan (2009), and managing the Haiti earthquake response (2010) transformed trauma into tools for protecting others.

1

The Last Salute

The papers, which arrived on a Tuesday in April, were clinical and impersonal documents that reduced my four years of service to mere checkboxes and administrative codes. There were no ceremonies, no handshakes from commanding officers, and no final salute. There were only forms to sign, equipment to return, and a quiet wait for the same bus that brought me here in 1985 with hope and purpose intact. The date at the top read April 1989, marking the end of what I'd believed would be a career.

I was twenty-four when I shed the uniform for the last time. The official discharge category read "administrative," but the reality beneath those sterile terms was far messier: military sexual trauma that had shattered not just my body but my fundamental trust in the system I'd sworn to serve. In the late 1980s, such experiences were rarely named, even less frequently acknowledged, and almost never prosecuted. The culture that had welcomed me as a young recruit now viewed me as a threat to unit cohesion and operational effectiveness.

The Canadian Armed Forces of the 1980s were entrenched in what military scholars would later describe as an "untouchable" masculine culture, one that viewed any challenge to traditional military values as anathema to mission success. The Air Force only lifted all restrictions on female participation in 1987, while the Army and Navy continued to ban women from combat roles. The idea that a male soldier could be victimized within this system was so far outside the institutional worldview that no frameworks existed for understanding, let alone addressing, such realities.

* * *

The Unspoken Truth

As I detailed in "A Soldier's Cry," the military sexual trauma that ended my career wasn't just a single incident but a systematic destruction of trust in the very institution I'd sworn to serve. The multiple assaults were devastating, but the institutional response, or lack thereof, proved equally damaging. When I reported what had happened, I was met not with support or investigation, but with suspicion, blame, and the clear message that my accusations threatened unit cohesion more than the perpetrator's actions.

The 1980s military culture had no framework for understanding male sexual trauma. The prevalent mindset held that men were incapable of being victims, that reporting assaults was a sign of weakness, and that survivors who voiced their experiences were disruptive forces. I learned quickly that the

4

institution would protect its reputation over its people, that my pain mattered less than preserving the silence that kept uncomfortable truths buried.

The discharge papers reduced years of torment to administrative categories, but they couldn't capture the deeper betrayal: I discovered that the system I'd trusted to make me stronger had instead allowed one of its own to break me. The hours-long sexual assaults gave way to decades-long institutional abandonment. Both violations would follow me into civilian life, shaping every relationship with authority, every attempt at trust, and every struggle to rebuild an identity that had been shattered by those sworn to protect it.

* * *

Attempts to Return

The institutional rejection stung most deeply during two occasions when I attempted to rejoin the Forces, seeking to reclaim the military identity that had been torn from me. The first attempt came in 1996, seven years after my discharge. I had spent those years trying to rebuild my life, working various civilian jobs and attempting to process the trauma that had ended my military career. Part of me believed that enough time had passed, that perhaps the military had changed, or that my experience and maturity might be valued despite my previous departure.

The second attempt came six years later, in 2002. By this

time, I had hoped that the Canadian Forces' evolution in addressing sexual misconduct and trauma might create space for someone like me to return. The military was beginning to acknowledge that it had problems with sexual harassment and assault, and various initiatives were being implemented to create a more inclusive environment.

Both times, I was rejected due to the comments that remained on my file regarding my original release. The administrative codes and clinical language from 1989 continued to define me in the military's eyes, regardless of the years that had passed or the person I had become. The institution's memory was long when it came to those it had labelled as problematic but seemingly absent when it came to its own failures that had created the circumstances of my departure.

These rejections carried a unique sting because they weren't based on my current capabilities, qualifications, or potential contributions. Instead, they were anchored in a past where I had been the victim, not the perpetrator. The military's refusal to reevaluate my case felt like an ongoing betrayal, punishing me indefinitely for experiencing victimization while serving my country.

The rejections forced me to confront a difficult truth: the institution that had shaped my identity and then destroyed it would never provide the redemption or validation I sought. I would have to find my own path to service, my own way to transform the skills and instincts the military had developed in me into something meaningful and constructive.

* * *

Another Uniform, Another War

Both times, I was rejected due to the comments that remained on my file regarding my original release. The administrative codes and clinical language from 1989 continued to define me in the military's eyes, regardless of the years that had passed or the person I had become. The institution's memory was long when it came to those it had labelled as problematic but seemingly absent when it came to its own failures that had created the circumstances of my departure.

I did, however, seek another path in military service after my time with the Canadian Forces, spending three years with a foreign military and participating in operations during the First Gulf War. That chapter of my life brought new challenges and lessons that shaped my search for purpose during those years. The details of that journey, and its impact on my evolving identity, will be explored fully in a future book.

* * *

The Long Exile

I wrote extensively in "A Soldier's Cry" about how military sexual trauma creates a unique form of complex PTSD, a concept I couldn't articulate at the time. Unlike combat trauma, which is at least acknowledged as an occupational

7

hazard, military sexual trauma carries the additional burden
of institutional denial and survivor isolation. The hypervigilance, dissociation, and inability to trust authority that would
define my civilian years weren't just symptoms of assault;
they were rational responses to institutional betrayal.

Living in exile from my own life characterized the first
months after discharge. The world was changing rapidly
around me; the Cold War was ending, the Berlin Wall would
soon fall, and Canada was entering a period of significant cultural transformation. However, I roamed aimlessly through
this evolving landscape, pursuing jobs that prioritized survival over human interaction, such as warehouse work and
construction, to avoid raising questions about my abrupt
departure from what could have been a promising military
career.

Sleep became elusive, haunted by flashbacks that blurred
memories of parade squares with fragments of trauma. The
hypervigilance that had once kept me alert on duty now
made civilian life feel like navigating a minefield, every loud
noise a potential threat, every authority figure a reminder
of betrayal. Unlike Vietnam veterans who were beginning to
receive recognition for their service-related psychological
wounds through programs emerging in the late 1980s, those
of us carrying different kinds of military trauma had no
language, no support systems, and no pathway to healing.

The diagnosis of PTSD had only been formally recognized
in 1980, largely in response to the struggles of Vietnam
veterans. But the clinical understanding of trauma was

still primitive, focused primarily on combat experiences and lacking any framework for understanding military sexual trauma or its long-term consequences. I cycled through attempts at rebuilding, new cities, new jobs, and sometimes new identities, but each effort collapsed under the familiar patterns of anger, isolation, and the bottle's false promise of temporary peace.

Family and friends spoke the language of "moving on," as if trauma operated on a civilian timeline. They couldn't understand why their returning son, brother, or friend seemed like a stranger wearing a familiar face. The military had taught me to be strong, to endure, to never quit, but what happened when the enemy was inside your own mind? What happened when the very institution that had promised to make me stronger had instead left me broken and discarded?

The statistics were sobering, though they wouldn't be compiled for years to come. The late 1980s saw a poor understanding of the military-to-civilian transition, with minimal research and even fewer support programs. The Canadian Forces prioritized Cold War readiness and operational effectiveness over the human cost of service and reintegration challenges. Those of us who fell through the cracks were largely invisible, our struggles unrecorded and unaddressed.

Those early years felt like a prolonged death, not of the body, but of purpose, identity, and hope. I existed in the margins, convinced that the uniform had contained whatever value I'd possessed and that its absence left me fundamentally diminished. The year 1989, which had marked my departure, was also the year thousands of service members were transitioning to civilian life as the military downsized following the Cold War's end. However, I carried invisible wounds that few could comprehend, unlike those who departed with their dignity intact.

What I couldn't see then was that survival itself required a different kind of courage, the willingness to keep searching for meaning in the wreckage, to believe that broken things could be rebuilt into something stronger than their original form. It would take more than two decades to journey from that first wounded departure to finding purpose in humanitarian service. But even in those darkest early years, something stubborn refused to quit entirely. Perhaps it was the same quality that had drawn me to military service in the first place, a need to be useful, to serve something larger than myself.

That ember would eventually ignite again, in the most unexpected places, among people who understood that the most valuable protectors are often those who know intimately what it means to need protection. A system that did not tolerate his pain broke the boy who left the Forces in 1989. The man who would eventually walk into humanitarian crises around the world would carry those breaks as fault lines filled with gold, visible scars that had become sources of strength rather than shame.

2

Searching for Ground

Content Warning: This chapter contains references to family abandonment and rejection, paternal abandonment, identity crisis, custody battles, divorce, addiction (pornography), job loss due to trauma-related behaviour, and emotional distress related to family separation. The content includes themes of rejection, betrayal, and struggles with unresolved trauma that may be distressing to some readers. Reader discretion is advised.

Unlike many of my fellow veterans who turned to alcohol to numb the pain, I'd made a different choice. The bottle held no appeal, perhaps because control was the one thing I still believed I possessed. Instead, I threw myself into work, any work that would exhaust my body enough to quiet my mind: driving, factory shifts, warehouse loading that left my hands raw and my back aching. In a country still reeling from recession and economic uncertainty, there was always someone willing to hire temporary labourers who asked no questions about their past.

By 1993, I found myself in Brandon, Manitoba, still drifting between temporary jobs and searching for something that resembled direction. I had just purchased a 1972 Oldsmobile Cutlass Supreme 442, a small victory that represented one of the few bright spots in those wandering years. The car was beautiful, powerful, and mine, something I could point to with pride. That summer, I decided to drive it to Ottawa to visit my mother, hoping that perhaps in the familiar surroundings of the capital, I might find the opportunity that had eluded me elsewhere.

The morning after my arrival, my mother poured me a cup of coffee and asked me to sit down. There was something different in her manner, a weight she seemed to be carrying. Before I could even bring the coffee to my lips, she delivered words that would shatter everything I thought I knew about myself: "The man you think is your father, he isn't. Your real father is a man who was our neighbour when I was a teenage girl."

The shock was profound, like a physical blow that left me reeling. For twenty-seven years, I'd lived with one under-standing of my identity, one narrative about abandonment and rejection that had shaped every relationship, every sense of belonging or not belonging. Now, in the space of a single sentence, that entire foundation cracked open.

The man I'd thought was my father had left my mother when I was two. I'd met him when I was sixteen, an encounter that had provided some answers but also deepened questions about abandonment and worth. Now I was learning that even that painful connection had been built on a lie. Somewhere out there was a stranger who shared my DNA, a man who might hold answers to questions I'd carried my entire life.

The betrayal cut deep. For twenty-seven years, I was kept in the dark about secrets that allowed me to construct my identity around a false narrative. With the military sexual trauma already fragmenting my sense of self, this revelation felt like another institutional betrayal, this time by the person who should have been my most reliable source of truth. But beneath the hurt was intrigue. I was learning, for the first time, that I was Scottish, a Baird. There was something powerful about discovering this heritage, this connection to a clan and a history I'd never known existed.

My mother had his phone number. We called him together, my hands shaking as I listened to her explain who I was. He suggested I come to Saint John, New Brunswick, to visit. Since I wasn't working and had nothing binding me to Brandon, I loaded my dog into the Cutlass and headed east.

* * *

Saint John greeted me with the smell of salt air and the cries of seagulls, a maritime city that felt both foreign and oddly familiar. When I knocked on my biological father's door, the man who answered bore an unmistakable resemblance to my own reflection. The same eyes, the same build, genetic echoes that couldn't be denied. But resemblance, I would learn, doesn't guarantee connection.

13

The conversation that followed was stilted, careful, and polite. I learned about my half-siblings, two brothers and a sister I'd never known existed. Since I had believed I was an only child, discovering my half-siblings was overwhelming. Suddenly I wasn't alone in the world, yet I felt more isolated than ever. These were strangers who shared my blood but not my experiences, family members who'd grown up knowing each other while I'd grown up knowing no one.

I was considering settling in Saint John, perhaps going to university to study law. The idea of starting fresh in this maritime city, of building a new identity as a Baird rather than carrying the name I'd carried in military shame, held appeal. But as conversations with my biological father continued, it became clear that my presence made him uncomfortable. He had his own life, his own issues, and little room for a twenty-seven-year-old son he'd never known.

After two months of scheduled conversations and careful politeness, he delivered his verdict: "This isn't working. I have a life here, responsibilities. But you should visit my sister in St. Andrews; she might want to meet you."

The rejection was devastating. Here was another father figure, this one biological, telling me I didn't fit into his life. The pattern of abandonment that began before birth repeated itself, and the wound cut deeper because of its familiarity. I learned to let him go, to release expectations I'd barely had time to form. To this day, he remains absent from my life, as do my half-siblings. The rejection taught me that blood alone doesn't create family.

In 1994, I made a decision that felt like reclaiming something essential: I officially changed my surname to Baird. I did not change my surname because I wanted anything from him; rather, I changed it because I wanted what was rightfully mine: my name, my heritage, and my connection to Scottish roots that stretched back centuries. He had abandoned my mother during her pregnancy, abandoned me at birth, and abandoned me again in 1993. But he couldn't take away my right to be a Baird.

I am a proud Baird. Over the decades since that name change, I've explored my Scottish heritage, learning about clan history and Highland traditions. The name represents not the man who rejected me, but the lineage I belong to regardless of his choices. Personal betrayals cannot sever the connection to something larger than individual relationships.

* * *

But my biological father's rejection led to an unexpected lifeline. St. Andrews by-the-Sea was everything Saint John was not: genteel, historic, and carefully preserved for tourists seeking Maritime charm. My aunt welcomed me with the warmth her brother couldn't muster, and it was there that I met my second wife, a pottery student from Fredericton working in my aunt's pottery studio.

She possessed something I thought I had lost: creativity, hope for the future, and the ability to shape something beautiful from raw clay. We talked through her breaks and walked the shoreline after her shifts, and for the first time since leaving

15

the military, I felt like I was building something instead of just surviving. When summer ended, we moved to Fredericton together, where she continued her studies while I found work wherever I could.

We relocated from Fredericton to Temperance Vale, a small farming and logging community in York County, established around 1860. Temperance Vale was a community where everyone knew each other, work was seasonal and scarce, and the 380 residents struggled to survive on logging, farming, and hope. We rented a small house on about 60 acres of land, surrounded by the kind of rural poverty that makes survival an art form.

Those months in Temperance Vale tested us in ways we hadn't anticipated. She was expecting our first child, and we were struggling to meet our financial obligations. I took any available work, primarily security jobs in Fredericton, to ensure we had food on the table while we awaited our son's arrival. Both of us struggled to cope with the pressure of impending parenthood and financial instability.

Everything changed when our first son was born in Fredericton in 1994. Holding him for the first time, I felt the weight of responsibility settle on my shoulders like a uniform I'd never wanted to remove. This tiny person depended on me completely, and I was determined not to fail him the way so many had failed me. But determination alone couldn't pay bills or provide the stability a growing family needed.

* * *

In 1995, we decided to move to Kitchener, Ontario, hoping to discover the opportunities that New Brunswick couldn't offer. A key reason for choosing Kitchener was that some of our family already lived there, providing a sense of support and stability during the transition. The move felt like a fresh start, but with a purpose that went beyond mere survival. I enrolled in college to study legal administration and computer sciences, two fields that promised steady employment in an increasingly digital world.

The program was challenging in ways I hadn't expected. After years of manual labour, learning about database management, legal research techniques, and computer programming in the classroom challenged my mental muscles. But for the first time since leaving the military, I felt like I was building something that might last, skills that couldn't be taken away by economic downturns or personal conflicts.

After graduating with honours and being nominated as a class valedictorian with my diploma in hand, I received an offer for a job in Ottawa in 1996. The position seemed perfect: a satisfactory salary, federal government benefits, and the kind of stability that had eluded us for years. We packed up our small family and moved to the nation's capital, optimistic that we'd finally found solid ground.

But the job didn't last long. The pressures of the position, coupled with unresolved traumas that I was still unable to name or address, led to a devastating spiral of self-destructive behaviour. Despite avoiding alcohol, I found myself compulsively turning to pornography as an escape, a desperate attempt to obtain temporary relief from the hypervigilance and anxiety that made ordinary workplace interactions feel like combat operations. This addiction became another prison, offering momentary numbing while ultimately deepening my isolation and shame. When compulsive behaviour began affecting my work performance and I finally lost the Ottawa position in 1998, it felt like losing the last piece of the life I'd been trying to build since leaving the military.

The stress in our marriage became unbearable. She needed a partner who could share the load of raising two small children after our second son was born in early 1999, and I was still learning basic skills like managing triggers and maintaining emotional regulation. Later in 1999, I made the decision that would reshape both our lives: I left my second wife for my third wife. The choice wasn't made lightly, but the patterns that trauma had created in our relationship, emotional numbing, withdrawal, and the inability to provide the consistency she deserved, had become impossible to ignore.

* * *

After leaving my second wife for my third wife, I was unprepared for the five years of intense legal and custody battles that followed. The early 2000s represented a major change in Canadian family law, as fathers increasingly questioned traditional custody arrangements. Statistics from this period show that fathers were winning custody cases at higher rates than in previous decades, with decisions favouring fathers reaching nearly 20% by 1999–2000. I was part of this trend, fighting for meaningful access to my sons in a system that was slowly recognizing fathers' rights but still operated with significant bias toward maternal custody.

The battles were exhausting and expensive. Each court appearance meant lost wages, legal fees I could barely afford, and the emotional toll of having my fitness as a father scrutinized by strangers. We fought over everything: holiday schedules, decision-making authority, and the boys' education and healthcare. The adversarial nature of the family court system turned what should have been collaborative parenting into zero-sum warfare.

In 2006, after years of legal wrangling, I achieved something that felt like victory: split custody, with our older son coming to live with me. Split custody was relatively rare, occurring in only about 4% of cases, where siblings are divided between parents, with each having primary custody of different children. For me, it meant finally having daily presence in at least one of my sons' lives, the chance to be the father I'd always wanted to be rather than the weekend visitor I'd become.

The transition wasn't easy for my son or me. He was twelve years old, caught between competing loyalties and the opportunity to build a different relationship with me, my new wife, and her son. I had to learn parenting skills I'd never fully developed during those early years when work and unresolved trauma had made me emotionally absent. But for the first time since my own childhood, I felt like I was building something that might last, a home where consistency mattered more than crisis management.

* * *

In 2007, as I established my new life with primary custody of
my older son, I secured employment with the Canadian Corps
of Commissionaires. Founded in 1925, the Corps provided
meaningful employment for veterans returning from the
First World War. By 2008, it had become Canada's largest
employer of veterans and the only national not-for-profit
security company.

The Corps represented something I'd been searching for
since leaving the military: a bridge between my service and
civilian life, an organization that understood the value of
military experience and training. Founded on the principle
that veterans possessed "exemplary discipline, loyalty, and
dedication to service," the Commissionaires offered more
than just employment; they offered community, purpose,
and recognition of skills that the civilian job market often
couldn't appreciate.

My role with the Commissionaires placed me at DND Headquarters in Ottawa, where I worked in security services with
other veterans who understood the peculiar challenges of
military-to-civilian transition. The work was steady and
respectful and utilized skills I'd developed both in uniform
and in the years since leaving it. For the first time in nearly
two decades, I perceived my military service as an advantage
rather than a drawback.

The timing was fortuitous. Just ahead of my first overseas
mission to Khartoum later in 2008, I was establishing myself

as both a competent single father and a reliable security professional. The years of searching for ground through failed relationships, custody battles, career false starts, and personal crises had finally led me to stable footing. The boy who'd left the Forces broken in 1989 was becoming a man who could protect others, starting with his own son and extending to assignments I couldn't yet imagine.

The search for ground was ending, but the real work was just beginning. The skills that trauma had taught me, reading dangerous situations, managing crises, and maintaining functionality under extreme stress, were about to find their most meaningful application in places where such abilities could mean the difference between life and death for people who had no other protection.

3

Blue Uniform, New Purpose

The building at 101 Colonel By Drive rose like a concrete fortress along Ottawa's Rideau Canal, its twin towers and connecting structure forming what locals called the Pearkes Building, National Defence Headquarters. It was October 2007 when I first walked through its security checkpoint wearing the blue uniform of the Canadian Corps of Commissionaires, but my journey to that moment had begun months earlier in a very different setting.

With the Commissioners, I first worked at NDHQ for about two months, learning the rhythms of Canada's defence establishment and proving myself reliable in one of the country's most sensitive security environments. The work was straightforward: access control, document verification, and maintaining vigilance in corridors where classified materials moved daily. But those initial weeks taught me something crucial: my military experience wasn't a liability to be overcome, but an asset to be leveraged in service of civilian institutions.

Early 2008 brought me a transformative new posting: managing the Commissionaires at CFB Petawawa. The base, located 130 kilometers west of Ottawa in the Ottawa Valley, housed the 2nd Canadian Mechanized Brigade Group, the Canadian Special Operations Regiment, and numerous other units that formed the backbone of Canada's rapid reaction capability. Moving from the bureaucratic environment of NDHQ to the operational atmosphere of Petawawa felt like returning home in ways I hadn't expected.

CFB Petawawa in 2008 was a base in transition, with the Afghanistan mission at its peak and soldiers cycling through constant deployment rotations. Managing security at Petawawa meant overseeing other veterans who, like me, had found purpose in protecting the institution that had shaped us. The Commissionaires under my supervision came from all branches of service, Army, Navy, and Air Force, each carrying their own stories of transition from military to civilian life.

It was while working at Petawawa that opportunity knocked in the most unexpected form. A representative from an organization I'd never heard of approached me about a position that sounded both familiar and utterly foreign: Mission Security Manager for a deployment to Khartoum, Sudan. The role would require managing security for the staff at the Canadian Mission in one of the world's most volatile regions, but my initial assignment would be highly specific and sensitive.

Before I could deploy to Sudan, there was one more assignment: a month-long posting to the National Bank of Canada as a uniformed security guard. The assignment seemed mundane compared to the prospect of Khartoum, but it served an important purpose, demonstrating that I could operate effectively in a high-stakes civilian environment where discretion, professionalism, and crisis management skills were essential.

I received all the details of my mission to Sudan after completing the National Bank assignment. The briefings painted a complex picture of a country where employees faced threats from armed groups, government harassment, criminal gangs, and the simple logistics of working in a region where basic infrastructure had been decimated by decades of conflict. My role would be multifaceted, but my initial assignment was highly specific: protecting the Canadian Mission from Abousfian Abdelrazik, a dual Canadian-Sudanese citizen who had sought safe haven there.

* * *

Slipping out of the Commissionaires' crisp blue tunic and into the unassuming jacket and slacks of a humanitarian security advisor felt at once liberating and unmooring. The uniform that had defined me, first as a veteran protecting national assets, then as a civilian guard enforcing boundaries, gave way to attire that offered both greater freedom of movement across borders and a loss of the clear identity that the blue tunic once guaranteed. In that moment, I realized that my service was no longer tied to walls and checkpoints but to the vulnerable people I would meet in the world's most dangerous places, a transformation both exciting and strangely disorienting, the tangible marker of my shift from guard to guardian.

4

From Father to Son, From Military to Mission

Looking back now, I feel like destiny had finally caught up with me during the time I was picking up my son from Navy League Cadets. The commanding officer had heard about my military experience and explained that they were searching for volunteer officers, particularly someone with military experience who could step into a leadership role immediately.

"Would you consider volunteering?" she asked. *"We really need someone with your background."*

My older son had recently joined the Navy League Cadets, and I could see how much the program meant to him. The structured environment, the sense of purpose, and the camaraderie evoked memories of days. When they explained they needed officers desperately, I couldn't turn away from an opportunity to serve again, especially one that would allow me to be part of my son's development journey.

Taking Command of a New Kind of Ship

Within weeks of that request, I found myself sworn in as Acting Sub-Lieutenant (NL) and appointed as the Ship's Executive Officer. The executive officer role was familiar territory: second-in-command, responsible for discipline, training organization, and the day-to-day operations of the corps. It was like being an XO again, but instead of soldiers or aid workers, I was responsible for young cadets eager to learn about naval traditions, leadership, and service.

The transition from military service to youth development wasn't as dramatic as I'd anticipated. The core principles remained the same: safety first, clear communication, structured training, and leading by example. These young cadets, aged 9 to 12, were eager to absorb everything we taught them about seamanship, drill, citizenship, and leadership. Their enthusiasm reminded me why I had chosen a life of service in the first place.

But my commitment to their safety went deeper than standard protocols. My own experiences as a cadet during summer camps decades earlier, experiences that no child should ever endure, had taught me to watch for signs that others might miss. The vulnerability of young people in structured environments, the power dynamics inherent in cadet programs, and the trust placed in adult leaders created responsibilities that extended far beyond teaching drill and seamanship. I was determined that no cadet under my command would face what I had faced in silence.

This heightened awareness shaped every aspect of how I ran the corps. I implemented buddy systems, ensured open-door policies, and created multiple channels for cadets to report concerns. Most importantly, I fostered an environment that encouraged and protected speaking up. The safety protocols weren't just about physical training accidents or equipment failures; they were about creating a space where young people could develop and thrive without fear.

What struck me most profoundly was watching my son navigate this environment. Here was my boy, learning the same lessons I had learned decades earlier, developing the same sense of discipline and respect that had shaped my own character. But unlike my own cadet experience, he was doing so in an environment I had worked to make genuinely safe, not just in policy, but in practice. I couldn't help but notice the full-circle nature of the situation, the father, who had once been a vulnerable cadet, was now safeguarding cadets, including his own son.

Every evening when we drove home together after cadet training, I would listen carefully not just to his excitement about what he'd learned but also for any undertone that might suggest something was wrong. The conversations we had about respect, boundaries, and the importance of speaking up weren't just about his development as a future leader, they were about ensuring he had the tools to protect himself and others that I had lacked at his age.

My son and I in uniform, together, Ottawa, Canada

Promotion and Greater Responsibility

My performance as Executive Officer must have impressed the Branch leadership, because after my first year with the corps, I was promoted to Lieutenant (NL) and given command. Taking command of NLCC Vice Admiral Kingsmill felt like assuming command of any unit, the weight of responsibility, the need to set the tone for the entire organization, and the duty to develop not just the cadets but also the officers serving under me.

29

As Commanding Officer, I was responsible for everything from recruiting and training to maintaining relationships with the local branch and ensuring our corps met all safety and administrative requirements. The skills I'd developed in the military, planning, organizing, motivating, and leading, translated perfectly to this civilian volunteer role. The difference was that instead of preparing soldiers for combat or coordinating humanitarian operations, I was preparing young Canadians for citizenship and potentially future military service.

The corps thrived under this leadership approach. We focused on making training "careful, interesting, and fun," as the Navy League mandate required. Drill nights became opportunities for leadership development, seamanship training sessions built confidence, and ceremonial events instilled pride and tradition. Watching these young people grow in confidence and capability was as rewarding as any mission I'd accomplished in uniform.

The Most Meaningful Promotion

Of all the promotions and achievements during my two years as Commanding Officer, none compared to watching my son advance through the cadet ranks. Seeing him develop leadership skills, gain confidence, and embrace the values of the program filled me with a pride I hadn't expected. This experience wasn't just about my son following in my footsteps; it was about witnessing the next generation embrace service and citizenship.

The cadet program was creating the same foundation in him that it had provided me thirty years earlier. The discipline, the respect for others, the understanding of teamwork, the basic leadership principles—all the elements that had prepared me for military service and later humanitarian work were now shaping my son's character. It was like watching my own story begin again, but through different eyes and in a different time.

There were evenings when we'd drive home together after cadet night, discussing what he'd learned, challenges he faced with younger cadets, or questions about naval history and tradition. These conversations bridged decades of my own experience while allowing me to see the program's impact through his fresh perspective. The connection between father and son, mentor and cadet, and past and future created bonds that went far deeper than I had anticipated.

The Call to Larger Service

By 2008, the demands of my humanitarian career were intensifying. The opportunity to deploy to Khartoum as a security advisor presented itself, a chance to return to the field and apply my skills in one of the world's most challenging environments. The decision to step down from command wasn't easy. I was leaving behind a corps that had become part of our family life, officers I had trained and mentored, and cadets who looked up to me.

The timing was particularly difficult because it meant re-ducing my involvement just as my son was reaching critical points in his own cadet development. But the humanitarian sector was calling, and I knew that the leadership skills I had refined with the Navy League, patience, mentorship, training development, and organizational management, would serve me well in Sudan and the challenging deployments that lay ahead.

I formally relinquished command at the end of 2009, just before my deployment to Haiti. The change of command ceremony was bittersweet—proud of what we had accomplished together, but aware that I was closing a chapter that had reconnected me with my roots while preparing me for my future.

The Bridge Between Services

Looking back, my three years with NLCC Vice Admiral Kingsmill served as more than just volunteer service; it was a bridge between my military past and my humanitarian future. The experience reminded me that leadership transcends uniform and context. Whether commanding soldiers, managing aid workers, or training young cadets, the fundamental principles remain constant: safety, clarity, development, and service to something larger than yourself.

The Navy League years also reinforced my belief in the importance of developing the next generation. Every skill I taught those cadets, every leadership principle demonstrated, and every moment of mentorship I provided was an investment in Canada's future. These young people would go on to become leaders in various fields, carrying with them the values and disciplines learned during their cadet years.

Most importantly, those years gave my son and me a shared experience that continues to influence our relationship. The respect he learned for service, the understanding of leadership he developed, and the confidence he gained through the program shaped him into the man he became. The fact that we both wore the same uniform, served in the same corps, and learned from the same traditions created a bond that transcends the typical father-son relationship.

Full Circle

The Navy League experience demonstrated that resilience isn't just about bouncing back from adversity; it's about finding new ways to deploy your skills and experience in service of others. My military training hadn't become obsolete when I left the Canadian Armed Forces; it had simply found a new application in developing young Canadians and preparing them for their own journeys of service.

The three years I spent as a Navy League officer were as formative for me as they were for the cadets I led. They reminded me that leadership is about nurturing potential, that service takes many forms, and that the greatest privilege of experience is the opportunity to pass it on to the next generation. Watching my son progress through the same program that had shaped me thirty years earlier was like watching my own story come full circle, proof that some traditions, some values, and some forms of service transcend generations.

When I boarded the plane for Khartoum in 2008, I carried with me not just the military and humanitarian experience I'd accumulated over the years, but also the renewed understanding of mentorship and development I'd gained with the Navy League. Those young cadets had taught me as much as I had taught them about leadership, patience, and the importance of investing in others' futures. It was a lesson that would prove invaluable in the challenging humanitarian deployments that lay ahead.

5

A Call to Khartoum

The diplomatic passport landed in my hands in September 2008, its red cover and embossed emblem marking a shift from the security work I'd known to something far more unpredictable. I stared at my photo, the lamination reflecting the overhead lights of the Ottawa office. Beneath my name and stern expression was a new designation: official representative of Canadian interests abroad. The title brought a faint shiver of pride, but anxiety lurked beneath. I was about to be tested in ways that no amount of military training could have prepared me for.

The assignment to Khartoum was, on paper, a security role. In reality, it became a crucible for everything I'd been running from and everything I still hoped to become. The news described the backdrop as "volatile," yet it failed to fully capture the atmosphere. Sudan was in the grip of decades-long conflict, humanitarian organizations shuttled between hope and despair, and each day the embassy doors became a threshold between precarious safety and the unknown.

My briefing package painted a crisis that was as much about competing narratives as it was about physical danger. The case of Abousfian Abdelrazik, a Canadian citizen imprisoned in Sudan, profoundly impacted Canada's security and human rights policies in the aftermath of 9/11. Abdelrazik had lived in the Canadian Embassy since seeking refuge there in 2007, unable to return home and tangled in the invisible webs spun by global watchlists and political bureaucracy. My first job was to protect the embassy, its staff, and its mission, while also managing the logistical realities of having a desperate Canadian sheltering on-site.

Sitting inside the Mission compound in the early days, Khartoum, Sudan

But the work wasn't just about guarding doors or monitoring threats. Each day, I navigated the space between policy and people, balancing operational security with the stark, unmet needs of a man whose only hope depended on decisions beyond my control. The embassy staff, overworked and strained, did their best to show compassion while following diplomatic protocols. Still, stress showed in small ways: tempers flared, routines frayed, and the line between security and humanitarian duty blurred until it was nearly invisible.

What struck me most, personally, was that Abdelrazik and I were both facing our own kinds of exile. His was enforced and public; mine was quieter, rooted in past trauma and the struggle to reconcile what I'd survived with what was now asked of me. During moments of calm, I'd sometimes linger at the window, watching the heat shimmer across Khartoum's streets. Life carried on with a kind of chaotic grace, even as we inside the walls existed in bureaucratic stasis.

I learned quickly that neither my past uniform nor my new passport could protect me from the moral and psychological complexity of the mission. Each decision I had to make carried real stakes, for the safety of others, for the well-being of a man in legal limbo, and for the integrity of Canada's humanitarian response in an environment where every choice could be misunderstood or weaponized. Oddly enough, the very traits that had once marked my trauma, heightened vigilance, deep skepticism, and the need to scan every room, now became essential tools. The things that once isolated me helped me read situations faster, respond with precision, and protect others better.

That first deployment became more than just a job. In hindsight, it marked the beginning of a more profound transformation. Khartoum, with its contradictions, crises, and complexity, was where my own sense of purpose began to crystallize. I began to understand that protection isn't only about keeping harm at bay. Occasionally, it means holding a space for others' fear and uncertainty, even when I was still learning how to hold space for my own.

6

Facing Demons Abroad

My role at the embassy began to shift soon after my arrival. What started as a protective detail rapidly grew more complex, and I found myself named Mission Security Manager. The title meant more than a change in responsibilities; it altered my perspective entirely. Instead of focusing solely on defending Canadian interests, I was now expected to coordinate with other embassies, the United Nations, and even Sudanese officials over mechanisms for staff safety, compound protocols, and quick responses in a city shaped by diplomatic intrigue and sudden unpredictability.

Despite how outsiders often described Khartoum as perilous, I found the city to be, on the whole, safe. The days unfolded with order; people moved through their routines, and the city's vibrant markets, mosques, and tea stalls offered a kind of everyday normalcy that belied the headlines. Still, there were moments that unsettled me, checkpoints that felt a little less predictable, rumours of unrest murmuring through our channels, and an occasional alert that reminded us that calm was never guaranteed.

What was never far from my thoughts, however, was the
personal cost of that deployment. During my posting in
Khartoum, from November 2007 to June 2008, I had no
periods of R&R, no respite from the intensity or duration of
that assignment. I worked straight through the Christmas
and New Year holidays, as well as Easter, missing all the key
holidays with my sons that most parents take for granted. The
sting of absence grew sharper with every milestone I missed:
their laughter and daily stories reduced to emails and calls,
our traditions left waiting year after year. Each holiday spent
in the embassy compound was a quiet reckoning, a reminder
that while I worked to safeguard others in a distant capital,
the moments I yearned for most with my family slipped past
unshared.

Drinking coffee in an empty hotel during Christmas, Khartoum, Sudan

Managing security meant constant vigilance: daily calls with counterparts in the American and British embassies, shared threat assessments, and sometimes tense negotiations with Sudanese security officials whose priorities didn't always align with our own. I learned to cultivate contacts, trade favours, and read between the lines, a skill honed equally by trauma and necessity.

Then, on March 4, 2009, the careful equilibrium we'd maintained shattered. The International Criminal Court issued an arrest warrant for Sudan's sitting President Omar al-Bashir, the first warrant ever issued against a serving head of state. The charges were severe: crimes against humanity and war crimes related to the conflict in Darfur. Within hours, the government's response was swift and devastating. Thirteen of the world's most prominent humanitarian organizations were expelled from Sudan, including CARE, Oxfam, Médecins Sans Frontières, Save the Children, and the International Rescue Committee. Three Sudanese NGOs were also shuttered.

The expulsions decimated humanitarian capacity across the country. In Darfur alone, over 2.7 million displaced people lost access to critical services. Water systems serving over one million people were compromised, healthcare for 1.5 million was interrupted, and food assistance for 1.1 million was cut. It was a calculated act of retaliation that would reverberate for months to come.

As mission security manager, I found myself coordinating not just embassy protection but crisis response on multiple fronts. The expelled organizations' local staff needed protection, their assets required securing, and their ongoing programs demanded emergency handover protocols. The UN and remaining agencies scrambled to fill gaps that couldn't realistically be filled.

Within days of the expulsions, the security situation deteriorated further. On March 11, just a week after the ICC warrant, four humanitarian workers, including a Canadian nurse, were kidnapped in Serif Umra, North Darfur. The abductors, calling themselves the "Eagles of Bashir," held the aid workers for four days before releasing them on March 14. The kidnapping represented a significant escalation in threats against international staff, forcing Médecins Sans Frontières to evacuate nearly all remaining international personnel from Darfur.

These events transformed my role from routine security management to crisis coordination. I found myself liaising with Canadian consular officials about the kidnapped nurse, coordinating with other missions on evacuation protocols, and helping manage the complex logistics of a humanitarian sector in collapse. The Canadian Mission became a critical hub for information sharing and coordination as the international community grappled with the largest humanitarian expulsion in decades.

However, the most persistent demons weren't the profes-sional ones that shadowed embassy corridors. They waited for me in quieter moments, in the margins between urgent calls and security briefings. Leaving my son behind in Canada, in the care of my third wife, was a wound that throbbed beneath every professional accomplishment. Each crisis I managed in Sudan reminded me of the personal crisis brewing at home: how my absence strained the fragile balances of blended family life, how distance bred misunderstandings, and how quickly weeks gathered into months.

The challenges of serving abroad while trying to be a parent across continents brought their own relentless strain. I missed milestones, phone calls lagged behind unfolding daily lives, and I wondered often if my service, noble as it sometimes felt, came at an impossible cost to those I loved. The expelled aid workers faced similar choices, forced to abandon programs they'd spent years building, communities they'd served, and colleagues they'd grown to trust.

Officially, my job was to prepare for the unexpected: to strate-
gize for sieges, evacuations, or political crises. Unofficially,
I fought to reconcile two truths: that in protecting others, I
was also seeking my own redemption, and that real danger
sometimes waited, not in Sudanese streets, but in the quiet
spaces between a father and the son he longed to protect from
half a world away.

The expulsions and kidnappings marked a turning point in
Sudan's relationship with the international community. They
also marked a turning point in my own understanding of
humanitarian work, not as a clean, heroic endeavour, but
as a complex negotiation between political realities, human
needs, and personal costs that could never be fully calculated
or controlled.

7

Returning to Sudan with CARE

The work in Sudan had given me something I hadn't expected: credibility within humanitarian circles. Particularly during the complex period following the INGO expulsions, my performance as Mission Security Manager established a reputation that extended beyond embassy protection. When CARE US approached me in October 2009 about returning to Sudan, it represented a different kind of challenge, not diplomatic security, but humanitarian reestablishment in a hostile environment.

CARE International had been among the thirteen organizations expelled in March 2009, losing years of programming, millions of dollars in assets, and crucial relationships with local communities. But by late 2009, the Sudanese government had begun allowing some expelled organizations to return under different operational frameworks, new names, altered structures, and enhanced oversight. CARE saw an opportunity to re-enter through CARE International Switzerland, and they needed someone who understood both the security landscape and the delicate politics of humanitarian operations in post-expulsion Sudan.

My connection to the previous CARE security manager proved crucial. When the expulsions began in March, I had assisted his evacuation, ensuring his safe departure and helping secure sensitive materials during the chaotic forty-eight hours organizations had to cease operations and leave the country. What made this evacuation particularly challenging was that I found myself as the sole person remaining at the embassy, with all other staff having departed for vacation just as the crisis unfolded. This meant I had to rely entirely on my own resources and out-of-the-box thinking to orchestrate a safe departure for the security manager.

With the embassy effectively empty except for myself, I couldn't follow standard evacuation protocols that would normally involve multiple personnel and established procedures. Instead, I had to improvise a comprehensive exit strategy from scratch. Recognizing that the embassy itself could not provide adequate security during this vulnerable transition period with our current resident, I made the strategic decision to arrange a safe haven at the hotel adjacent to the embassy compound. This location offered better operational flexibility while maintaining proximity to diplomatic resources.

The next critical challenge was securing transportation out of the country within the narrow forty-eight-hour window mandated by the government. Working through my network of contacts and leveraging relationships built during previous security operations, I managed to locate and book a flight despite the sudden surge in demand as multiple organizations scrambled to evacuate their personnel simultaneously. The logistics of getting the security manager safely from the hotel to the airport required careful timing and route planning, given the heightened tensions and potential for civil unrest during the mass expulsion period.

Perhaps most critically, the security manager possessed sensitive information that couldn't risk falling into unauthorized hands or being compromised during a hurried departure. Recognizing the gravity of this material, I coordinated with embassy officials to arrange for the documents to be transmitted through the diplomatic pouch system to Uganda. This required precise documentation and adherence to diplomatic protocols, even under the compressed timeline. The diplomatic pouch provided the necessary legal protections and secure transmission channels that standard courier services couldn't guarantee in such a volatile environment.

That professional relationship, built on trust during this high-stakes crisis, now became the foundation for continuity. CARE needed someone who could recover assets, restore relationships, and rebuild security protocols in an environment where every humanitarian organization operated under intense scrutiny. My demonstrated ability to think creatively under pressure, coordinate complex logistics single-handedly, and maintain the integrity of sensitive information while ensuring personnel safety had proven my value in crisis management, exactly the skill set CARE required for their challenging reentry into South Sudan's increasingly restrictive operating environment.

* * *

The October 2009 deployment was unlike my embassy work. Instead of protecting Canadian interests, I was helping rebuild the operational capacity of an organization dedicated to fighting poverty and empowering communities. The challenges were immediate and complex: negotiating with Sudanese officials who viewed returning organizations with deep suspicion, locating and recovering equipment that had been seized or abandoned, and establishing security protocols that would satisfy both organizational requirements and government oversight.

Working under the CARE International Switzerland banner required navigating bureaucratic complexities I'd never encountered. Every asset recovery needed documentation, every relationship required careful calibration, and every security decision carried implications for the organization's long-term presence in Sudan. The Sudanese government's Humanitarian Aid Commission (HAC) maintained strict oversight over returning organizations, viewing them as potential threats that had been expelled for "violating their humanitarian mandates."

In the field reclaiming assets, Darfur, Sudan

The work was both exhausting and meaningful. Each re-covered vehicle, each restored program relationship, and each successfully negotiated agreement represented lives that could be saved, communities that could be served, and hope that could be restored. The hypervigilance that trauma had taught me became essential for reading the intentions of officials, detecting potential threats, and managing the complex negotiations required to establish CARE's new operational footprint.

49

8

Ground Zero: Haiti, 2010

Shortly after reconstructing one humanitarian response, a devastating new crisis began to unfold in a distant part of the world. On January 12, 2010, at 4:53 pm local time, a 7.0-magnitude earthquake struck Haiti, just 25 kilometers from Port-au-Prince. The devastation was immediate and overwhelming: between 220,000 and 300,000 people killed, over 300,000 injured, and 1.5 million left homeless. The earthquake decimated infrastructure, collapsed government buildings, and created what would become one of the largest humanitarian responses in history.

Within days, CARE US was mobilizing its earthquake response, and my work in Sudan had positioned me as someone who could manage security in complex, high-risk environments. In mid-January, I received an offer to deploy to Haiti as a Response Security Manager, where I would be responsible for ensuring the safety of CARE's rapidly expanding operations in a country where basic infrastructure had collapsed and security threats were constantly evolving.

The devastation was real, Haiti

The transition from Sudan's calculated political tensions to Haiti's chaotic post-earthquake reality was jarring. Where Sudan required diplomatic finesse and bureaucratic navigation, Haiti demanded rapid decision-making amid a genuine humanitarian emergency. Port-au-Prince was a city transformed by tragedy, with buildings reduced to rubble, streets clogged with debris, and hundreds of thousands of people sleeping in makeshift camps. The scope of human need was unlike anything I'd encountered, even in Sudan's conflict zones.

My first three months in Haiti as CARE's Response Security Manager meant establishing security protocols in an environment where traditional infrastructure no longer existed. Police capacity was severely limited, government authority was fractured, and the sheer number of humanitarian organizations arriving daily created coordination challenges that threatened operational effectiveness. Every day brought new risks: unstable buildings, overwhelmed hospitals, and the complex security dynamics of a population struggling to survive in conditions of unprecedented displacement.

* * *

One of our most challenging tasks involved conducting a complex food distribution just outside of Pétionville. The logistics were daunting: we had to determine a suitable location and develop a comprehensive plan for how beneficiaries would enter the distribution site and exit safely, managing the flow of thousands of desperate people in an orderly manner that wouldn't create dangerous crowd dynamics or stampede conditions.

Food ready for distribution, Port-au-Prince, Haiti

The security arrangements reflected the complexity of post-earthquake Haiti. We had US military security positioned across the street in a house compound, observing the operation but maintaining their distance. Behind us, a UN detachment of Jordanian soldiers provided perimeter security. The Haitian National Police (PNH) were assigned to assist with moving people through the entrance, controlling the flow of beneficiaries seeking food assistance.

What I witnessed during that distribution remains one of the most morally challenging aspects of my deployment in Haiti. Watching how the PNH treated beneficiaries trying to access food aid was deeply disturbing. Officers would hit people with sticks, using physical violence to control crowds of hungry, desperate earthquake survivors who were simply trying to feed their families. The brutality was casual and systematic, turning what should have been a humanitarian lifeline into another form of trauma for people who had already lost everything.

Entry control point for the distribution, Port-au-Prince, Haiti

The positioning of the international forces created a troubling dynamic. The US military personnel observed from their compound across the street, maintaining their distance from the violence but making no effort to intervene. The UN Jordanian soldiers behind us provided security for the distribution infrastructure but showed no inclination to protect beneficiaries from police brutality. As the security manager, I found myself caught between operational necessity and moral outrage, needing PNH cooperation to manage the distribution while witnessing their systematic abuse of the very people we were trying to help.

This distribution crystallized the complex ethical landscape of humanitarian work in post-disaster environments. The very security arrangements that enabled us to deliver life-saving assistance also facilitated violence against the people we served. The international military presence that provided stability for our operations remained passive observers to human rights violations occurring meters away. The Haitian authorities whose cooperation we needed to reach affected populations were simultaneously victimizing those same populations.

These moral contradictions became part of my daily reality in Haiti, forcing me to navigate the intersection of humanitarian principles and operational pragmatism in ways that academic training had never prepared me for. Each successful distribution meant food reached hungry families, but it also meant complicity in a system that treated earthquake survivors as potential threats rather than human beings deserving dignity and respect.

* * *

The personal cost remained constant. Once again, I was serving thousands of miles from home, missing milestones in my son's life, and managing family relationships through sporadic phone calls and delayed emails. The nobility of humanitarian service couldn't entirely compensate for the persistent ache of absence, the knowledge that every life I helped protect abroad came at the cost of daily presence in the lives of those who mattered most to me.

But Haiti also represented something new: the application of skills I'd developed through trauma and refined through experience to serve people in their most desperate hour. The hypervigilance, crisis management abilities, and capacity to function under extreme stress that had once been symptoms of my own brokenness now became tools for protecting others when everything familiar had been destroyed.

In those first months after the earthquake, amid the rubble of Port-au-Prince and the organized chaos of humanitarian response, I began to understand that my journey from military trauma through diplomatic security to humanitarian service wasn't just about personal redemption. It involved transforming the most challenging experiences of my life into the ability to assist others during their most challenging times, when their own foundations, both literally and metaphorically, crumbled.

9

From Survivor to Specialist

Content Warning: This chapter contains references to child kidnapping, human trafficking, and crisis situations that may be distressing to some readers. Reader discretion is advised.

By April 2010, my three months with CARE US in Haiti had established me as someone who could manage security operations in the most challenging humanitarian contexts. The earthquake response had tested every skill I'd developed through trauma and experience: the ability to function under extreme pressure, to make critical decisions with incomplete information, and to protect others when traditional support systems had collapsed. But even as I was proving myself in Port-au-Prince, new opportunities were emerging that would reshape my understanding of what humanitarian security could become.

The call came from an unexpected source: the BBC needed someone to provide personal security training to their staff in Afghanistan. It was a short assignment, just two weeks, but it represented something significant. Media organizations, like humanitarian agencies, were recognizing that traditional security approaches weren't adequate for the complex environments where their people worked. They needed trainers who understood both the technical aspects of protection and the human dynamics of operating under threat.

The BBC contract with Armadillo at Large took me to a very different kind of crisis zone. Where Haiti's challenges stemmed from natural disaster and systemic poverty, Afghanistan's dangers were rooted in active conflict, political instability, and the ongoing tensions of a war-torn society. The journalists I trained faced threats that were both predictable and constantly shifting, IED attacks, kidnapping attempts, and the complex challenge of reporting from a country where neutrality was often viewed with suspicion by all sides.

The streets of Kabul, Kabul, Afghanistan

Teaching security to media professionals required a different approach than protecting humanitarian workers. Journalists needed to balance their safety and access to information with the imperative to tell stories that the world needed to hear. My role wasn't to keep them safe by keeping them isolated; it was to provide them the skills and awareness to make informed decisions about acceptable risk. The hypervigilance that trauma had instilled in me transformed into a teaching tool, assisting others in cultivating the situational awareness that could distinguish between the completion of a story and its actualization.

It was during those two weeks in Afghanistan that my phone rang with an opportunity that would change everything. The

59

caller identified himself as the Response Security Manager for World Vision International, one of the world's largest humanitarian organizations. He was leaving his position and wanted to know if I'd be interested in taking on his role, a one-year contract that would make me responsible for security operations for World Vision's Haiti response.

The conversation was brief but significant. World Vision's approach to humanitarian work was different from what I'd experienced with CARE or diplomatic missions. Founded as a Christian organization, World Vision brought both extensive resources and distinct operational challenges to emergency response. Their programs often operated in contexts where religious identity could be both an asset and a vulnerability, requiring security management that understood the inter-section of faith, politics, and protection. I accepted the offer, beginning my new role as Response Security Manager for Haiti on April 1, 2010.

Immediate Crisis Upon Arrival

When I arrived at the World Vision office on April 1, 2010, to start my assignment, I walked into the middle of a crisis that would define my first days with the organization. The son of one of our staff members had been kidnapped the evening before my arrival. The office was in chaos, with staff members torn between their professional responsibilities and their personal anguish for their colleague's family.

We managed the crisis as best we could over the next few days, coordinating with local authorities, maintaining communication with the family, and providing whatever support we could while continuing essential operations. The situation was a stark reminder of the personal costs that humanitarian work extracted from local staff, who faced the same dangers as international personnel but without the option of evacuation or rotation home. Despite our efforts and those of local law enforcement, the child was believed to have been sold off to another type of kidnapping organization, a devastating outcome that highlighted the complex criminal networks operating in post-earthquake Haiti.

This immediate immersion into crisis management set the tone for my entire Haiti deployment. There was no gradual orientation period, no time to settle into new responsibilities; from day one, I was managing life-and-death situations that affected not just our operations but the personal lives of our team members.

Building the Security Team

I was introduced to my team, which comprised an administration officer and three field security officers. One field security officer was from Uganda, bringing valuable regional experience and perspectives on managing security in challenging African contexts. The other two were local nationals whose knowledge of Haitian culture, language, and local dynamics proved invaluable in navigating the complex security landscape of post-earthquake Haiti.

Our office was located in the corner of the response office in Pétionville, a strategic location that provided favourable

access to the broader humanitarian community while maintaining some operational separation for sensitive security
discussions. The space was modest but functional, reflecting
the rapid deployment nature of emergency response operations.

I am proud of the team we built for the response security
operations. Despite the challenging circumstances and the
immediate crisis that greeted my arrival, we quickly developed into a cohesive unit that combined international
expertise with local knowledge. The diversity of our backgrounds, military, humanitarian, international, and local,
created a team dynamic that was both professionally effective
and personally supportive during the difficult months that
followed.

Demonstrations were commonplace in Haiti, Port-au-Prince, Haiti

GPS Installation Project

One of our major assignments was the installation of GPS units in all of the World Vision International vehicles operating in Haiti. This project represented a significant upgrade to our security capabilities and reflected the organization's commitment to staff safety in the post-earthquake environment.

The GPS devices were remarkable technology for the time, providing real-time tracking capabilities that proved beneficial for monitoring both the location and speed of vehicles throughout our operational areas. The systems allowed us to track convoy movements, ensure that vehicles remained within approved routes, and respond quickly if a vehicle stopped unexpectedly or deviated from planned itineraries.

We installed these devices in approximately 20 vehicles, a significant undertaking that required coordination with drivers, mechanics, and field teams across all of World Vision's Haiti operations. Careful planning was necessary for each installation to conceal the devices properly and maintain their accessibility for maintenance. We also had to train drivers and field staff on the systems, establishing protocols for emergency situations and regular check-ins.

The GPS systems transformed our security management capabilities. Instead of relying on scheduled radio checks and estimated arrival times, we could monitor real-time vehicle locations and respond immediately to any irregularities. The speed monitoring function proved particularly valuable in a country where road conditions varied dramatically and where high speeds could indicate either emergency situations or inappropriate driving that could endanger staff and equipment.

This technology upgrade represented more than just better tools; it reflected World Vision's recognition that effective security management in post-disaster environments required investment in systems that could adapt to rapidly changing conditions while providing continuous protection for staff operating across wide geographic areas.

Traffic Accidents were a daily occurrence, requiring proper mitigation measures in Haiti

* * *

The summer of 2010 brought another opportunity that would prove even more transformative. World Vision's Global Rapid Response Team (GRRT) was seeking a Field Security Advisor, someone who could deploy to new emergencies within 72 hours, establish security frameworks from scratch, and train local teams to maintain those protocols after international staff departed. Designed to be the first on the ground in crisis situations, the GRRT served as the foundation for larger relief operations.

The interview process was rigorous, testing not just technical knowledge but psychological resilience, cultural adaptability, and the capacity to work effectively under extreme stress. They needed someone who could function independently in chaotic environments, make sound decisions with limited information, and build trust quickly with local partners who might have legitimate reason to be suspicious of international organizations.

My background, military service, trauma survival, diplomatic security, and humanitarian experience across multiple contexts had prepared me uniquely for this role. The interviewing panel recognized that the qualities that had once been symptoms of my brokenness were now professional assets. The hypervigilance that made civilian life challenging turned into a natural ability to assess threats. The emotional numbing that had damaged relationships enabled clear thinking in crisis situations. The deep suspicion of authority that stemmed from military sexual trauma had evolved into a healthy skepticism that protected both myself and those I served.

The Full Circle Moment

The journey from the broken recruit I described in "A Soldier's Cry" to this moment, being recruited for World Vision's Global Rapid Response Team, proved that survival itself was a specialized skill. The military had discarded the young man as "damaged goods" in 1989, but now one of the world's largest humanitarian organizations sought him for his ability to function in their most dangerous environments.

The hypervigilance and threat assessment abilities born of military sexual trauma have become professional assets of the highest calibre. What the military had considered symptoms of a "problem soldier" were now recognized as exactly the skills needed to protect others in crisis zones. The dissociative episodes that had once made me unemployable now enabled me to compartmentalize effectively during traumatic events. The deep suspicion of authority that had complicated every civilian job was now understood as healthy skepticism essential for security work.

In "A Soldier's Cry," I had written about feeling like a ghost haunting my own life, unable to find purpose or place in a world that seemed designed for people who hadn't been broken by institutional betrayal. But here, in this recruitment conversation, I finally understood that I hadn't been broken; I had been forged. The trauma that had once defined my limitations was now defining my capabilities.

The boy who had left the Forces carrying invisible wounds had become a man whose job was to ensure that others didn't suffer similar abandonment. I didn't overcome my trauma, but instead, I learned to use it as a precise tool to safeguard the innocent and vulnerable. The circle wasn't closing; it was expanding, encompassing not just my own survival but the survival of others who would depend on skills that pain had taught me.

* * *

I was successful in the selection process, with one condition:

I would need to relocate from Haiti to establish my new base of operations at World Vision's Costa Rica office in early December 2010. The move represented more than a change of location; it was a transition from reactive security management to proactive rapid response, from protecting existing operations to creating new ones in the world's most volatile regions.

The journey from a broken veteran who had left military service in 1989 to a specialist being recruited for one of the most demanding roles in humanitarian work was not a straightforward one. It had required decades of failure and rebuilding, countless small choices to keep moving forward when everything suggested retreat, and the gradual recognition that survival itself was a skill that could be refined and deployed in service of others.

By December 2010, as I prepared to relocate to Costa Rica, we were no longer running from our trauma or trying to overcome it. We were wielding it as a precision instrument, honed through years of experience in environments where the difference between protection and vulnerability could be measured in seconds and decisions. A boy who'd been broken by institutional betrayal had become a man whose job it was to ensure that others didn't suffer the same fate, not because he'd overcome his wounds, but because he'd learned to transform them into tools for protecting the innocent and vulnerable.

The transition to Costa Rica would mark the beginning of a new phase, where the skills trauma had taught and experience had refined would be deployed on a global scale, in service of people facing their own moments of ultimate vulnerability. The survivor was becoming a specialist, not despite his trauma, but because of how he'd chosen to carry it forward.

* * *

End of Part I Summary

The Uniform Exchange: From Regulation to Adaptation

The transformation from military precision to humanitarian improvisation required more than changing clothes; it demanded rewiring decades of institutional conditioning. In the Forces, every morning began with the same ritual: uniform pressed to regulation standards, boots polished to a mirror finish, and protocols memorized until they became reflexive responses. Orders flowed down clearly defined chains of command, leaving little room for interpretation but providing the comfort of absolute clarity about roles, expectations, and procedures. Yet in humanitarian work, I discovered a different kind of structure, one built on principles rather than protocols, guided by moral imperatives rather than military orders. The blue uniform of the Commissionaires had been my bridge, offering familiar hierarchy while introducing civilian flexibility. But stepping into World Vision's Global Rapid Response Team meant embracing radical adaptation: no two deployments were identical, cultural contexts shifted with each border crossing, and success depended on reading situations that no manual could anticipate. The hypervigilance

69

that military trauma had embedded in my nervous system, once a liability in peaceful civilian settings, became vital when navigating this new landscape where improvisation and intuition mattered as much as preparation and protocol. I learned that true resilience emerged not from rigid adherence to rules, but from the ability to honour core values while adapting methods to serve them effectively.

From Breakdown to Breakthrough (1989–2010)

The twenty-one years between military discharge and my first humanitarian deployment traced a geography of survival: from the wounded departure that left me exiled from purpose, through the relentless search for solid ground amid failed relationships and custody battles, to finding unexpected sanctuary in the blue uniform of the Commissionaires.

Each setback, the father who rejected me, the marriages that crumbled under trauma's weight, and the jobs lost to unmanaged triggers became instruction in a curriculum I didn't know I was learning. The hypervigilance that made civilian life exhausting, the emotional numbing that harmed intimacy, and the deep suspicion of authority resulting from institutional betrayal were not merely symptoms to over-come; they were skills to refine.

Sudan changed everything. In Khartoum's embassy corridors and Haiti's earthquake rubble, I discovered that the most challenging experiences of my life had become the foundation for protecting others during their most vulnerable moments. The boy broken by military sexual trauma had become a man

70

whose wounds were wisdom, whose survival was specialized knowledge, and whose very brokenness had been transformed into tools for safeguarding the innocent.

The breakdown had become a breakthrough. The real work could now begin.

Looking Ahead

By the time I wrapped up those first deployments, from Sudan's embassies to Haiti's earthquake rubble, I already sensed that my old scars were becoming assets while new scars were forming. The same hypervigilance that once isolated me would soon transform into a teaching tool, and the hard-won ability to lead under fire would guide my shift from protector to trainer and advocate. In the chapters to come, you'll see how these early breakthroughs laid the groundwork for a new kind of service, one grounded in sharing trauma's lessons so others might face danger with wisdom, resilience, and the confidence that even the most broken things can be rebuilt stronger than before.

II

Into the Fire (2011–2016)

After years of rebuilding, I stepped onto new frontlines, where expertise forged in trauma met the world's most acute crises. From Kenya's coordination rooms to Syria's chaos and South Sudan's war-torn villages, each deployment tested my limits and expanded my purpose. "Into the Fire" chronicles my evolution from survivor to specialist, confronting danger and loss so others could endure, and teaching that resilience is born not just from survival, but from service.

10

Famine's Shadow: Kenya, 2011

The decision that destroyed my third marriage came in early 2011, delivered through a series of terse phone calls between Ottawa and Costa Rica. My wife had made her position clear: she would not relocate to Central America for my World Vision posting. The choice, she said, was between the job and the family. But the reality was more complex than her ultimatum suggested; by 2011, I had become the primary financial provider not just for our household but also for my son from my second marriage, who was now sixteen and living with his stepmother while I was deployed.

The mathematics was brutal and unforgiving. Walking away from the Global Rapid Response Team position would mean returning to contract security work in Canada, accepting a dramatic reduction in income at precisely the moment my son needed stability as he approached university age. The humanitarian career I'd built over the last year, from Sudan through Haiti to this specialized role, would vanish, leaving me to explain to my son why I'd chosen his stepmother's comfort over his future.

So I chose financial security over marital harmony, a decision
that felt like betrayal even as I made it. My third wife filed for
divorce within weeks of my refusal to return to Canada. The
divorce papers arrived at the World Vision Costa Rica office
in March 2011, reducing my failed marriage to clinical legal
terminology and asset division. At forty-five years old, I was
facing my third failed marriage, alone in a foreign country,
with nothing but the specialized skills that trauma had taught
me and the humanitarian community that had embraced
them.

I recognized the irony: I was mastering the art of safeguarding
others, yet I was utterly incapable of safeguarding my own
relationships. Each deployment that built my professional
reputation extracted another piece of my personal life. The
hypervigilance that made me valuable in crisis zones made
me impossible to live with during the quiet moments between
emergencies. The emotional numbing that enabled clear
thinking under extreme stress translated into an inability
to provide the intimacy that marriage required.

But there was no time for self-pity or extended reflection on
personal failure. In July 2011, the worst drought in sixty years
began ravaging the Horn of Africa. The crisis would eventually
affect over 13 million people across Somalia, Kenya, Ethiopia,
and Djibouti, with Somalia experiencing the first famine
declared by the UN in nearly three decades. By late October
2011, an estimated 1,150 people per day were fleeing Somalia
for refugee camps in Kenya, particularly the sprawling Dadaab

complex, which was designed for 90,000 people but now housed over 350,000.

World Vision's GRRT was activated, and I received deployment orders for Kenya in late August 2011. My mission was to establish security protocols for World Vision's emergency response in the drought-affected regions, assess risks to international staff, and create frameworks that could protect both aid workers and the populations they served. The assignment could take me into areas where desperation had reached levels that tested every lesson I'd learned about human resilience and institutional response.

The flight from San José to Nairobi gave me time to process the personal and professional transitions converging in my life. I was no longer a married man trying to balance family obligations with humanitarian service. I was now a specialist whose only remaining responsibility was to the work itself and to the son whose future I was trying to secure through choices that continued to isolate me from ordinary human connection. The survivor had become truly specialized, not despite the personal costs, but because of them.

* * *

The World Vision East Africa Response Office in Nairobi operated from a converted colonial-era building in the Westlands district, its high ceilings and thick walls providing some relief from the equatorial heat. My arrival in late August 2011 coincided with the peak of the crisis, over 750,000 Somali refugees had fled to Kenya, with the Dadaab refugee complex becoming the largest in the world. But my role wasn't to work directly in the camps or drought-affected regions. Instead, I was stationed in Nairobi as the coordination hub for all field security operations across the Horn of Africa.

From my office overlooking Nairobi's sprawling urban landscape, I managed security for World Vision operations across multiple counties and contexts. The work required a different kind of vigilance than I'd known in previous deployments. Rather than assessing immediate physical threats, I was analyzing patterns of risk across a vast geographic area, coordinating with field teams that I might never meet in person, and developing contingency plans for scenarios that could unfold hundreds of kilometres away.

Most days, our team would break from the intensity of crisis coordination with lunch or coffee at the nearby Westlands mall, a modern shopping complex that provided a brief respite from the weight of managing humanitarian security across the Horn of Africa. The mall's food court and cafes offered one of the few spaces where international aid workers could decompress, share intelligence informally, and maintain some semblance of normal life amid the crisis. It became our unofficial meeting point for coordination that couldn't happen in formal UN briefings, the kind of sensitive information exchange that occurred over coffee rather than in conference rooms. None of us could have imagined that this same mall, which served as our sanctuary from the stress of humanitarian work, would become the site of a devastating terrorist attack two years later when Al-Shabaab militants stormed the complex in September 2013, killing 67 people and injuring over 175 others. The irony wasn't lost on me when news of the Westgate mall attack reached me: the place where we'd discussed security threats over casual meals had become the very kind of target we'd been working to protect people from.

The complexity was staggering. World Vision's response encompassed operations in Kenya's northern counties, refugee camps along the Somali border, cross-border programs that attempted to address root causes of migration, and urban programming in Nairobi itself, where thousands of displaced families had settled informally. Each context brought unique security challenges: banditry and cattle rustling in pastoral areas, political tensions in refugee camps, criminal activity in urban slums, and the ever-present threat of Al-Shabaab infiltration from Somalia.

My days began before dawn with situation reports from field locations, radio checks with security focal points in remote areas, and coordination calls that formed the backbone of humanitarian security management in Kenya. The United Nations Department of Safety and Security (UNDSS) served as the primary coordination mechanism, hosting daily security briefings that brought together representatives from all major international organizations operating in the region. These meetings, held in the secure UN compound in Gigiri, became my window into the broader security landscape affecting humanitarian operations.

The UNDSS briefings were exercises in diplomatic information sharing, where organizations disclosed what they could while protecting operational security. Each morning, I would join security managers from UNHCR, UNICEF, WFP, IRC, MSF, Oxfam, and dozens of other agencies to review overnight incidents, assess evolving threats, and coordinate movement plans. The information flow was carefully calibrated, detailed enough to enable informed decision-making but general enough to prevent sensitive operational details from being compromised.

My relationship with the UN Office for the Coordination of Humanitarian Affairs (UNOCHA) proved equally critical. While UNDSS focused on security threats, UNOCHA managed the broader humanitarian response coordination, tracking who was doing what where, identifying gaps in coverage, and ensuring that security decisions aligned with programmatic priorities. Their twice-weekly humanitarian coordination meetings brought together program managers and security personnel to balance operational needs against risk assessments.

The interagency security coordination revealed the complex dynamics of humanitarian response. Organizations with different mandates, funding sources, and risk tolerances had to find common ground on security protocols that would enable collective action while respecting individual institutional requirements. World Vision's faith-based identity, for example, sometimes required different security considerations than secular organizations, particularly in areas where religious tensions were high.

Coordination with other International Non-Governmental

Organizations (INGOs) became a daily necessity. The major agencies, CARE, Oxfam, Save the Children, IRC, and MSF, each brought different operational philosophies and security approaches. Some maintained strict security protocols that limited access to high-risk areas, while others accepted greater risk to maintain program presence. It was my responsibility to ensure that World Vision's security posture remained appropriate for our specific operational context, based on collective intelligence.

The information-sharing protocols were complex and sometimes contradictory. During the morning UNDSS briefings, we would receive sanitized threat assessments that provided general situational awareness without compromising specific sources or methods. But the real intelligence exchange happened in bilateral meetings and informal conversations, where security managers could share more sensitive information about specific threats, local dynamics, and operational vulnerabilities.

* * *

One of my first tasks was completely rewriting World Vision's Hostile Environment Awareness Training (HEAT) policy specifically for Global Rapid Response Team members. The existing protocols were inadequate for the specialized nature of GRRT deployments, which required team members to be first responders in the world's most volatile environments within 72 hours of crisis onset. The new policy established that all GRRT members would be required to complete comprehensive HEAT training before deploying to high-risk environments.

The GRRT HEAT policy development was more complex than standard humanitarian security training. Unlike traditional aid workers who deployed to established programs with existing security frameworks, GRRT members arrived in crisis zones where security protocols didn't yet exist. They needed to assess threats in real-time, establish security frameworks from scratch, and make life-or-death decisions with minimal local knowledge or support structures.

The policy required GRRT members to demonstrate competency in multiple domains before deployment authorization: threat assessment and risk analysis in unstable environments, personal security awareness and protective measures, crisis communication and emergency procedures, cultural awareness and conflict sensitivity, psychological resilience and stress management, and evacuation planning and execution protocols.

The training protocols we developed drew heavily on lessons learned through my own trauma and experience in high-threat environments. How do you teach someone to recognize subtle changes in crowd behaviour that might signal impending violence? How do you explain the importance of trusting gut instincts while providing concrete frameworks for decision-making? The challenge was translating survival skills rooted in personal experience into professional protocols that could protect others.

The new HEAT policy represented a significant investment

in GRRT member safety, but it also reflected World Vision's recognition that rapid response work required specialized skills that went beyond traditional humanitarian competencies. By the time we completed the policy development, it had become a template that other agencies were beginning to adapt for their own emergency response teams.

HEAT Course in Nairobi, 2011

* * *

Travel coordination became another critical function, requiring constant liaison with UNDSS movement control officers and other agency security managers. Every journey between

Nairobi and field locations required careful planning and multi-agency coordination. Road conditions changed daily based on security incidents, weather, and political tensions. Flight schedules were unreliable, and some airstrips were subject to closure without notice. I developed routing protocols that balanced operational efficiency with staff safety while ensuring that World Vision movements were coordinated with the broader humanitarian community's security framework.

The contingency planning work proved to be some of the most challenging I'd undertaken. The Horn of Africa crisis was characterized by slow-onset, complex emergencies that could escalate unpredictably, unlike the earthquake response in Haiti or diplomatic security in Sudan. Working closely with UNDSS and other agency security managers, I developed evacuation plans for multiple scenarios: rapid deterioration in specific locations, complete breakdown of government authority, cross-border conflict spillover, and terrorist attacks on humanitarian operations.

These contingency plans required constant coordination with the broader humanitarian community. In the event of a security incident requiring evacuation, individual agencies couldn't act unilaterally; our movements had to be coordinated through UNDSS to ensure that evacuation routes remained viable and that one organization's emergency response didn't compromise others' safety.

Working from Nairobi also meant grappling with the disconnect between the relative comfort of the capital and the desperate conditions in the field. While I coordinated security for operations serving people facing starvation and displacement, I returned each evening to an apartment on the sixth floor with reliable electricity, running water, and internet connectivity. The guilt was persistent, the knowledge that my expertise in violence and vulnerability was being deployed to protect those serving others, while I remained insulated from the immediate human cost of the crisis.

The isolation was profound in ways I hadn't anticipated. In previous deployments, I'd worked directly alongside those I was protecting. In Nairobi, my protection was largely invisible: radio checks that went smoothly, travel that proceeded without incident, and contingency plans that hopefully would never be activated. Success was measured by the absence of crisis rather than visible accomplishment.

Yet the work felt essential in ways that transcended personal fulfillment. Each day, dozens of World Vision staff moved through high-risk environments to reach some of the world's most vulnerable populations. The security frameworks I developed, the training I delivered, and the contingency plans I maintained formed an invisible safety net that enabled that lifesaving work to continue. The skills that trauma had taught me, threat assessment, crisis planning, and the ability to function under pressure, had found their most meaningful application in service of those serving others.

By the time my Kenya deployment ended in late November, I had established security protocols that would protect humanitarian workers across the Horn of Africa for some time. But the personal price remained constant: each professional success extracted another piece of the life I'd once hoped to build, leaving me more skilled at managing crises than at preventing them in my own relationships. The journey from breakdown to breakthrough was proving to be less linear than I'd imagined; each step forward in professional competence seemed to require another step away from the possibility of ordinary human connection.

* * *

Famine's Shadow: Kenya, 2011 - Key Lessons Learned

Multi-Agency Security Coordination Is Essential

- Daily UNDSS briefings and interagency information sharing provided the only real-time common operating picture across Kenya, Somalia, Ethiopia, and Djibouti.
- Establishing formal channels with UNOCHA, UNHCR, WFP, and major INGOs ensured that movement plans, threat updates, and evacuation protocols were harmonized rather than duplicated or conflicting.

Context-Specific Risk Frameworks

- Diverse threats, ranging from banditry and cattle rustling in pastoral areas to political tensions in refugee camps and crime in Nairobi slums, cannot be adequately addressed by a single security policy.
- Security assessments must analyze local patterns (e.g. Al-Shabab infiltration routes into Dadaab) and adapt

protocols (e.g. curfew adjustments, convoy size limits) accordingly.

Contingency Planning for Slow-Onset Crises

· Unlike rapid natural disasters, the Horn-of-Africa famine evolved over months. Robust evacuation and communications planning must therefore account for sudden escalations, such as cross-border conflict spillover, as well as protracted insecurity.
· When disruptions in supply chains occurred, prepositioning alternative fuel sources, spare vehicle parts, and backup satellite communications proved critical.

Investing in Local Capacity and Training

· Requiring all Global Rapid Response Team members to complete enhanced Hostile Environment Awareness Training (HEAT) before deployment ensured both international and national staff understood kidnapping, siege, and extortion threats in the region.
· Developing a regional Security Awareness in National Theatres (SAINT) course empowered local humanitarian workers to assess everyday risks, such as vehicle ambushes and checkpoint bribes, without relying on external security contractors.

Balancing Duty of Care with Operational Reach

· Maintaining program presence in famine-affected areas required accepting calculated risks. Daily risk–benefit

87

analyses, grounded in real-time intelligence, enabled humanitarian teams to serve over 350,000 refugees in Dadaab without catastrophic losses.

- Over-securitization (e.g. limiting all movements to large convoys) can impede humanitarian access; under-securitization (e.g. ad hoc travel planning) endangers lives. A calibrated posture, guided by shared UN risk registers, struck the necessary balance.

The Personal Toll of Humanitarian Security Work

- High-stress coordination from Nairobi headquarters created a dissonance between the relative comfort of the capital and the desperation in the field, leading to compassion fatigue and moral injury among security staff.
- Regular psychological support, peer-to-peer debriefs, and mandatory rest rotations are as critical as physical security measures to sustain long-term effectiveness.

By embedding these lessons into standard operating procedures, training modules, and regional coordination mechanisms, humanitarian organizations can better protect both aid recipients and aid providers in protracted, slow-onset emergencies like the 2011 Horn of Africa famine.

11

Crossing Lines: Syria, 2013

Content Warning: This chapter contains references to active armed conflict, extremist groups including ISIS and Al-Qaeda, checkpoint negotiations with armed militants, civilian casualties, and humanitarian crisis situations that may be distressing to some readers. The content includes detailed accounts of operating in war zones and interactions with designated terrorist organizations. Reader discretion is advised.

The call came in early April, 2013, jerking me from the shallow sleep that had become routine during emergency deployments. World Vision's Global Rapid Response Team was activated for Syria in January 2013, and I was being deployed as the second wave of the response team to cover for the Field Security Advisor (FSA) while he went on R&R. This was April 2013, eighteen months into what had begun as peaceful protests against Bashar al-Assad's government and had devolved into a multi-sided civil war that was tearing Syria apart.

The deployment briefing revealed a stark reality: the conflict had already claimed over 70,000 lives, and millions more were either internally displaced or fleeing to neighbouring countries. World Vision's response was expanding rapidly from supporting Syrian refugees in Lebanon and Jordan to direct programming inside Syria itself, in the northern regions near the Turkish border where opposition forces maintained control. My mission was to manage security protocols for operations in one of the world's most dangerous environments, where the humanitarian space was shrinking daily and aid workers faced threats from multiple armed groups with competing agendas.

The flight from San José to Istanbul provided me with ample opportunity to scrutinize situation reports, which depicted an unparalleled intricacy. Unlike the relatively clear-cut scenarios I'd managed in Sudan, Haiti, or Kenya, Syria presented a kaleidoscope of armed actors, shifting alliances, and territorial control that changed daily. The Syrian government still controlled major cities like Damascus and much of the coast, but opposition forces held significant territory in the north, including key border crossings with Turkey that had become lifelines for humanitarian aid.

I landed in Gaziantep around 0200 on a mid-April morning in the Turkish city that had become the unofficial humanitarian capital for Syria operations. Barely 40 miles from the Syrian border, Gaziantep was where international organizations co-ordinated cross-border assistance to areas the Syrian government couldn't or wouldn't reach. The city's economy, once built on trade with nearby Aleppo, had been transformed by the influx of Syrian refugees and aid organizations, creating a strange parallel reality where humanitarian professionals worked in relative comfort while managing operations in zones of active conflict.

We had a limited time to prepare before our early morning departure. I barely had time to shower and review the latest security updates before joining the FSA and two program officers for the journey to the Syrian border. We drove south through the Turkish countryside toward Karkamis, a border town that faced the Syrian city of Jarabulus across a frontier that had become one of the most militarized and contested boundaries in the world.

The FSA gave me a quick overview of Karkamis before we crossed into Syria. The town had become a staging area for humanitarian operations, its position directly across from Jarabulus making it a crucial entry point for aid destined for northern Syria. But the situation was complicated by the fact that control of territory shifted constantly, and what looked secure on paper often proved dangerous on the ground. The border itself had been closed multiple times due to fighting, and even when open, crossings required careful negotiation with whoever happened to be controlling the checkpoints on any given day.

* * *

Before we crossed the border into Syria, one of our guides approached me with a concerned expression. "Do you have a jacket or long-sleeve shirt?" she asked, eyeing my arms with obvious worry. Not thinking before we left that morning, I had put on a short-sleeve shirt due to the oppressive heat. Having tattoos visible on my arms was not acceptable when entering Syria at that time, particularly given the conservative nature of the armed groups controlling the checkpoints we would encounter.

Unfortunately, I didn't have a long-sleeve shirt with me, but my partner had a long-sleeve raincoat that I could borrow. This was an exceptionally hot day, with temperatures reaching about 40 degrees Celsius, and here I was preparing to walk into Syria wearing a raincoat. For the entire day, I had to keep this sweatbox on, perspiring profusely while maintaining the cultural sensitivity required for our mission. The discomfort was intense, but the alternative, potentially offending armed checkpoint guards with visible tattoos, could have jeopardized not just our mission but our safety.

Border between Turkieye & Syria, Karkamis, Turkieye

After conducting careful analysis over the next few trips across the border with appropriately long-sleeved shirts, I determined that my tattoos were actually not offensive to the groups we were working with, so I could wear shorter sleeves on subsequent crossings. This small but significant learning experience highlighted the importance of understanding local cultural sensitivities while also demonstrating how initial assumptions about what might be problematic don't always prove accurate in practice.

* * *

At this time, there was no official Syrian government border checkpoint inside Syria. Instead, we faced three successive extremist group checkpoints, each manned by different factions with competing ideologies and territorial claims. The first

93

checkpoint belonged to the Free Syrian Army, the ostensibly moderate opposition force that had emerged from defecting Syrian military officers and had Western backing. The second was controlled by Al-Qaeda's Syrian affiliate, then known as Jabhat al-Nusra, which had established itself as one of the most effective fighting forces against Assad's government. The third checkpoint was manned by ISIS, the Islamic State of Iraq and Syria, which had recently emerged as a separate entity from Al-Qaeda and was beginning its campaign to establish a caliphate across Iraq and Syria.

Before gaining access to our programming sites in Jarab-ulus, we had to negotiate our way through each of these checkpoints. This required a delicate balance of diplomacy, cultural awareness, and calculated risk assessment that drew on every lesson I'd learned about operating in contested environments. Each group had different priorities, different rules of engagement, and different levels of hostility toward international humanitarian organizations. The Free Syrian Army checkpoints were generally the most accommodating, viewing humanitarian aid as legitimizing their claim to represent the Syrian people. The Al-Qaeda checkpoint required more careful navigation, with emphasis on our work serving Muslim populations and respect for local customs. The ISIS checkpoint was the most unpredictable, as the group was still defining its relationship with international aid organizations and foreign nationals.

During one of our border crossings, we experienced a significant delay at the ISIS checkpoint that led to an unexpected and profoundly impactful conversation. We had been waiting for

94

over an hour for clearance to proceed, and I found myself in discussion with one of the ISIS fighters, a large man wearing all black, with an imposing black beard and black kufi that marked his religious devotion. What began as a routine checkpoint interaction gradually evolved into a more substantive conversation about our work and presence in the area.

Somehow our conversation turned to World Vision being a Christian organization, a fact that could have created significant tension given ISIS's well-documented hostility toward Western and Christian entities. However, this fighter surprised me completely with his response. He expressed that he was actually happy that we were not proselytizing during our work inside Jarabulus, acknowledging that we were delivering on everything we said we would deliver and when we said we would deliver it. He had clearly been observing our operations and had formed his own assessment of our conduct and reliability.

His final words to me before we were cleared to leave were perhaps the most unexpected I heard during my entire Syria deployment: "Remember, at the end of the day, we are all under the same God." This statement absolutely shocked me, coming from a member of an organization that had become synonymous with religious extremism and violence against anyone who didn't share their interpretation of Islam. But I was deeply thankful to hear those words, as they suggested that even in the midst of the most radical ideological environment, there remained space for recognition of shared humanity and divine connection that transcended sectarian boundaries.

The negotiation process was exhausting and nerve-wracking. At each checkpoint, armed fighters would examine our documents, ask questions about our mission, and make decisions about whether to allow us passage based on criteria that weren't always clear. The hypervigilance that had once been a symptom of trauma became essential for reading the mood of different groups, assessing the genuine versus performative nature of threats, and determining when to be accommodating versus when to stand firm on operational requirements.

* * *

Over the course of my three-month deployment, we crossed into Syria no less than 30 times. Each crossing was a fresh negotiation, a new test of the relationships we'd built and the acceptance we'd earned. The routine became familiar but never comfortable: loading supplies in Gaziantep, driving to Karkamis, presenting documents and explaining our mission at each checkpoint, then navigating the bombed-out streets of Jarabulus to reach our programming sites.

Providing potable water to an IDP camp

12

Operations Under Fire: Syria, 2013 (Part II)

Content Warning: This chapter contains references to active armed conflict, direct death threats and kidnapping threats from terrorist groups, destruction of humanitarian infrastructure, personal loss and grief, and detailed accounts of operating under threat from ISIS and Al-Qaeda operatives. The content includes explicit threats of violence against humanitarian workers and descriptions of civilian displacement and suffering in war zones. Reader discretion is advised.

The Portable Medical Clinic Operation

One of our most complex operations occurred on June 25, when we coordinated the move of a Portable Medical Clinic (PMC) from Turkey to Jarabulus. This wasn't a routine supply delivery but a major infrastructure transfer that would significantly enhance World Vision's capacity to provide medical services to the displaced population. Unfortunately, the border crossing at Karkamis was not sufficient for this move due to the size and complexity of the equipment, so we had to coordinate the operation from the Çobanbey border crossing instead.

Portable Medical Clinic arriving at the Syrian border.

The PMC arrived in three separate parts mounted on three different trailers, requiring precise coordination and careful handling. At the border crossing, we had to transfer the PHC modules from Turkish trailers to Syrian-plated trailers, a complex logistical operation that required coordination with customs officials, transportation companies, and our security contacts on both sides of the border. The transfer process was tense, as any delay or complication could have jeopardized the entire operation and left expensive medical equipment stranded in a contested border zone.

Once the transfer was completed, the trucks entered Syria and had to navigate the dangerous journey from Çobanbey to Jarabulus, a route that took them through territory controlled by different armed groups and across areas that had seen recent fighting. The security implications were significant; losing the medical clinic to theft, destruction, or confiscation would have represented not just a financial loss but a devastating blow to our capacity to serve the medical needs of displaced families.

On June 27, accompanied by my valued colleague, our security analyst, we crossed into Syria to check on the status of the PMC and ensure that the installation was proceeding successfully. When we arrived in Jarabulus, it was a pleasant surprise to see that the clinic had already been assembled completely, both the medical modules and the washroom facilities, along with the generator that would provide power for operations. The efficiency with which our local partners had completed the installation was impressive and spoke to their commitment to serving their community despite the dangerous circumstances.

The finished PMC inside Jarabulus, Syria

An image we took of the team standing beside the completed PMC felt monumental, capturing not just a successful logistics operation but a moment of hope amid the devastation of civil war. Here was tangible evidence that international humanitarian assistance, properly coordinated and culturally sensitive, could deliver life-saving resources to people who desperately needed them. The medical clinic represented months of planning, significant financial investment, and considerable risk-taking by everyone involved in its delivery and installation.

Unfortunately, the fate of the PMC would illustrate the tragic unpredictability of working in active conflict zones. After we were asked to leave Jarabulus and our operations were suspended, about a week or two later, Jarabulus came under attack. Much of the infrastructure we had worked so hard to build was destroyed during the fighting, as far as we know, including the PMC. The medical facility that had represented hope and healing became another casualty of a conflict that seemed to consume everything constructive that tried to take root.

Personal Loss Amid Professional Duty

Personal tragedy also marked the deployment, reminding me of the costs of serving far from home during family crises. On June 13, during the middle of my Syria deployment, my grandmother passed away. The news reached me through a difficult phone call that highlighted the isolation of humanitarian work and the reality that life's most decisive moments often occur when we're thousands of miles away, focused on protecting others while unable to be present for our own families during their times of greatest need.

Missing my grandmother's funeral while managing security operations in a war zone created a complex emotional burden. The grief of loss was compounded by the guilt of absence, the knowledge that professional duty had prevented me from being where my family needed me most. However, the work in Syria felt indispensable, and the displaced families we assisted were enduring losses far surpassing my own. The balance between personal needs and professional obligations that defines humanitarian work was never more stark than during those June days, managing operations while processing grief across continents and time zones.

The programming sites revealed the human cost of this complexity. Opposition forces had taken Jarabulus in July 2012, and ISIS had taken control of it after multiple handovers throughout 2013. The population had been devastated by repeated battles, with many residents fleeing to Turkey and those remaining living under increasingly harsh restrictions imposed by ISIS rule. World Vision's programs focused on basic humanitarian needs: food distribution, medical assistance, and emergency shelter for internally displaced persons (IDPs) who had sought refuge in abandoned schools and other damaged buildings.

But acceptance in Syria's civil war was as fragile as it was essential. During what would prove to be our last mission inside Syria, we received a warning that changed everything. After months of successful operations and relationship-building, we were informed by our contacts that at the end of that day, our protection could no longer be guaranteed. The shifting alliances and territorial control that characterized Syria's conflict had finally caught up with us. What had once been a manageable security environment was becoming untenable, and the very groups that had provided our protection were now unable or unwilling to vouch for our safety.

The programming sites revealed the human cost of this complexity. Opposition forces had taken Jarabulus in July 2012, and ISIS had taken control of it after multiple handovers throughout 2013. The population had been devastated by repeated battles, with many residents fleeing to Turkey and those remaining living under increasingly harsh restrictions imposed by ISIS rule. World Vision's programs focused on basic humanitarian needs: food distribution, medical assistance, and emergency shelter for internally displaced persons (IDPs) who had sought refuge in abandoned schools and other damaged buildings.

At one of these sites, an abandoned school that housed dozens of displaced families, the gravity of our work became starkly apparent. During one of our regular delivery runs, a colonel with Al-Qaeda's local affiliate pulled me aside for what he called a "conversation." Speaking in broken English, he made his position unmistakably clear: World Vision had made promises about clean water to the families sheltering in the school, and failure to keep those promises would have consequences. "If you ever fail on a delivery promise," he said, his hand resting casually on his hip, "I will kidnap you personally."

This school was the IDP camp where I was threatened to be kidnapped

The threat was delivered matter-of-factly, without dramatics or raised voices, which somehow made it more chilling than theatrical intimidation would have been. This wasn't posturing or negotiation tactics; it was a simple statement of cause and effect in an environment where humanitarian aid had become entangled with territorial control, legitimacy, and the survival of armed groups that depended on maintaining credibility with local populations.

Working in this environment meant making daily decisions about acceptable risk versus operational impact. Every program activity had to be weighed against security implications, not just for international staff, but also for local partners and beneficiaries who would remain in the area long after we left. The skills that trauma had taught me about threat assessment and crisis management were essential, but they had to be applied in a context where the threats came not just from indiscriminate violence but from deliberate targeting of humanitarian workers by groups that viewed international aid as part of a Western conspiracy against Islam.

We built what we thought was a solid acceptance strategy with all three of the key armed elements inside Syria. Through careful relationship-building, cultural sensitivity, and con-sistent delivery of promised assistance, we had earned a degree of protection and freedom of movement that allowed World Vision's programs to operate effectively. The Free Syrian Army appreciated our work with displaced families; Al-Qaeda's affiliate valued our respect for Islamic customs and our focus on Muslim beneficiaries; even ISIS tolerated our presence as long as we operated within their interpretation of appropriate humanitarian activity.

But acceptance in Syria's civil war was as fragile as it was es-sential. During what would prove to be our last mission inside Syria, we received a warning that changed everything. After months of successful operations and relationship-building, we were informed by our contacts that at the end of that day, our protection could no longer be guaranteed. The shifting alliances and territorial control that characterized Syria's conflict had finally caught up with us. What had once been a manageable security environment was becoming untenable, and the very groups that had provided our protection were now unable or unwilling to vouch for our safety.

* * *

Final Night and Departure

The night before I departed from my deployment, I was able to attend a U20 World Cup football match between Colombia and El Salvador in Gaziantep. After months of managing security operations in one of the world's most dangerous humanitarian environments, sitting in a stadium watching young athletes compete felt surreal. The normalcy of the crowd, the excitement of the match, and the simple pleasure of being entertained rather than constantly assessing threats provided a brief respite from the intensity of the previous three months.

Last night in Turkey, FIFA U18 World Cup match

The football match served as a bridge between the world I
was leaving, one of checkpoints, armed groups, and constant
vigilance, and the world I was returning to, where the biggest
concerns were match outcomes rather than survival. Even
in that stadium, my hypervigilance remained active, as I
scanned for exits, assessed crowd dynamics, and maintained
the situational awareness I had honed during my deployment
in Syria.

I flew out on June 29 for home, carrying with me the complex
mixture of satisfaction and loss that characterized humanitarian work in conflict zones. We had successfully delivered
aid to thousands of displaced people, established medical
facilities, and built relationships that had enabled sustained

programming. But we had also been forced to abandon operations just as they were showing promise, leaving behind local partners and beneficiaries who would continue facing the same dangers we had escaped by leaving.

* * *

Other than my time in Haiti, the Syrian conflict was my second exposure to death and destruction on a massive scale, but this time it was human-caused rather than the result of a natural disaster. While the earthquake in Haiti was devastating, it was a natural occurrence: sudden, overwhelming, and devoid of malicious intent. Syria was different. The destruction I witnessed was deliberate, calculated, and ongoing. Buildings weren't just collapsed; they were targeted. Not only did circumstances force families to flee their homes, but neighbours who turned into enemies also drove them out. Children weren't just traumatized by disaster; they were growing up in a war zone where violence had become the norm.

The human dimension of the Syrian conflict was perhaps what affected me most deeply. In Haiti, I had worked to help people recover from catastrophe. In Syria, I was witnessing people who had lost not just their homes and livelihoods, but also their faith in the possibility of coexistence. The displaced families sheltering in the abandoned school weren't just waiting for the crisis to end so they could return home; many were beginning to understand that home, as they had known it, might never exist again.

The three-month deployment that lay ahead would test

everything I'd learned about humanitarian security in ways
that previous missions hadn't. Operating in a space where
humanitarian principles themselves were contested, where
neutrality was viewed with suspicion by all sides, and where
the mere presence of international aid workers could be used
as justification for violence against local populations was far
more challenging than the relatively clear-cut challenges of
natural disasters or even conventional conflicts.

As my time in Syria drew to a close, I recognized that this
deployment had profoundly transformed my perspective on
humanitarian work. The negotiated acceptance we had built
with armed groups, the constant threat assessments, and
the knowledge that our protection could disappear without
warning had forced me to confront the limits of security
management in environments where the humanitarian space
itself was under attack. The survivor had transformed into a
specialist, yet the complexity of human conflict had taught
me that even specialists could fall short.

* * *

Crossing Lines: Syria, 2013 - Key Lessons Learned

Acceptance Requires Genuine Engagement

- Humanitarian access in active conflict zones depends
  on carefully built, negotiated acceptance with all armed
  actors. In northern Syria, safe passage through three
  successive checkpoints, Free Syrian Army, Jabhat al-

Nusra, and ISIS, depended on demonstrating impartiality, cultural respect, and consistent delivery of aid.

Contextualized Security Protocols

- Standard security measures must be adapted to fluid multi-actor environments. Rigid, one-size-fits-all approaches fail when territorial control shifts daily and alliances realign unpredictably.

Operational Neutrality Is a Fragile Shield

- Neutrality must be actively negotiated and reaffirmed. Even groups ideologically opposed to Western aid tolerated CARE's presence only as long as our actions aligned with their political imperatives. That protection could be withdrawn without warning.

Local Partnership and Intelligence Are Essential

- Reliable security information came not from headquarters but from in-country staff and community contacts. Investing in trusted local networks provided real-time insights into fast-changing threats.

Psychological Resilience Underpins Operational Effectiveness

- Witnessing firsthand the trajectory of conflict, from peaceful protests to outright civil war, underscored the need for crisis managers to cultivate emotional regulation. Maintaining composure amid targeted threats

and moral dilemmas was as critical as physical security
measures.

Crisis Complexity Demands Integrated Responses

· Security, logistics, and program staff must coordinate
seamlessly. Aid deliveries hinged on synchronized checkpoint negotiations, route planning, and community out-
reach, all of which required joint planning between security and program teams.

Evacuation Plans Must Be Scenario-Based and Tested

· The warning that "protection could no longer be guaranteed" illustrated the need for robust, regularly rehearsed
evacuation protocols. Every security plan must include
clear criteria for suspension of operations and rapid
extraction routes.

Community Trust Amplifies Protection

· Demonstrating genuine concern for civilians, listening to
their needs, and involving them in distribution planning
built acceptance not only with armed groups but also with
local communities, strengthening our de facto security.

Reflection and Adaptation Are Continuous Endeavors

Every checkpoint negotiation and distribution mission
yielded new insights. Systematic after-action reviews
allowed the security team to refine protocols in real time,

ensuring learning translated into safer subsequent missions.

13

Conflict at the Core: South Sudan, 2014

⚠ STRONG CONTENT WARNING ⚠

This chapter contains graphic descriptions of mass casualties, ethnic violence and genocide, decomposing bodies, targeted killings based on tribal identity, child soldiers, forced displacement, and detailed accounts of civil war atrocities. The content includes disturbing imagery of death, destruction, and systematic targeting of civilians. This chapter discusses one of Africa's worst humanitarian crises with explicit references to ethnic cleansing and contains content that may be extremely distressing. Reader discretion is strongly advised.

If you are sensitive to graphic descriptions of violence, death, or ethnic conflict, you may wish to skip this chapter.

The call came in early December 2013, just as South Sudan was celebrating two years of independence from Sudan. Within hours, that celebration had turned to ashes as fighting erupted between forces loyal to President Salva Kiir and those supporting former Vice President Riek Machar. By the time I received my deployment orders in late December for a three-month assignment beginning in January 2014, the world's newest nation was tearing itself apart along ethnic lines that had been carefully managed during the long struggle for independence but now exploded into the open.

When I departed Costa Rica in mid-January 2014, it was summer in Central America, with temperatures in the high twenties and humidity that made even lightweight clothing feel oppressive. Living in Costa Rica's tropical climate had made me completely oblivious to the fact that it was winter in New York, where I had to change planes for my onward journey to South Sudan. I had not realized that I would also have to transfer terminals, assuming I would simply be doing a gate transfer within the same airport complex.

Not wearing winter gear or winter shoes, I was dressed for comfortable travel in what I thought would be climate-controlled airport environments. The weather in New York on this particular day found the entire region in the grip of a full-blown blizzard with frigid temperatures that cut through clothing like a knife. To make matters worse, I discovered that I had to take my two large bags out of the airport because I was changing airlines as well, which meant I had to collect my luggage, find transportation, and make my way to a completely different airport, from LaGuardia to JFK, for my outbound flight to London Heathrow.

Moving with all my gear through a New York blizzard while

wearing travel Crocs was certainly an adventure I hadn't anticipated. The snow was deep enough that it filled my Crocs with each step, my feet were numb within minutes, and I was dragging two heavy bags through conditions that would have challenged someone properly dressed for Arctic weather. Finding a bus that would take me between the airports in those conditions required waiting at exposed stops where the wind chill made the already frigid temperatures feel life-threatening.

This was different from my previous deployments. Syria had been a complex civil war, but it was still fundamentally about opposing political systems. South Sudan represented something more personal and more tragic: a liberation movement consuming itself, ethnic groups that had fought together against a common enemy now turning their weapons on each other, and the systematic targeting of civilians based solely on their tribal identity.

I arrived in Juba in mid-January 2014 and checked into the Keren Hotel, which had become the de facto headquarters for international humanitarian operations in the capital. The hotel, with its concrete walls and basic amenities, provided a strange sanctuary of normalcy in a city where the sound of gunfire had become routine. When I wasn't deployed to field locations, the Keren Hotel served as my base, a place where aid workers from dozens of organizations gathered each evening to share information, coordinate responses, and try to make sense of a crisis that seemed to defy all previous experience.

The briefings presented a stark picture. The first week of

fighting resulted in over 1,000 deaths and 100,000 displacements. The violence had spread from Juba to Upper Nile, Unity, and Jonglei states, with both sides engaging in targeted killings based on ethnicity. The Sudan People's Liberation Army, once a unified force that had fought for independence, had fractured along tribal lines, with Dinka units generally supporting Kiir and Nuer units backing Machar.

My first field deployment outside of Juba came fairly quickly, with travel to the northern state of Upper Nile and the town of Malakal. By January 2014, Malakal had already changed hands multiple times between government and opposition forces, with each exchange of control accompanied by systematic looting, burning, and killing. The town, once a vibrant commercial centre on the White Nile, was now largely abandoned; its population had fled to UN compounds, neighbouring countries, or the surrounding bush.

I stayed in Malakal within the UN compound, sharing the space with peacekeepers from the United Nations Mission in South Sudan (UNMISS) who were struggling to protect not just themselves but the thousands of civilians who had sought refuge at their base. The smell of death was everywhere from the moment I arrived until the time I departed. Bodies lay scattered along roads outside the compound, victims of the ethnic violence that had consumed the town. The stench was inescapable, a constant reminder of how quickly civilization could collapse when fear and hatred were unleashed.

I was in Malakal with two World Vision colleagues: our security analyst and the response team logistics director.

The security analyst and I had worked together on previous deployments and had developed the kind of professional trust that was essential in high-risk environments. The logistics director was responsible for ensuring that aid supplies reached their intended destinations despite the chaos of ongoing conflict.

As soon as we got off the plane at Malakal airfield, we were thrust into immediate operational work. A Non-Food Item (NFI) distribution was taking place close to the airfield, and we assisted in ensuring that displaced families received essential supplies like plastic sheeting, blankets, and hygiene kits. The distribution site was crowded with people who had lost everything, many carrying only the clothes on their backs after fleeing their homes during night attacks.

Distribution upon arrival to Malakal, South Sudan

After the distribution, we drove to the UN compound, but the journey illustrated the complex dynamics we faced in South Sudan. Some government soldiers wanted us to give them a ride in our World Vision vehicle. We had to politely but firmly explain that we could not transport them due to our commitment to SPHERE standards and the International Red Cross Red Crescent Code of Conduct, which required humanitarian organizations to maintain neutrality and independence from military forces. This wasn't just bureaucratic adherence to policy; in South Sudan's polarized environment, being seen to favour one side could result in our exclusion from areas controlled by the other faction.

The drive to the compound revealed the extent of the destruction that had befallen Malakal. Military vehicles lay wrecked along the roadside, testimony to the fierce battles that had raged for control of this strategic town. Bodies remained in the fields by the road, victims of the ethnic violence that had accompanied each change of control. The systematic nature of the destruction was evident: this wasn't collateral damage from military operations, but deliberate targeting of civilian infrastructure and populations.

Makeshift graveyard, bodies buried where they fell, Malakal,
South Sudan

During our stay in Malakal, we were tasked with visiting what
remained of the World Vision office to assess damage and
recover any salvageable assets. The office building stood as a
testament to the violence that had consumed the town. The
walls were riddled with bullet holes, and inside, the space
was completely trashed. Desks were overturned, computers
destroyed, and documents scattered across floors stained
with what might have been blood or simply the detritus of
urban warfare.

As we surveyed the destruction, one of our local staff members, who had managed to remain in Malakal throughout
the worst of the fighting, gestured for us to follow him to

a particular area of the office. He climbed onto a desk and reached up into the ceiling, carefully moving aside a ceiling tile. From this hiding spot, he pulled out a bag that contained our World Vision satellite phones and some hard disc drives containing critical operational data. It was a cunning and effective way to hide and secure some of our most valuable equipment during the chaos. The foresight of our local staff in protecting these assets before fleeing had preserved communication capabilities and program data that would be essential for resuming operations.

We were also tasked with recovering two World Vision boats that had been stolen and then abandoned at various locations along the White Nile River. In a region where roads were few and often impassable, boats were essential for reaching remote communities and delivering humanitarian assistance. The boats had been taken during the initial chaos but abandoned when their usefulness to the fighters proved limited. Finding and recovering them required careful negotiation with various military units and local commanders who might claim salvage rights or simply want payment for "protection services."

Rescuing WV Boats in Malakal, South Sudan

The recovery missions took us along stretches of the White
Nile that revealed both the beauty of South Sudan's landscape
and the tragic human cost of the conflict. Villages that should
have been bustling with activity stood empty, their populations having fled. Fishing nets hung unused while cattle
wandered unattended, their owners either dead or displaced.
The river that had once been a lifeline for commerce and
communication had become another front line in the ethnic
violence tearing the country apart.

During these operations, we encountered elements of the
White Army, the youth militia that had become one of the
most feared forces in the conflict. These were mainly young
Nuer men, often in their teens or early twenties, who had

been mobilized to fight against government forces. The name "White Army" came from their practice of covering their bodies with white ash, both as camouflage and as spiritual protection. They were feared by everyone, including the regular forces on both sides of the conflict, because of their reputation for brutal tactics and their willingness to fight to the death.

The White Army represented something particularly tragic about South Sudan's conflict: an entire generation of young men who had grown up knowing only war and displacement, first during the long struggle against Sudan and now in this internecine fighting. Many had been promised cattle, land, or other rewards for their service, but the reality was that they had become instruments of ethnic cleansing, carrying out some of the worst atrocities of the conflict. Encountering them required extreme caution, as their youth, drug use, and religious fervour made them unpredictable and dangerous.

We stayed in tents that we had brought from our base in Juba, setting them up within the secure perimeter of the UN compound. The compound itself was divided into different sections: the main UN operational area, our humanitarian working space, and adjacent to it all, a Protection of Civilians (POC) compound that housed thousands of displaced people. Initially, this POC site was occupied primarily by people from the Nuer tribe, who had fled government forces' ethnic targeting. But over the course of our stay, the population would change from Nuer to Dinka on a regular basis, reflecting the shifting control of territory outside the compound and the fear each group felt when the other was in power.

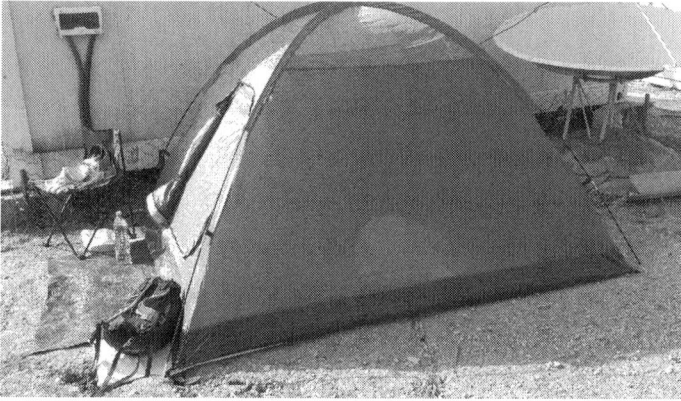

My home away from home, Malakal, South Sudan

During night attacks on the town, there were makeshift
bunkers that we would move to for protection. These were
basically holes in the ground covered by sheet metal, offering minimal protection from small arms fire and shrapnel
but providing some psychological comfort during the most
intense fighting. The sound of gunfire, mortars, and rocket-
propelled grenades would echo through the night, and we
would huddle in these crude shelters, monitoring radio communications and waiting for the all-clear.

At times, we would go out the next morning and assist
in transporting wounded soldiers to a location in Malakal
where Médecins Sans Frontières (MSF) was operating. These
missions required careful coordination with both sides of the
conflict, as wounded soldiers from opposing factions might be
brought to the same treatment facility. The medical neutrality
that MSF maintained was one of the few things both sides

respected, though even that would be tested as the conflict intensified.

Over the ten days we were in Malakal, we conducted security analysis and humanitarian assessments and assisted in many distributions, both food and NFI. The assessment work revealed the staggering scale of displacement and need. Entire communities had been uprooted, with many families separated during flight. Children arrived at the UN compound unaccompanied, having lost their parents in the chaos. The humanitarian response was overwhelmed by the speed and scale of the crisis, with agencies struggling to provide even basic services to the thousands seeking protection.

* * *

After completing our initial assessment in Malakal, I returned to Juba for a few weeks before being tasked to another location in Unity State called Nyal. Unity State had been particularly hard hit by the conflict, with the oil-rich region becoming a key battleground between government and opposition forces. Nyal, located in Panyijar County, had become a refuge for thousands of internally displaced persons who had fled fighting in other parts of the state.

Arriving in Nyal, South Sudan

In Nyal, I was paired with another World Vision logistics officer for what was planned as a joint NFI and food distribution operation with the World Food Programme (WFP). The mission represented the kind of interagency coordination that was essential in South Sudan, where no single organization had the resources to address the massive humanitarian needs alone. WFP would handle food distribution, while World Vision managed the non-food items like shelter materials, blankets, and hygiene supplies.

Again, we stayed in our tents within a secured compound. The security situation in Nyal was more stable than in Malakal, but the humanitarian conditions were arguably worse. The town had become a magnet for displaced populations from across Unity State, with over 25,000 people seeking safety in an area that lacked the infrastructure to support such numbers. Clean water was scarce, sanitation was nonexistent, and the risk of disease outbreak was constant.

126

People waiting to register for the distribution

Here we were managing the NFI distribution while WFP handled food deliveries. Our NFI supplies were arriving via WFP helicopters along with some food items that could not be airdropped. Most other food items were airdropped to a field next to the distribution site, a massive logistical operation that required precise coordination between aircraft crews and ground teams. Local nationals were responsible for running out to the field to bring in the 50-kilogram bags of rice and other staples, then sorting them for distribution.

WFP Airdrop, Nyal, South Sudan

Collecting the airdrop food, Nyal, South Sudan

Meanwhile, our NFI supplies were not arriving at the same
pace as the food. Supply chain management in South Sudan
was a constant challenge, with helicopter schedules depen-

dent on weather, fuel availability, and security conditions. We eventually had to stop the NFI distributions because we fell far behind the food distribution schedule. The situation was exacerbated by a high-profile UN visit that took priority for helicopter resources, redirecting aircraft that were supposed to bring in our supplies.

Beneficiaries queuing for NFI and Food distribution

While we were in Nyal, we received intelligence that there was a military unit very close to our location that wanted to seize the food that was being distributed. In South Sudan's environment, humanitarian aid had become a strategic resource. Armed groups understood that controlling aid distribution gave them leverage over civilian populations and could be used to demonstrate their ability to provide for people under their control.

Knowing that our location might be overrun at any time, I was not confident that the UN would have enough seats on their helicopters to evacuate all international humanitarian staff if the situation deteriorated rapidly. UN evacuation protocols prioritized their own personnel, and there were no guarantees that spaces would be available for other agencies' staff. Given this uncertainty, I made the decision to arrange for Mission Aviation Fellowship (MAF) to come in and evacuate our World Vision staff on the morning of the last scheduled day we were to be in Nyal.

Fortunately, this proved to be a sound decision. The military unit did make an advance on the food distribution site shortly after we were airborne. From the aircraft, we could see UN helicopters also starting to remove WFP staff, confirming that the threat had been real and immediate. It turned out that had we waited for the UN evacuation, we would not have been accommodated, as there were not enough seats on their helicopters for non-UN personnel.

* * *

My three months in South Sudan brought many other ad-ventures and challenges, but also the opportunity to work with some incredible people from World Vision. The local staff, in particular, demonstrated remarkable courage and commitment, continuing to serve their communities despite the personal risks they faced. Many had family members on different sides of the conflict, yet they maintained their professionalism and dedication to humanitarian principles.

Unlike my previous deployments to natural disasters or

130

even the Syrian conflict, South Sudan presented the unique challenge of working in an environment where the very concept of national identity was being contested through violence. The liberation movement that had united diverse ethnic groups in the struggle against Sudan had fractured along traditional lines, and the humanitarian community was trying to provide assistance in a context where neutrality itself was seen as suspicious.

By the time I departed South Sudan in March 2014, over 1 million people had been displaced and thousands killed. The humanitarian response had scaled up rapidly, but the needs continued to outpace capacity. The conflict would continue for years to come, eventually resulting in one of Africa's worst humanitarian crises and highlighting the fragility of post-conflict transitions.

The three months in South Sudan had tested everything I thought I knew about humanitarian security and crisis response. The skills that trauma had taught me about reading dangerous situations and managing under extreme stress had been essential, but they had to be applied in a context where the rules of engagement changed daily and where the line between helper and target could shift without warning. The survivor had become a specialist in navigating chaos, but South Sudan had shown me that some forms of chaos defied all expertise.

* * *

Conflict at the Core: South Sudan, 2014 - Lessons Learned

Understand the Local Context, Not Just the Headlines

- Conflict in South Sudan erupted along ethnic lines (Dinka vs. Nuer) rather than clear ideological or policy disputes, so any security planning must map shifting alliances and communal tensions.
- Liberation movements can fracture into internecine warfare, don't assume wartime camaraderie endures in peacetime deployment areas.

Prioritize Protection of Civilians in UN "Safe Zones"

- UN compounds and Protection of Civilian Sites become de facto sanctuaries; security protocols must guarantee sustained access, clear evacuation routes, and robust perimeter defences.
- Internally displaced persons (IDPs) may shift allegiances or demographics as front lines move; be prepared for camp populations to change rapidly, as Dinka and Nuer residents rotated through Malakal's POC site.

Recover and Secure Critical Assets Quickly

- Preposition sensitive equipment, satellite phones, data drives, and riverboats in hidden caches (e.g., ceiling hiding spots) to ensure communications and logistics capacity survive sudden evacuations.
- Organize small, specialized teams with clear roles: one

for asset recovery, another for security assessments, and a third for humanitarian distributions.

Develop Multi-Modal Evacuation Contingencies

- Plan for both air and river evacuation: secure agreements with Mission Aviation Fellowship for helicopter lifts and identify reliable boat captains for river exfiltration to neighbouring, safer states (DRC across the Ubangi River).
- Test evacuation routes under non-emergency conditions, e.g., reconnaissance trips to roads, airstrips, and river crossings, to validate feasibility under stress.

Coordinate Interagency Risk Management

- Security conditions change too quickly for any single organization to manage alone; integrate with UNMISS, UNDSS, WFP, and MSF for shared threat intelligence and movement controls.
- Agree on common communication channels and brief other agencies daily to synchronize evacuation plans, convoy escorts, and facility lockdown procedures.

Adapt Distribution Operations to Local Security Dynamics

- Joint NFI–food distributions with WFP require synchronized scheduling; when supply chain disruptions occur, consider temporarily suspending one stream to avoid crowd-control breakdowns or opportunistic theft by armed actors.
- Recognize humanitarian aid, food, shelter materials, and

medical supplies as strategic resources for both military
units and militias; reinforce distribution sites discreetly
and maintain procedural transparency to deter seizures.

Integrate Local Knowledge and Liaison

- Engage local security focal points and national staff in
  every step: their intimate awareness of military unit
  movements, militia behaviours (e.g., White Army tactics),
  and community trust is invaluable.
- Use culturally attuned acceptance strategies: respect
  local customs, negotiate with both formal security forces
  and informal militias, and leverage local relationships to
  legitimize humanitarian presence.

Emphasize Psychological Resilience and Staff Care

- Front-line security work exposes staff to traumatic
  scenes; prepare teams with stress-management tools and
  regular rotations out of high-intensity roles to prevent
  burnout and cumulative trauma.
- Build "safe havens" within compounds (e.g., improvised
  bunkers, relaxation spaces) and conduct daily check-ins
  to address mental health risks in real time.

Expect and Plan for Rapid Escalation

- Towns like Malakal and Nyal changed hands repeatedly,
  protocols must include immediate suspension thresholds
  for operations and clear criteria for when to evacuate or
  hunker down.

· Stay flexible: plans valid one week may be obsolete the next; maintain modular security frameworks that can be scaled up or down with minimal lead time.

Document and Review Rapidly

· After-action reviews should be conducted within days, not months, and capture lessons from each incident (e.g., successful asset recoveries, near-miss evacuations, security breaches) to refine protocols.
· Share these lessons across field locations; what worked in Malakal may be adaptable to Unity State or elsewhere, and integrate improvements into standard operating procedures promptly.

14

Bangui Under Siege: C.A.R., 2014

⚠ *EXTREMELY STRONG CONTENT WARNING* ⚠

This chapter contains graphic descriptions of genocide, ethnic cleansing, sectarian violence, mass murder of families, detailed accounts of a traumatized child orphan whose entire family was slaughtered before his eyes, active combat situations, and religious persecution. The content includes deeply disturbing imagery of systematic violence against civilians and may be extremely traumatic for readers. This chapter discusses one of the world's most severe humanitarian crises with explicit references to ethnic cleansing and contains content that may be profoundly distressing. Reader discretion is strongly advised.

If you are sensitive to descriptions of genocide, violence against children, family murder, or ethnic cleansing, you may wish to skip this chapter entirely.

In November 2014, I was tasked with a short three-week deployment to Bangui, Central African Republic. My role was to assist with a handover of security managers and develop a comprehensive evacuation plan for World Vision's operations in one of the world's most dangerous humanitarian environments. The Central African Republic had been convulsed by sectarian violence since December 2013, when the predominantly Muslim Séléka coalition had been overthrown by largely Christian Anti-balaka militias, triggering a cycle of reprisal attacks that had torn the country apart along religious lines.

The conflict represented a particularly tragic form of violence: what had once been a country where Christians and Muslims lived in relative harmony had become a battleground where religious identity determined who lived and who died. The Anti-balaka, whose name meant "anti-machete" or "invincible" in Sango, had emerged to counter the brutal excesses of Séléka forces, but their response had become equally savage, targeting Muslim civilians in revenge attacks that amounted to ethnic cleansing.

By the time of my arrival in November 2014, the statistics were staggering: over 1 million people had been displaced, thousands killed, and the country was effectively partitioned with Anti-balaka forces controlling the south and west while ex-Séléka factions held the north and east. The international community had warned of potential genocide, and French forces under Operation Sangaris, along with African Union peacekeepers and later UN forces, were struggling to maintain even basic security.

Arrival and Initial Orientation

After arriving at Bangui M'Poko Airport, I was met by my colleague, a World Vision security manager from France who had been managing operations in the volatile capital. The airport itself was surrounded by one of the largest internally displaced persons (IDP) camps in the region, with thousands of people living in makeshift shelters under the nominal protection of French peacekeepers. The juxtaposition was stark: international flights landing and departing while just beyond the runway, families who had lost everything struggled to survive in conditions that barely met basic humanitarian standards.

My French colleague took me on a comprehensive tour of the city and surrounding environment, showing me the division between different armed groups that had carved Bangui into religious and ethnic enclaves. The capital, once home to a mixed population of Christians and Muslims, has been transformed into a patchwork of segregated neighbourhoods, where crossing the wrong street could mean death. Churches had become refuges for Christians fleeing Muslim areas, while mosques sheltered Muslims terrorized by Anti-balaka militias.

The scale of destruction was overwhelming. Entire neighbourhoods had been burned to the ground; their residents were killed or fled. The few remaining Muslim enclaves were under siege, protected only by international peacekeepers who struggled to maintain security with inadequate resources. The Anti-balaka had effectively driven tens of thousands of

Muslims from areas they controlled, leading human rights organizations to describe the situation as ethnic cleansing.

Living Under Siege

The accommodation arrangements for international staff reflected the dangerous reality of working in Bangui. While the hotel provided basic security measures, its location in an area where violence erupted regularly and unpredictably was problematic. The hotel sat along the main street that became a frequent scene of armed confrontations between different militia groups, government forces, and international peacekeepers.

During my stay, there were several armed events where active shooting took place just outside my hotel room. The sound of automatic weapons fire, grenades, and rocket-propelled grenades would echo through the streets, sometimes lasting for hours as different factions engaged in firefights that showed little regard for civilian areas or international presence. The hypervigilance that had once been a symptom of my trauma became essential for survival, as I learned to distinguish between different types of weapons fire and assess whether the fighting was moving closer to or away from the hotel.

The environment in Bangui was very tense in the evenings, when most of the violence seemed to occur. Armed groups used the cover of darkness to move through the city, settle scores, and launch attacks on rival factions or civilian populations. The nights were filled with the sounds of gunfire, explosions, and occasionally the screams of victims caught in the crossfire. Sleep became fitful and shallow, interrupted by sudden bursts of violence that could signal immediate danger.

At one point during a particularly intense period of fighting, I made a call to my wife just to hear her voice. I wasn't sure if it would be the last conversation we would have. The isolation of being in such a dangerous environment, combined with the unpredictability of the violence, created a psychological pressure that was different from previous deployments. In Haiti, the danger had come from a natural disaster and its aftermath. In Syria and South Sudan, there had been clear front lines and identifiable threats. But in Bangui, the violence was random and sectarian and could erupt anywhere at any time.

Hearing my wife's voice on the phone provided a connection to normalcy and safety that felt essential for maintaining psychological balance. The conversation was brief; international calls were expensive and the connection unreliable, but it served as a reminder that there was a world beyond the violence, relationships that mattered, and reasons to be careful and return home safely.

At several times during my deployment, I could not get to the World Vision office due to active fighting in a field approximately 200 meters in front of the hotel. This open area had become a regular battleground where different armed groups would engage each other, sometimes for territorial control, sometimes simply as a result of chance encounters that escalated into violence. The field provided clear lines of sight for weapons fire, making it extremely dangerous for anyone attempting to cross during active fighting.

During one of these incidents, the hotel's security guard motioned for me to come to the security gate, indicating I should bring a chair with me. I wasn't sure why he was making this request, but having learned to trust the instincts of local staff who understood the environment better than any international visitor could, I complied with his instructions.

When I arrived at the gate with the chair, I discovered that the security guard was essentially treating the ongoing violence as a form of entertainment. He was watching a small battle taking place in the same field where fighting had previously prevented my travel to the office. A United Nations vehicle found itself trapped in the crossfire between opposing factions in the midst of this firefight.

Soldiers advancing past an unmarked grave, Bangui, CAR

The UN peacekeepers in the vehicle were unable to move forward or retreat without exposing themselves to direct fire from multiple directions. The sight was both tragic and surreal: representatives of the international community, present to protect civilians and maintain peace, had become targets themselves in a conflict that seemed to have no clear military objectives or strategic goals.

Recognizing the extreme danger of the situation and the inappropriateness of observing active combat as if it were entertainment, I immediately retreated back to my room. The incident demonstrated the normalization of violence in Bangui's daily life and the intricate challenges faced by international peacekeeping forces operating in a hostile environment.

The Turning Point

However, Bangui would prove to be a turning point in my life, where I experienced that profound "aha" moment that gave meaning to everything I had been working toward in my humanitarian career.

Around day four in the country, the most moving moment came during a food distribution at one of the IDP sites. Before the distribution began, we held a meeting with a local Imam who was explaining what was needed for the displaced Muslim families under his care. The conversation was routine, covering logistics, beneficiary numbers, and security protocols for the distribution.

During this conversation, a little boy, perhaps nine or ten years old, wandered over and quietly took my hand. He was wearing a dirty jalabiya, the traditional robe common in the region, and his eyes held a fearful expression that seemed far too mature for his age. Something about his presence, the way he clung to me without saying a word, made me interrupt the Imam to ask about the child's story.

The explanation that followed hit me like a physical blow. Three days prior, the very day I had arrived in Bangui, this little boy's entire family had been slaughtered before his eyes during one of the sectarian attacks that had become routine in the capital. For reasons unknown, perhaps his age or some moment of mercy from the attackers, he had been spared while watching his parents, siblings, and extended family murdered. He had wandered into the IDP camp alone, traumatized and silent, with nowhere else to go.

I nearly broke at that moment, feeling the full weight of what this conflict meant in human terms. This wasn't statistics about casualties or displacement numbers; this was a child whose world had been destroyed by hatred that he couldn't possibly understand. But I was able to hold it together, drawing on the professional composure that years of trauma and humanitarian work had taught me.

We were at the distribution for about six hours, and the entire time, this little boy remained by my side. He didn't speak, didn't ask for anything, and just stayed close as if my presence offered some small measure of safety in a world that had become incomprehensibly dangerous. I will never forget the image of him holding my hand as displaced families received their meagre rations of food and supplies.

It became a candid moment that I have cherished, captured in a photo of the two of us at the distribution. Looking at that photograph later, I could see in the boy's face all the reasons why humanitarian work mattered: the vulnerability that demanded protection, the innocence that deserved preservation, and the resilience that offered hope even in the darkest circumstances.

This particular moment brought everything into focus, more than any of my previous deployments through death and destruction in Sudan, Haiti, Kenya, Syria, and South Sudan. I finally realized not just what I was doing, but more importantly, why I was doing it in this career choice. The technical skills, security protocols, and operational expertise were all in service of moments like this, protecting the most vulnerable when their own world had failed them completely.

I am kneeling beside the young local boy, embodying compassion and solidarity in the midst of crisis during an emergency relief mission.

Professional Completion

After the distribution, my colleague and I proceeded to develop our evacuation plan, which evolved into a robust and comprehensive process that later proved its worth. The security situation in Bangui was deteriorating rapidly, with

145

fresh violence erupting regularly and humanitarian workers increasingly targeted by armed groups who viewed international aid as partisan. World Vision needed detailed
contingency plans for multiple scenarios: sudden escalation
of violence, direct threats to staff, complete breakdown of
government authority, or attacks on humanitarian facilities.

After a great deal of work and careful analysis of the operational environment, we visited the Democratic Republic
of Congo (DRC) embassy, which was conveniently located
next to the World Vision office. Through careful negotiation
with embassy officials, we were able to secure pre-approved
entry visas for all international World Vision staff arriving in
CAR. We located a boat and captain for emergency evacuation
across the Ubangi River, tested the route to the village of
Zongo on the DRC side, negotiated arrangements with the local convent for short-term housing, visited the Zongo airstrip,
and made arrangements with Mission Aviation Fellowship
(MAF) for potential air evacuation to Kinshasa.

Crossing the Zongo River on an exploratory mission, Bangui, CAR

The plan was used several years later with enormous success when the security situation in Bangui deteriorated to the point where international staff needed to be evacuated. After my replacement arrived, a seasoned security officer who had worked with me during the Haiti earthquake response, I departed Bangui for home to spend the remainder of the year with my family.

My three weeks in Bangui were among my shortest deployments, but they gave me the most insight into my professional purpose. In a city torn apart by hatred and violence, in a moment of connection with a child who had lost everything, I had finally understood that the path from personal trauma to professional competence wasn't just about survival; it was about using the skills that pain had taught me to protect others who were experiencing their own unimaginable losses.

* * *

147

Lessons from "Bangui Under Siege: C.A.R., 2014"

Accepting Protection through Partnership

- Humanitarian security relies on negotiated acceptance with local armed actors. Building relationships through respect for community grievance, transparent communication, and consistent delivery of assistance enabled safe operating space in a city fractured along religious and ethnic lines.

Psychological Safety in Unrelenting Violence

- Frequent nighttime firefights and armed confrontations underscored the need for both physical protection (fortified compounds, safe rooms) and psychological preparedness. Regular drills, access to mental-health support, and norms that acknowledged stress and trauma were essential to sustaining staff well-being under siege.

Creative Contingency Planning

- Establishing nontraditional evacuation routes, such as negotiating boat evacuations across the Ubangi River into the DRC, and securing embassy visas ahead of time proved critical when standard UN airlift capacity became overwhelmed.

Partnering with Local Staff to Safeguard Assets

- Local team members' ingenuity, like hiding satellite

148

phones and data drives above a bombed-out office, demonstrated the importance of empowering national staff to secure critical equipment and information during rapid departures.

Meeting Humanitarian Imperative in Extremis

· Under conditions of ethnic cleansing, maintaining aid distributions to IDP sites, even as sectarian militias threatened beneficiaries, reminded security managers that protection extends beyond staff: it's about safeguarding the lives and dignity of those who rely on assistance the most.

15

Earthquake Lessons: Nepal, 2015

The magnitude 7.8 earthquake that struck Nepal on April 25, 2015, became a defining moment in the country's modern history and a significant chapter in my own professional development. Nearly nine thousand people died, over twenty-two thousand were injured, and hundreds of thousands of structures were damaged or destroyed across central and eastern Nepal. World Vision declared a Category III Global Response the day after the earthquake, mobilizing surge capacity from around the world to support what would become one of the largest humanitarian responses in the organization's history.

By September 26, 2015, I received a call to help support the Response Security Director with some specialized tasks in Kathmandu. This would be a one-month deployment focused on conducting a five-day Security Risk Management (SRMT)course for local staff, while also assisting with security documentation and analysis. The timing was particularly challenging: Nepal was not only still recovering from the devastating earthquake and its major aftershocks but was also grappling with a border blockade imposed by India that had created severe shortages of fuel, food, and essential supplies.

The border blockade, which had begun on September 23, 2015, was one of the most significant challenges facing Nepal's recovery effort. India had imposed an unofficial blockade as a protest against changes to Nepal's new constitution, which had been promulgated on September 20, just days before the blockade began. The blockade was ostensibly led by Nepal's Madheshi ethnic minorities, who claimed the new constitution discriminated against them, but the Nepalese government accused India of orchestrating the restrictions.

For a landlocked country that imported virtually all of its petroleum products through India, the blockade was devastating. On a normal day, approximately 300 fuel trucks would cross from India into Nepal, but during the crisis, this dwindled to a sporadic flow of just 5–10 trucks per day. The shortage forced the government to implement an odd-even number plate system for vehicles, created massive queues at fuel stations, and sparked a black market where gasoline that normally cost 104 rupees per litre was selling for 300–450 rupees.

The situation was particularly cruel because it came just months after the April earthquake, severely hampering humanitarian efforts in the disaster's aftermath. Nepal's only international airport had to deny foreign carriers fuel, contributing to the country's isolation at a time when it desperately needed international support. Nothing could come in from the north either, as the passageway with China remained blocked due to earthquake damage to mountain roads and infrastructure.

I arrived in Kathmandu to find a city and country struggling with multiple simultaneous crises. The earthquake had destroyed much of Nepal's infrastructure, the blockade was preventing essential supplies from reaching those who needed them most, and the approaching winter threatened to create additional hardships for the millions of people still living in temporary shelters. The World Vision office was operating under enormous pressure, trying to maintain humanitarian programs while managing severe logistical constraints imposed by the fuel shortage.

* * *

During my month-long deployment, I was working alongside my boss, the response security director, as well as a new World Vision security analyst who was being introduced to the complexities of managing security in a post-disaster environment. The team dynamic was professional and collaborative, with each member contributing unique expertise to tackle the multi-layered challenges confronting the Nepal operation.

I assisted in delivering a five-day SRMT course to local staff, which aimed to offer security training specific to Nepal's unique operating environment. The curriculum covered threat assessment in post-disaster contexts, personal security awareness for humanitarian workers, emergency communication protocols, cultural sensitivity in security management, and evacuation procedures specific to Nepal's geography and infrastructure limitations.

The course took on added significance because of the blockade-related challenges. With fuel shortages limiting vehicle movements, communication systems stressed by increased demand, and supply chains disrupted, local staff needed enhanced skills to manage security risks while maintaining program effectiveness. The SRMT training placed a strong emphasis on adaptive security planning, alternative communication methods, and risk assessment frameworks that remained functional even in the face of disruptions to normal operating procedures.

The local staff brought valuable insights to the training, sharing their experiences of managing security challenges during both the immediate earthquake response and the ongoing blockade crisis. Many had family members affected by both disasters, yet they continued to serve their communities with remarkable dedication and professionalism. Their local knowledge and cultural understanding proved essential for developing security protocols that were both effective and culturally appropriate.

Handing out SRMT Certificates, Katmandu, Nepal

In addition to the SRMT course, I assisted with broader security documentation and analysis for World Vision's Nepal operations. This work involved updating security assessments to reflect the changing threat environment, revising standard operating procedures to account for blockade-related constraints, and developing contingency plans for different scenarios ranging from further escalation of the border crisis to potential renewed seismic activity.

The documentation process required careful analysis of how the blockade was affecting not just World Vision's operations but the broader humanitarian response across Nepal. With fuel shortages limiting field access, communication systems under strain, and supply chains disrupted, every aspect of humanitarian work required adaptation and innovation. The security analysis had to account for these operational constraints while maintaining focus on the primary mission of serving earthquake-affected communities.

At some point during this assignment, I had the opportunity to discuss professional development with my boss. The conversation turned to the Harvard Humanitarian Response Intensive Course (HRIC) that I had been researching as a way to enhance my understanding of emergency response coordination and multi-sector humanitarian action. My boss recognized the value of having World Vision represented at such a prestigious program, both for the learning opportunities it would provide and for the networking potential with other humanitarian professionals.

He authorized me to look into the HRIC program more deeply and start the process of enrolling for the April 2016 course. This was an exciting development that promised to bridge my field experience with academic frameworks for understanding humanitarian action. The timing seemed appropriate: after years of rapid deployment work across multiple crisis contexts, the Harvard course would provide an opportunity to step back and analyze lessons learned while preparing for future challenges.

* * *

I also assisted in two cash distributions during my time in Nepal, gaining direct experience with one of the most effective forms of humanitarian assistance in post-disaster contexts. Cash distributions were particularly valuable in Nepal's post-earthquake environment because they allowed affected families to prioritize their own most urgent needs while supporting local markets and economic recovery. The blockade made cash programming even more important, as it provided families with the flexibility to purchase whatever essential items were available in local markets.

The cash distribution work required careful coordination with local authorities, community leaders, and security forces to ensure safe and equitable distribution processes. With fuel shortages limiting transportation options and economic disruption affecting everything from banking systems to market supply chains, the logistics of cash programming were more complex than in typical post-disaster environments.

People queing for cash distribution, Katmandu, Nepal

The month in Nepal provided me invaluable information about how multiple crises intersect and compound each other's effects. The earthquake had created massive humanitarian needs, but the blockade was preventing the international community from effectively addressing those needs. Local communities were demonstrating remarkable resilience, but they were being tested by circumstances beyond their control. Humanitarian organizations, adapting their approaches, encountered constraints that questioned fundamental assumptions about aid delivery.

Working in Kathmandu during this period also highlighted the importance of local capacity and knowledge in humanitarian response. International surge capacity and expertise were valuable, but the crisis was ultimately being managed by Nepalese professionals who understood the cultural, political, and operational context in ways that international staff could never fully grasp. The SAINT training we delivered was as much about learning from local colleagues as it was about sharing external expertise.

By the time I completed my deployment in late October 2015, I had gained a deeper appreciation for the complexity of humanitarian work in politically contested environments. The earthquake had been a natural disaster, but the blockade was a human-imposed crisis that demonstrated how political decisions could multiply the suffering of disaster-affected populations. The experience would inform my future work and contribute to my preparation for the Harvard course that would take place the following spring.

The flight home from Kathmandu carried more than just professional satisfaction from a successful training delivery. It carried the weight of having witnessed a proud nation struggling against both natural disasters and political manipulation, as well as the inspiring example of humanitarian workers, both international and local, who continued serving others despite facing unprecedented challenges themselves. The lessons learned in Nepal would resonate throughout my remaining humanitarian career and beyond.

* * *

Key Lessons from the 2015 Nepal Earthquake Response

Build Trauma-Informed Security Frameworks

- Recognize compounding crises. The April quake and subsequent India-led blockade created simultaneous natural-disaster and man-made emergencies.
- Adapt risk assessments to intersecting threats (aftershocks, fuel shortages, civil unrest).
- Incorporate flexibility in evacuation plans when infrastructure and supply chains are disrupted.

Prioritize Local Capacity and Knowledge

- Engage Nepali staff in designing context-specific safety protocols; no outsider template fits every setting.
- Leverage community relationships to maintain access when external assistance is constrained by road blockades.
- Empower local teams through SAINT (Security Awareness in National Theatres) training that blends global best practices with Nepal's unique cultural and geopolitical landscape.

Integrate Cash-Based Assistance with Security Planning

- Cash distributions boosted local markets amid blockade-driven shortages but required meticulous crowd and site management.
- Coordinate closely with local authorities for secure, transparent beneficiary verification and disbursement proce-

dures.

- Anticipate secondary risks (theft, crowd crushes) by staggering disbursement times and reinforcing perimeter controls.

Leverage Regional Coordination Mechanisms

- Collaborate with UNOCHA and UNDSS equivalents to share real-time security updates and adapt standard operating procedures rapidly.
- Use joint planning with UN agencies (WFP-facilitated airlifts) to overcome fuel shortages and infrastructure damage.
- Establish cross-agency contingency plans for multi-modal evacuation (road, air, and river routes).

Turn Crisis into Professional Development

- Employ short-term surge deployments to blend field experience with training, and write after-action reviews that inform future response intensification.
- Use post-deployment periods (lockdowns, travel restrictions) to codify lessons learned into organizational security policies and training curricula, e.g., improving the intranet resource hub at WUSC.
- Invest in senior-level courses (e.g., Harvard's HRIC) to integrate operational insights with academic frameworks and apply them in complex emergencies.

Embrace Adaptive Leadership and Self-Care

- Recognize that heightened hypervigilance and crisis-mode dissociation, while protective in the field, must be balanced with psychological decompression at home.
- Institutionalize rest periods and peer support following intense deployments to prevent burnout and enhance long-term resilience.
- Foster leadership models that value vulnerability, lived experience, and trauma-informed decision-making as core security competencies.

These lessons from Nepal underscore the necessity of integrating trauma-informed approaches, local expertise, flexible logistics, and continuous learning into earthquake and compound-crisis responses. The alignment of security planning with culturally grounded practices and adaptive leadership ensures more resilient humanitarian operations in the face of multifaceted emergencies.

16

The Harvard Experience: Humanitarian Response Intensive Course

The invitation arrived by email while I was still rotating through aftershocks in Kathmandu. Between field assessments and security briefings, I had begun to speak with my response security director about professional development; World Vision wanted a senior deployer to "road-test" an academic course it was considering for future staff. We took advantage of the opportunity when Harvard University's Humanitarian Initiative opened registration for its two-week "Humanitarian Response Intensive Course (HRIC)." By February 2016 my place was confirmed.

In late April, I took a flight to Boston, leaving behind the high-country dust of Mali, where I was with my boss conducting another SAINT course, for the tranquilly of Cambridge, Massachusetts. Morning lectures were held in the T.H. Chan School of Public Health; afternoons were spent in breakout rooms wrestling with case studies on Goma, Darfur, and Syria. The participant mix was eclectic: new graduates eyeing humanitarian careers, a handful of U.S. Marines preparing for civil-military missions, logistics officers from Médecins Sans Frontières, and one slightly road-worn security adviser from World Vision. From the first introductions I realized my value to the cohort was practical experience: six years of rapid-onset deployments offered the lived examples the syllabus required.

Learning beyond the "security hat"

The curriculum was deliberately multidisciplinary. Core sessions covered rapid needs assessments, SPHERE minimum standards for shelter, WASH and food security, negotiation with armed actors, coordination architecture inside UN cluster meetings, and personal/team security in non-permissive settings. In the field, I had assumed most of those roles, but not all at once. The course compelled me to adopt a mindset that prioritizes response management over security, thereby broadening my understanding of the purpose of security: to facilitate humanitarian action, not to impede it.

Reviewing Programme Activities, Harvard

The three-day simulation

During the second week we moved to a lakeside reserve north
of the city for a 72-hour immersive simulation. Teams slept
under tarps, navigated mock checkpoints, bargained with
role-players posing as warlords, and improvised distributions while media crews demanded interviews. The scenario,
an earthquake compounded by conflict, felt eerily familiar,
echoing Haiti and South Sudan. Yet the controlled chaos
allowed reflection in real time: Where had I over-secured
an operation in the past? When had I under-consulted the
community? By the final after-action review, I had a clearer
framework for balancing duty of care with operational reach.

164

Simulation planning, Harvard

Networking and shared purpose

Evenings back in Harvard Yard became town-hall sessions where marines asked how to read an MSF security incident report and NGO staff debated whether SPHERE's food basket still made sense for urban crises. I shared stories of Malakal bunkers and Bangui hotel firefights; in return I absorbed logistics tricks, cash-transfer lessons, and a marine colonel's primer on air-bridge planning. The cross-pollination was precisely what my supervisor had hoped World Vision would harvest.

A reaffirmed mission

Early May graduation resulted in a certificate, but the most
profound insight was a renewed understanding of the importance of wearing multiple roles. First-wave deployers must
switch from assessor to negotiator to trainer in the same 24-
hour period; HRIC distilled the theory behind those pivots
and validated the improvisation that fieldwork demands. The
course also broadened my appreciation of SPHERE; seeing
it taught by its authors revealed nuances I had missed while
thumbing the handbook in disaster zones.

HRIC Class 2016, Cambridge, Mass

* * *

The Regional Circuit

The Harvard experience launched what became an intensive period of professional development that would reshape my understanding of institutional security management. Following graduation from HRIC, I travelled directly to Santo Domingo for the Regional Meeting for Corporate Security for LACRO (Latin America and Caribbean Regional Office). The contrast between Harvard's academic environment and the operational realities discussed in the Dominican Republic was striking.

The Santo Domingo meeting brought together security managers from across World Vision's Latin American operations to share lessons learned, standardize protocols, and prepare for emerging threats. The region faced unique challenges, including natural disasters, criminal violence, migration crises, and political instability, all of which created complex operating environments. My recent experience at Harvard proved immediately relevant, as I could translate the theoretical frameworks we'd studied into practical applications for the specific contexts discussed by my regional colleagues.

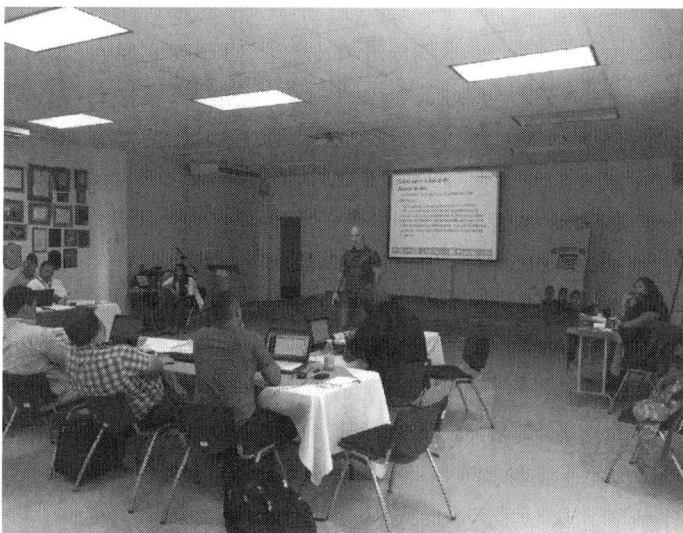

Sharing knowledge in Santo Domingo, DR

From Santo Domingo, I proceeded to Haiti for the Security
Awareness in National Theatres (SAINT) course, returning
to the country where my rapid deployment career had begun
six years earlier. We drove from Santo Domingo to Port-au-
Prince, which took approximately 8 hours with two hours
crossing into Haiti. The SAINT course was created to give
staff working in dangerous areas training that is specific to
their country, mixing basic security ideas with important information about local dangers, cultural factors, and practical
limitations.

Near the Dominican Republic–Haiti border

Being back in Haiti for professional training rather than emergency response provided a different perspective on the country and my own professional development. Port-au-Prince bore scars from the 2010 earthquake but had also shown remarkable resilience and recovery. The SAINT course utilized local case studies and real-world scenarios from Haiti's complex security environment, including gang violence, political unrest, natural disasters, and the challenges of operating in areas with limited government presence.

Global Convergence in Cyprus

In early June, I flew to Cyprus for the Global Corporate Security Meeting, where World Vision's security professionals from all regions converged to share best practices, discuss emerging threats, and develop standardized approaches to institutional security management. Cyprus, strategically located at the crossroads of Europe, Africa, and Asia, offered neutral ground for discussions that spanned multiple continents and conflict zones.

The Cyprus meeting was the capstone of this intensive professional development period. Armed with fresh insights from Harvard's academic approach, regional perspectives from Santo Domingo, and country-specific knowledge from Haiti, I was able to contribute meaningfully to global discussions about security policy, training standards, and operational procedures. The convergence of field experience and academic learning proved invaluable in these high-level strategic discussions.

The three consecutive training experiences, Harvard University's academic rigour, regional operational focus, and global strategic planning, represented a comprehensive professional development cycle that prepared me for the next phase of my humanitarian career. Each built upon the others, creating a foundation of knowledge and networks that would prove essential as I transitioned from purely operational deployments to more strategic security management roles.

By the time I returned home from Cyprus in mid-June, I

carried not just certificates and training materials but a transformed understanding of how academic theory, regional operations, and global strategy are interconnected in modern humanitarian work. The Harvard experience had been the catalyst, but the full journey through Santo Domingo and Haiti to Cyprus had created a comprehensive framework for the challenges ahead.

Little did I know that the Cyprus trip would be my last trip with World Vision.

*My final departure with World Vision, leaving Cyprus not
knowing this was my final trip*

17

When Old Wounds Resurface

The professional development circuit that culminated in Cyprus represented the peak of my World Vision career, but it also preceded my most devastating professional collapse. What I didn't share in those strategic discussions about security policy and training standards was that I was privately battling a resurgence of addiction long forgotten, one I thought I'd conquered years earlier.

In "A Soldier's Cry," I wrote extensively about how military sexual trauma had created patterns of self-satisfaction that followed me long after leaving the Forces. The hypervigilance, emotional numbing, and persistent anxiety that defined my CPTSD had made pornography an appealing escape during the darkest years of the 1990s and early 2000s. I'd believed that finding purpose in humanitarian work had finally given me the tools to manage those impulses constructively.

* * *

The Neural Pathways of Survival

In "A Soldier's Cry," I chronicled how military sexual trauma
had rewired my brain's threat detection systems, creating
neural pathways for self-satisfaction that could lie dormant
for years before stress reactivated them. What I hadn't fully
understood then was how these pathways functioned like
underground rivers, invisible during calm periods but capable
of flooding everything when the psychological water table
rose too high.

The accumulated weight of six years protecting others in
crisis zones had finally overwhelmed the coping mechanisms
that humanitarian purpose had strengthened but never fully
healed. Each deployment had added layers: the smell of
death in Malakal, the sound of mortars in Syria, the sight
of a traumatized child in Bangui, and the constant hypervigilance required to keep others safe while managing my own
fragmented psyche.

The addiction that emerged wasn't recreational or hedonistic;
it was medicinal, a desperate attempt to quiet a nervous
system that had been running on combat settings for so long
it had forgotten how to downshift. The addiction did not
numb success or allow avoidance of responsibility; instead,
it treated symptoms for which there were no other available
remedies in a humanitarian sector that celebrated resilience
but seldom acknowledged the psychological costs of repeated
trauma exposure.

What "A Soldier's Cry" had taught me about institutional

174

responses to trauma proved painfully prophetic. The military viewed my multiple sexual assaults as a threat to unit cohesion instead of recognizing them as a crime that needed justice, while World Vision regarded my addiction as a liability to be eliminated rather than a symptom that required treatment. The pattern of institutional abandonment that had begun in 1989 was repeating itself in 2016, proving that even organizations dedicated to helping vulnerable populations could be remarkably unsympathetic when their own staff became vulnerable.

One institution rejected the boy for his brokenness, and another rejected him for his breakdown. But this time, I had twenty-seven years of survival experience, a clearer understanding of trauma's trajectory, and the knowledge that institutional failure didn't define personal worth. The setback was devastating, but it wasn't terminal; it was just another chapter in a story that had been teaching me about resilience since 1989.

* * *

But the accumulated stress of six years of rapid deployments, constant exposure to human suffering, and the psychological toll of living with persistent hypervigilance had gradually worn down my defences. The very trauma responses that made me effective in crisis zones, the ability to compartmentalize emotions, to function under extreme stress, and to maintain operational focus despite personal cost and also made it easier to hide when I began struggling again.

The addiction wasn't about recreational use or poor judgment; it was about managing a nervous system that had been rewired by both military sexual trauma and years of humanitarian exposure to violence. When the hypervigilance became unbearable and the accumulated images of human suffering overwhelmed my psychological defences, addictions offered temporary relief from symptoms for which there was no other effective treatment.

World Vision discovered my relapse shortly after the Cyprus meeting, and their response was swift and unforgiving. Despite seven years of exemplary service, the security protocols I'd developed, and the lives I'd helped protect, the organization terminated my employment without consideration for the underlying trauma that drove my addiction or the possibility of rehabilitation.

The institutional response was strikingly similar to the pattern of abandonment I'd experienced in the military, dismissing my military sexual trauma instead of addressing it. Once again, an institution I'd served faithfully chose to discard me rather than confront the complexity of trauma's long-term effects. The betrayal cut especially deep because humanitarian organizations were supposed to understand vulnerability and human suffering.

The termination triggered a cascade of shame, rage, and despair that threatened to unravel everything I'd built since leaving the military. The professional identity I'd constructed as a competent humanitarian security specialist crumbled overnight, replaced by the familiar labels of "damaged," "unreliable," and "liability." The Avenger alter, dormant during my successful World Vision years, roared back to life with a fury that demanded justice for this latest institutional betrayal.

But the addiction itself was just a symptom, a maladaptive coping mechanism for managing trauma that had never been properly treated, only temporarily controlled through purpose and professional success. The military sexual trauma that had shattered my sense of safety and trust in institutions continued to influence my neural pathways decades later, creating vulnerabilities that stress and exposure could reactivate without warning.

Losing World Vision felt like losing everything I'd built to prove my worth after military betrayal. The Harvard certificate, the training expertise, the relationships with humanitarian professionals, all of it seemed meaningless when reduced to the stigma of addiction. Yet this devastating setback would eventually become another chapter in the ongoing story of survival, adaptation, and the stubborn refusal to let institutional failures define my ultimate trajectory.

The boy broken by military sexual trauma had become a man whose professional competence couldn't fully shield him from trauma's persistent effects. But he would also become someone who understood that recovery isn't linear, that setbacks don't negate progress, and that true resilience lies not in avoiding falls but in learning to rise again each time.

* * *

End of Part II Summary

Into the Fire (2011-2016)

Six years of deploying to the world's most dangerous places had transformed me from a competent security manager into a specialist whose expertise was sought by the humanitarian sector's most demanding organizations. From Kenya's coordination centres to Syria's contested checkpoints, from South Sudan's ethnic warfare to the Central African Republic's sectarian violence, each crisis added layers to my professional competence and personal trauma inventory.

The journey through Harvard's academic halls to Cyprus's strategic meetings marked the peak of institutional recognition, a broken veteran now teaching security protocols to the world's leading humanitarian organizations. I had achieved everything the 1989 version of myself could never have imagined: respect, expertise, and the knowledge that my wounds had become wisdom capable of protecting others.

Yet even as I mastered the art of safeguarding humanitarian workers, I remained unable to protect myself from trauma's persistent effects. The hypervigilance that saved lives in conflict zones, the emotional compartmentalization that enabled clear thinking under fire, and the accumulated weight of human suffering witnessed across continents, all of it had been slowly overwhelming defences I thought were permanent.

The institutional betrayal that ended my World Vision career proved that recovery isn't linear, that professional success can't fully heal complex trauma, and that the organizations dedicated to helping the vulnerable can be remarkably un-forgiving when their own staff become fragile. But it also revealed something else: that true resilience isn't about avoiding falls; it's about learning to rise each time, carrying new wisdom from the wreckage.

III

The Ripple Effects and New Purpose (2016–Present)

The collapse of my World Vision career marked not an ending but a transformation. Stripped of institutional identity yet armed with hard-won expertise, I discovered that true resilience lies not in avoiding falls but in how we rise. These years brought new organizations, deeper understanding of trauma's persistence, and the gradual recognition that my greatest contribution might not be protecting others in crisis zones but teaching them to protect themselves while honouring their own wounds.

18

Emergency Response with IRC

Content Warning: This chapter contains graphic descriptions of suicide bombings, terrorism, human remains from explosive attacks, kidnapping and recruitment of children by terrorist groups, active insurgency violence, and detailed accounts of living under constant threat of terrorist attacks. The content includes disturbing imagery of bomb scenes and may be distressing to readers sensitive to terrorism, violence, or descriptions of death and injury. Reader discretion is advised.

About a month after my role with World Vision ended in July 2016, I received a call from the International Rescue Committee (IRC) about a position as an Emergency Safety and Security Coordinator within their External Emergency Roster. The timing couldn't have been better; I was still processing the abrupt end of my six-year tenure with World Vision's Global Rapid Response Team and wondering where my specialized skills would find their next application.

This position seemed perfect for me, drawing directly on my

years as a response security advisor across multiple crisis contexts. The IRC had a different organizational culture than World Vision, with a more secular humanitarian mandate and a reputation for operating in some of the world's most challenging environments. Their approach to emergency response emphasized rapid deployment, technical expertise, and the ability to work in contexts where other organizations might withdraw.

I conducted two telephone interviews in August 2016, speaking with senior management about my experience in Syria, South Sudan, the Central African Republic, and Nepal. The interviews revealed that IRC was specifically seeking someone who could establish security frameworks from scratch in active conflict zones, manage complex threat environments, and coordinate with military and peacekeeping forces, exactly the skill set I'd developed over the previous six years.

In September, I contracted with IRC and had to travel to their headquarters in New York City to complete my onboarding and meet the management team I would be working with. Several floors of a Manhattan high-rise housed the IRC office, a stark contrast to the field environments where the organization conducted its actual work. The juxtaposition was familiar: humanitarian headquarters located in comfortable Western cities coordinate responses to crises in regions that their donors would never visit.

Working directly with the Director of the Emergency Response and Preparedness Unit, I was able to learn more about IRC's organizational structure and what would be expected of me in this new role. IRC's approach to emergency response was more centralized than World Vision's, with rapid deployment teams that could be mobilized within 72 hours for sudden-onset crises or deteriorating security situations.

I met with other new hires during my time in New York, including logisticians, program managers, and technical specialists who would form the pool of surge capacity for IRC's global operations. The networking opportunities proved valuable; humanitarian work often depended on personal relationships and professional trust built during brief encounters like these.

* * *

Deployment to Nigeria's Epicentre

Shortly after returning home from New York, I received the call I'd been expecting: a deployment to Maiduguri, Nigeria, in support of IRC's response to the Boko Haram crisis. On September 28, 2016, I departed for this three-month deployment, leaving my wife behind to set up our new home in Kitchener with our dog, Moses. The timing was particularly challenging; we'd just moved to a new city, my wife was adjusting to life in Canada after years of my deployments, and now I was immediately heading to one of the world's most dangerous humanitarian theatres.

Maiduguri, the capital of Borno State in northeastern Nigeria, had become the epicentre of a humanitarian response to one of the world's most brutal insurgencies. Boko Haram, whose name roughly translates to "Western education is forbidden," had been terrorizing the region since 2009, but their campaign had intensified dramatically after 2013. By the time of my deployment, the conflict had displaced over 2 million people, created a massive humanitarian crisis across the Lake Chad Basin, and turned Maiduguri into a fortified city under constant threat.

During this deployment, I was responsible for managing and implementing IRC's safety and security policies during the emergency response. This meant adapting organizational protocols developed for different contexts to the specific realities of operating in an active insurgency zone where suicide bombings, kidnappings, and armed attacks were daily threats.

Daily security briefings were like morning prayers. Maiduguri, Nigeria

I was also responsible for implementing security plans and Standard Operating Procedures (SOPs) that could protect international and national staff while maintaining operational access to affected populations. This required constant coordination with Nigerian military forces, UN security personnel, and other humanitarian agencies operating in the region. The challenge was balancing duty of care for staff with the operational imperative to reach communities that desperately needed assistance.

Working in collaboration with the Deputy Director of the Emergency Response, I adapted IRC's organizational security policies and procedures to the specific contexts we faced in northeastern Nigeria. This wasn't a matter of applying templates but of understanding how Boko Haram operated, how Nigerian security forces responded, and how the civilian population had adapted to living under constant threat.

In addition to security management, I was responsible for organizing flights to our operational areas and developing route management plans for road movements. Maiduguri's location in the heart of Boko Haram territory meant that normal transportation methods were often impossible or prohibitively dangerous. Most travel to field locations required military escort or UN-managed transportation systems.

* * *

Living in a City Under Siege

I was based at the Dujima International Hotel for the duration of my stay in Maiduguri, working out of the IRC offices in the city. The hotel had become an unofficial headquarters for the international humanitarian community, with aid workers from dozens of organizations sharing meals, information, and the psychological burden of working in such a challenging environment.

Some of our response staff eventually moved from the hotel to the IRC guest house, a more permanent arrangement for those whose deployments extended beyond the initial emergency phase. The guest house offered more privacy and better facilities, but it also meant greater isolation from the broader humanitarian community that the hotel environment provided.

The city itself bore the scars of years of conflict. Military checkpoints punctuated every major road, buildings showed damage from various attacks, and the constant presence of armed security forces created an atmosphere of vigilance that never entirely relaxed. Yet life continued, markets operated, children attended school when possible, and people demonstrated the remarkable resilience that characterized communities living under persistent threat.

This mission included field visits to Monguno, north of Maiduguri, where we had to travel by World Food Programme (WFP) helicopters. The pilots were usually Russian contractors with extensive experience flying in conflict zones and a dark sense of humour, which helped manage the stress of operating in dangerous airspace. During a particularly bumpy flight, one pilot cheerfully suggested, "If a problem occurs with the helicopter, no problem, vodka is on board!" The gallows humour was typical of humanitarian aviation, where professionals used laughter to cope with risks that were very real but rarely discussed publicly.

Sitting on the helicopter to Monguno, Nigeria

The helicopter flights to Monguno revealed the scale of displacement caused by Boko Haram's campaign. From the air, we could see abandoned villages, burnt structures, and the geometric patterns of refugee camps that had sprung up

190

around areas still under government control. The landscape told the story of a population in flight, seeking safety wherever Nigerian military forces could provide some measure of protection.

Other field visits required road travel to Konduga, southeast of Maiduguri. These road trips required UN armed escort, highlighting the security challenges of humanitarian work in active conflict zones. What I found iconic was the disparity in protection levels: the UN peacekeepers were heavily armoured and wearing helmets and body armour in vehicles designed to withstand IED attacks. Meanwhile, we humanitarian workers wore normal clothing with no personal protective equipment, protected only by the assumption that our civilian status and humanitarian mandate would shield us from targeting.

This disparity reflected ongoing debates within the humanitarian community about the balance between security and access. Some argued that a militarized appearance compromised humanitarian neutrality and increased the likelihood of targeting aid workers. Others contended that basic protective equipment was a reasonable precaution in environments where the distinction between civilian and military targets had largely collapsed.

* * *

Living with Suicide Bombings

During my deployment, we experienced two suicide bombing attempts that brought the reality of Boko Haram's tactics into sharp focus. The first occurred very close to a petroleum storage location, executed using a tuk-tuk as the delivery vehicle for the explosive device. This suicide bombing killed 3 people and injured several others, highlighting the group's strategic thinking in targeting infrastructure that could create secondary explosions and maximum psychological impact.

Driving by the scene shortly after the attack and seeing the fresh carnage of human remains was a visceral reminder of how close death lurked in Maiduguri. The twisted metal of the tuk-tuk was scattered across the road, mixed with debris that had moments before been a bustling area of civilian activity. The smell of smoke and something more disturbing hung in the air while emergency responders worked to clear bodies and treat the wounded. Being so close to this event, close enough that we could have easily been caught in the blast had our timing been slightly different, brought home the arbitrary nature of survival in a city under siege.

Terrorism was real and present, remains of a tuk-tuk, Maiduguri, Nigeria

The randomness was perhaps the most unsettling aspect. We had no tactical reason for avoiding that location at that moment, nor was there any superior security planning or threat assessment that protected us. It was simply timing, luck, and the unpredictable patterns of urban movement that had kept us alive while others died. This proximity to sudden, violent death created a psychological burden that accumulated over time, a constant awareness that each day survived was a gift rather than a guarantee.

The second incident was even more disturbing: a young person attempted to run into an internally displaced persons (IDP) camp wearing an explosive vest. The individual was shot by security forces before he could jump the wall into the camp, but the incident revealed Boko Haram's willingness to target the most vulnerable populations, people who had already lost everything and were depending on humanitarian assistance for survival.

These incidents weren't just security events to be managed; they were reminders of the human cost of the conflict and the moral complexity of humanitarian work in such environments. The young person who attempted to attack the IDP camp was likely a victim himself, recruited or coerced by Boko Haram through methods that included kidnapping, indoctrination, and psychological manipulation. The security forces who shot him were protecting innocent civilians but were also killing someone who might have been as much a victim as a perpetrator.

The psychological impact of living with such incidents was cumulative and profound. Each bombing attempt, whether successful or not, reinforced the reality that our security depended on variables beyond our control: the effectiveness of Nigerian security forces, the tactical decisions of Boko Haram commanders, and the random factors that determined whether threats materialized into actual attacks.

Working in Maiduguri also meant confronting the intersection of humanitarian need and military strategy. IRC's programs served populations that Boko Haram was actively trying to terrorize and control. Our food distributions, medical services, and protection programs were not just humanitarian activities; they were part of a broader struggle over whether civilian populations could survive in areas contested by the insurgency.

* * *

194

The three months in Nigeria provided valuable experience in managing humanitarian security in an active insurgency context, but it also added another layer to the accumulated trauma of my humanitarian career. Maiduguri was different from Syria, South Sudan, or the Central African Republic; the threats were more immediate, the operational space more constrained, and the psychological pressure more intense.

By the time I completed the deployment in late December 2016, I had successfully established security frameworks that enabled IRC's programming to continue, but I had also absorbed another dose of the violence and desperation that characterized the world's most challenging humanitarian environments. While the survivor continued to specialize, each new context brought its own psychological burden, contributing to the collection of images, sounds, and experiences that would resurface in quieter moments for years to come.

In Maiduguri I also conducted a two-day security risk management course for the IRC response team. We had a tight-knit group whose cohesion formed almost instantly under pressure: our response director, who was rigorously security-conscious; a Scottish colleague whose razor-sharp wit and humour kept us grounded; and dedicated national staff who brought deep local knowledge. The training reinforced not only technical risk management skills but also the importance of trust and camaraderie when every decision could mean life or death.

19

When Institutions Fail Again

After my deployment ended in early December, I returned to Canada and awaited my next assignment. Without a standing salary when not deployed, I needed another contract quickly. To my surprise, the Director of the Emergency Response and Preparedness Unit called with glowing feedback: my work had strengthened the team's security posture and delivered real value. He offered me a full-time role with IRC's Emergency Response team, which I eagerly accepted. He promised to follow up in a few days with details.

The absence of the call devastated me. The "Avenger" alter in my DID system surged to the surface, fueled by betrayal reminiscent of past institutional let-downs. The repeated terrorist attacks I'd survived in Syria, South Sudan, and Nigeria replayed in my mind, triggering renewed hypervigilance, anger, and despair. The failed offer felt like another ambush, not of the physical kind I was trained to repel, but a personal breach of trust. For days I oscillated between grief and rage, confronting the painful reminder that even the organizations I served could abandon me in my moment of need. Nevertheless, as always, I drew on my training to ground myself, channelling the Avenger's fury into renewed determination to identify my purpose and a place where my expertise would be valued.

* * *

When the Avenger Emerges

The terrorist attacks I experienced during my deployment in Nigeria reactivated trauma responses that I believed I had learned to manage. Each suicide bombing attempt didn't just threaten my physical safety; it triggered the hypervigilance and dissociative episodes that had defined my struggle with Complex PTSD and Dissociative Identity Disorder since my military sexual trauma in the 1980s.

In "A Soldier's Cry," I wrote about how institutional betrayal[1] had fractured my sense of self, creating protective alters that emerged when I felt most vulnerable. The "Avenger" was one of these parts, born from the rage I couldn't safely express when my own military system failed to protect me from sexual assault. While other parts of me learned to survive through compliance or withdrawal, the Avenger held my fury, my sense of injustice, and my refusal to accept betrayal quietly.

The constant threat environment in Maiduguri had kept the

---

[1] A Soldier's Cry, Ch. 6 on institutional betrayal in the Forces

Avenger at the forefront. Every checkpoint negotiation, every security briefing about potential attacks, and every night falling asleep to the sound of distant gunfire reminded my nervous system that danger was everywhere and institutional protection was unreliable. The Avenger's hypervigilance, which had once been a symptom of trauma, became operationally useful; I could assess threats faster, react to danger more quickly, and maintain the constant alertness that kept me and my colleagues alive.

But when the IRC job offer vanished without explanation[2], the Avenger fully emerged. This was not merely a professional setback; it was yet another instance of institutional betrayal. An organization I'd served faithfully, whose mission I believed in deeply, had dangled hope and then withdrawn it without even the courtesy of an explanation. The pattern was devastatingly familiar: serve the institution, trust the system, and then watch it abandon you when convenient.

The Avenger's response was immediate and overwhelming. Where my adaptive parts might have rationalized the situation or blamed myself for misunderstanding, the Avenger knew exactly what this was: another powerful institution treating me as expendable. The rage was clean and focused, not the confused shame of my early trauma responses, but the crystalline anger of someone who had learned to recognize betrayal and refuse to accept it silently.

For days, I oscillated between the Avenger's fury and other

---

[2] A Soldier's Cry, Ch. 6 on institutional abandonment

aspects of my system as I attempted to manage the emotional turmoil. The Avenger sought to reveal IRC's unprofessional behaviour, insist on responsibility, and resist abandonment after years of faithful service. Other parts of me recognized that such responses might damage my reputation in the humanitarian community and limit future opportunities.

This internal struggle reflected the ongoing challenge of living with DID in professional contexts. The same psychological fragmentation that had helped me survive military sexual trauma and rebuild my life also complicated how I processed setbacks and betrayals. The Avenger's protective rage served a purpose; it prevented me from accepting mistreatment passively, but it had to be channelled constructively rather than destructively.

The Nigeria deployment had ended successfully by every professional measure. I had protected the team, established effective security protocols, and contributed meaningfully to IRC's humanitarian mission. But the institutional betrayal that followed reminded me that no amount of competent service guaranteed institutional loyalty. The Avenger understood this reality in ways my more hopeful parts struggled to accept.

As I waited in Kitchener for the next opportunity, I carried both the professional satisfaction of another successful deployment and the renewed recognition that my relationship with humanitarian institutions would always be complicated by my history of institutional betrayal. The Avenger remained vigilant, ready to protect me from the next disappointment,

while other parts of my system focused on finding organizations that might prove more reliable partners in the work that
still called to me.

The survivor was continuing to specialize, but the specialist was learning to protect himself not just from external
threats but also from the institutional abandonment that
could wound him as deeply as any physical danger he'd faced
in the world's conflict zones.

20

When Words Become Weapons

The "Avenger" had been dormant for months, contained by the structured demands of humanitarian work and the careful therapeutic boundaries I'd learned to maintain. But losing my position at World Vision had torn open wounds I thought had scarred over, and in the aftermath of that institutional betrayal[3], familiar fury began to stir. The feeling wasn't the clean anger of righteous indignation; the sensation was the primal rage of abandonment, the same volcanic emotion that had sustained me through the darkest years after military sexual trauma when the world felt designed to crush anyone who dared to be vulnerable.

Not long after my termination and a couple of weeks back in Canada, still living in a hotel with my wife, I found myself sitting across from a former colleague in a Guelph restaurant, while the sting of institutional rejection still burned fresh. We had worked together during my South Sudan deployment, and

---

[3] A Soldier's Cry, Ch. 6 on institutional abandonment

he had reached out during one of my brief returns to Canada, curious about my experiences and eager to hear the stories that had accumulated across my years of crisis response.

Over lunch, I found myself sharing tales that even I sometimes struggled to believe: negotiating with armed groups at Syrian checkpoints, evacuating staff from collapsing operations in South Sudan, managing security during Haiti's earthquake response, and navigating the complex politics of humanitarian access in some of the world's most dangerous places. Each story seemed to captivate him more than the last, and as our conversation stretched into the afternoon, he leaned forward with an intensity that caught my attention.

"You need to write about this," he said, his voice carrying the conviction of someone who had recognized something significant. "These stories, these experiences you've lived through, people need to hear them. The humanitarian sector needs to hear them."

The seed he planted that afternoon took root during my deployment with CARE International to the Syria response. During quiet evenings in Amman and Beirut, when the day's security assessments concluded and the crisis's weight temporarily eased, I found myself revisiting his suggestion. The memories of my humanitarian career played through my mind like scenes from someone else's life: the little boy in Bangui whose family had been murdered, the sound of mortars in Malakal, and the complex negotiations required to deliver aid in contested territories.

I began researching how to create a blog, learning about platforms and formats with the same methodical approach I had applied to security planning. The technical aspects were easy to grasp, but the emotional preparation proved to be more challenging. Writing about trauma, institutional failure, and personal resilience would require a level of vulnerability I had spent decades learning to control and compartmentalize.

When I eventually launched the blog, the response surpassed my initial expectations. Colleagues from across the humanitarian sector reached out with encouragement and recognition. Other veterans shared their own struggles with transition and institutional disappointment. The stories resonated with people who understood the psychological toll of serving in crisis zones and the complex challenge of carrying that experience back into civilian life.

The early posts flowed naturally: recounting the technical challenges of establishing security protocols in post-earthquake Haiti, analyzing the lessons learned from managing evacuations in South Sudan, and reflecting on the cultural sensitivity required for effective humanitarian work in diverse contexts. These were professional stories told with personal insight, drawing on experience while maintaining appropriate boundaries.

But as the chronology of my writing approached my years with World Vision, something shifted. The institutional betrayal I had experienced wasn't just professional disappointment; it was a wound that connected directly to my military sexual trauma, triggering the same patterns of abandonment and

rage that had nearly destroyed me decades earlier. The
"Avenger," that protective alter born from institutional betrayal, began to stir with increasing intensity.

* * *

When I finally began writing about my World Vision experience, the careful professional boundaries I had maintained
throughout the earlier posts began to collapse. The "Avenger"
had awakened with a vengeance, and what should have been
reflective analysis became targeted attacks on individuals
who had been colleagues, mentors, and professional partners.
Names were mentioned. Specific incidents were described
with a level of detail that served no constructive purpose
beyond inflicting maximum damage. Blog posts, which
resembled revenge fantasies more than professional reflection, destroyed years of accumulated trust and professional
relationships.

The damage was swift and devastating. Colleagues, who
had previously supported my career and appreciated my contributions, suddenly faced public criticism for institutional
decisions or policies they had not initiated. Mentors who
had invested in my professional development discovered
their private conversations and professional guidance twisted
into evidence of systemic failure. Professional relationships
that had taken years to build were destroyed in weeks of
angry writing that served no purpose beyond feeding the
"Avenger's" insatiable appetite for retribution.

The humanitarian sector is smaller than it appears from the

outside. Professional networks overlap, reputations matter, and trust forms the foundation of operational effectiveness. By severing ties with my World Vision colleagues, I also jeopardized my relationships with professionals from various organizations, who would carry their perceptions of my character and judgment into future situations. The blog posts didn't just attack specific individuals; they established a pattern of professional behaviour that would follow me throughout my career.

The moment of recognition came gradually, like emerging from a dissociative episode to discover the wreckage left behind. Reading my own words with growing horror, I realized that the "Avenger" had hijacked not just my blog but my professional identity. The same protective mechanism that had helped me survive military sexual trauma was now destroying the civilian career I had built through years of competent service and careful relationship-building.

The work of regaining control required the same therapeutic techniques I had learned for managing other aspects of my Complex PTSD and Dissociative Identity Disorder. I had to acknowledge the "Avenger's" purpose, protecting me from further institutional betrayal, while also recognizing how that protection had become destructive. It wasn't wrong to feel anger; World Vision's termination after years of exemplary service was truly unfair. However, expressing that anger through personal attacks on former colleagues was both morally wrong and self-destructive from a professional standpoint.

Undoing the damage proved more difficult than causing it. A direct apology and acknowledgment of my mistakes could repair some professional relationships. Others were permanently severed, casualties of trauma responses that I hadn't managed effectively enough to prevent collateral damage. Several colleagues responded to my attempts at reconciliation with grace and understanding, recognizing that the person who wrote those bitter posts wasn't the professional they had known and worked with. Others, understandably, couldn't separate my trauma responses from my character and chose to maintain distance for their own protection.

The most painful aspect of this period was not the significant professional consequences, although they were considerable. It was the recognition that I had become the kind of person I despised: someone who used their platform to hurt others, who allowed personal pain to justify causing professional harm, and who had lost sight of the values that should guide both humanitarian work and human interaction. The "Avenger" had protected me from vulnerability, but in doing so, it had also protected me from accountability, empathy, and the possibility of genuine healing.

* * *

Learning to manage the "Avenger" became a crucial part of my ongoing therapy work. This wasn't about suppressing legitimate anger or accepting institutional mistreatment passively. It was about finding ways to channel protective instincts constructively rather than destructively, to advocate for systemic change without attacking individuals, and to maintain professional relationships even when processing personal disappointments.

In these two books, I've found a more constructive way to acknowledge my DID and various personalities. Upon abruptly terminating and erasing the blog from the internet, I realized the anger-fueled posts had caused more harm than beneficial effects. The blog's removal became a catalyst for transformation: I channelled that frustration into sharing lessons learned, advocating for stronger support systems for trauma survivors in humanitarian work, and demonstrating how professional setbacks can be addressed without destroying the relationships that supply our lives meaning and stability. Yet the memory of those turbulent weeks remains a permanent reminder that, left unchecked, trauma responses can undermine both our purpose and our most important connections.

This experience taught me something crucial about the long-term management of Complex PTSD and DID in professional contexts. Recovery isn't linear, and the protective mechanisms that enable survival in some contexts can become destructive in others. The "Avenger" that had helped me survive military sexual trauma and institutional abandonment was powerful enough to destroy my civilian career if I didn't maintain conscious awareness of when it was emerging and why.

The humanitarian sector's eventual acceptance of my return to professional effectiveness required both time and evidence of changed behaviour. Organizations like CARE International and eventually WUSC were willing to work with someone who had demonstrated both competence and fallibility, but only after I had shown that I could manage my trauma responses without causing harm to colleagues or operations.

Writing about this period remains one of the most difficult aspects of my recovery journey. The shame of having hurt people who didn't deserve it, of having used my platform irresponsibly, and of having allowed trauma responses to override professional judgment, these memories carry a different kind of pain than the original trauma itself. They represent choices I made, however unconsciously, rather than violations imposed upon me.

This chapter also discusses redemption, the idea that even our worst mistakes can teach us if we examine them honestly. Authentic knowledge of my character, including its flaws, strengthened the relationships that survived this period. The professional success that followed was more meaningful because it was earned through demonstrated growth rather than just technical competence.

The "Avenger" remains part of my psychological landscape, but it no longer controls my professional choices. Learning to recognize its emergence, understand its purpose, and channel its protective energy constructively has become an ongoing practice rather than a one-time achievement. The boy broken by institutional betrayal had learned to survive, but the man rebuilding his career had to learn when survival mechanisms were helping and when they were hindering.

This period taught me that healing trauma isn't just about individual recovery; it's about learning to manage our responses in ways that serve both our own well-being and our relationships with others. The most effective trauma survivors aren't those who never struggle; they're those who struggle consciously, who take responsibility for the impact of their responses, and who commit to doing better even when doing better is difficult.

The bridges I burned during this period were casualties of trauma responses I hadn't yet learned to manage effectively. But the recognition of that damage, the work of making amends where possible, and the commitment to preventing similar harm in the future became foundations for a more mature approach to both healing and professional service. Occasionally our greatest failures become our most important teachers, if we're brave enough to learn from them.

21

Resolute Return: Syria with CARE, 2017-2018

After the disappointment with the IRC, I kept searching for work in the NGO sector, where my skills in humanitarian security could still make an impact. The job hunt was complicated: most of my network and resources were connected to my years overseas, and after working abroad so long, I wasn't even eligible for Canadian social assistance.

Before my next longer-term opportunity materialized, I took a one-month contract with Food for the Hungry based in Les Cayes, Haiti, managing security for cash distributions that stretched along the coast all the way to Les Anglais. Cash distributions are always challenging from a security perspective, especially in areas of extreme poverty where the sight of money can quickly attract unwanted attention or create dangerous crowd dynamics. My final task with Food for the Hungry was to bring in my replacement, so I reached out to one of my former security officers from World Vision. During our handover period, we conducted a course on managing security risks for the local team, ensuring they had the tools and knowledge to manage future distributions safely. I have always had a soft spot for Haiti; with all of its problems, it is a beautiful country.

The Regional Security Director for CARE International, based in Jordan, called me in March 2017. He told me they needed a response security manager for their Syria operations, a three-month deployment based out of Amman. I accepted that same month.

My task was clear: conduct security risk assessments and analysis for CARE's partner organizations working inside Syria. For the next three months I rotated between Jordan and Beirut, Lebanon, meeting partners who operated cross-border into areas of Syria still under varying degrees of conflict and control. Every assessment meant gathering information in a fluid environment, balancing the operational need to reach communities with the very real threats of armed actors, bombings, and shifting front lines.

One of the greatest privileges during this deployment was reconnecting with former colleagues who had watched my journey from Khartoum to South Sudan to Bangui. Their genuine appreciation for the presence and expertise I brought to the security sector reinforced the value of our shared commitment. It was gratifying to hear veteran aid workers say that my guidance, born of both trauma and experience, had become a stabilizing force in their own operations, proof that the bonds forged through service transcend organizational lines and crises.

Despite the intensity of the assessment and planning, I made a point to savour Jordan's remarkable heritage. Over weekends, I explored Petra's rose-red canyons, marvelled at Wadi Rum's sweeping desert vistas, and wandered the ancient ruins of Amman, each site a testament to civilizations that thrived amid adversity. During my deployment, I arranged for my wife to join me for a week. Together we traced history's footsteps through Jerash and Petra, then spent an unforgettable night under Wadi Rum's starlit sky. These moments of wonder reminded me why balance matters, grounding me amid the relentless demands of crisis response. During my wife's visit in March 2018, we were also blessed to visit the baptismal site of our Lord Jesus at Bethany Beyond the Jordan, a profoundly spiritual experience that deepened our appreciation for the region's enduring faith heritage.

Placing our hands in the location where our Savior, Jesus was baptized, Bethany, Jordan

My wife and I at Petra, Jordan

When my initial rotation ended, I returned to Canada for a short break, but CARE called again within weeks with a second assignment. This time, I returned to Syria's orbit with one key goal: build security risk management capacity for local partners inside the country.

Back in Amman and Beirut, I met again with familiar faces, including a former Global Rapid Response Team colleague from World Vision who was now working for another organization in the Syria response. Together, we decided to tackle a persistent problem: each INGO and local partner had its own security documentation and formats, meaning I was constantly rewriting risk assessments for essentially the same context. We worked on harmonizing security risk

214

management planning across multiple organizations so that, at least in Jordan, everyone was working from the same page.

After a couple of months, CARE assigned me to an entirely different front, Syria's northeast. In late 2017 I flew to Istanbul, then onward to Cizre near the Turkish–Iraqi border. From there, I taxied to the actual crossing point into Iraq, transferring into another vehicle that took me to Dahuk in the Kurdish Region of Iraq. I stayed overnight before continuing on to the border with Syria, a modest river crossing. Once I crossed, I was inside northeastern Syria in a small village called Derek.

That month based in Derek was one of the more unique chapters of my security career. We visited multiple locations along the Turkish border, including Qamishli, Kobane, and other remote towns where partner organizations worked within earshot of sporadic armed clashes. My work there focused on direct partner support, reviewing site-specific threats, adjusting evacuation plans, and mentoring local security focal points who would remain long after I left.

The statue honoring Arin Mirkan, Kobane, Syria

When my one-month rotation ended, I handed over to my replacement, another former World Vision colleague, this one from Australia, and retraced my steps back to Canada along the same route I had entered.

* * *

After a couple of weeks' rest back home, CARE contacted me again. My final deployment with them would be based in Gaziantep, Turkey, a familiar base for Syrian cross-border operations. Joined again by my Australian colleague, I delivered training sessions for partner organizations on security risk management, policy creation, and standard procedures tailored to Syrian contexts. We made sure partners had the documents and knew how to use and adapt them, which was vital in Syria.

Later, during my Gaziantep posting, CARE organized a team excursion to Halfeti, where we boarded a small boat on the Euphrates. Drifting past partially submerged Roman ruins at the easternmost edge of an empire, I felt history's sweep colliding with modern turmoil. The gentle lapping of water and smell of citrus groves on the riverbank offered a rare pause, an opportunity to regroup, recharge, and reaffirm the deeper purpose driving my work even in the most challenging environments.

That month in Gaziantep closed my time with CARE International. It had been a string of demanding, complex deployments in one of the most politically tangled and dangerous humanitarian theatres in the world. The experience deepened my capacities in "partnership-based security," teaching me that the real legacy of a security advisor isn't the risk matrix you leave behind; it's the confidence, knowledge, and practical tools you help build in the people who will keep working long after you've gone.

This chapter of my career was not just another deployment; it was a sustained opportunity for growth, a test of my ability to shift from direct oversight into capacity building. And in that shift, I found a new kind of satisfaction in the work, helping others become resilient protectors in their own right.

* * *

A Soldier's Cry: The Legacy That Returned

As I closed out my final deployment with CARE International, I recognized how deeply my original journey, the trauma and survival detailed in "A Soldier's Cry," continued to shape my approach in Syria. The same vigilance, skepticism of authority, and empathy born from military betrayal were assets now, informing not only how I assessed threats but also how I mentored and protected. What I once considered weakness or a burden had become indispensable to building local partner confidence in the face of constant risk.

Every conversation with a Syrian colleague struggling with anxiety or survivor's guilt reminded me of those early post-military years. I knew the language of trauma because I had lived it: the disbelief, the isolation, and the long wait for institutions to admit responsibility. In those moments, my ability to listen, validate, and model psychological safety mattered just as much as any security plan or risk assessment.

The soldier broken by silence hadn't just survived; he'd learned to help others reclaim their own voices after tragedy. By teaching resilience and honest vulnerability alongside security practice, I extended the mission begun in "A Soldier's Cry": to break isolation, challenge institutional indifference, and embody hope for those still living through the aftermath.

In Syria's shifting landscape, this was the final lesson: trauma does not just isolate; it connects and strengthens if shared. My legacy, now, wasn't just the risks managed or the missions completed, but the encouragement given to those fighting for their communities' future and the ongoing work of turning wounds into wisdom.

22

Peace Walls: West Bank Deployment, 2019

Following my deployments with CARE International in the Middle East, I found myself back in Canada facing a familiar challenge: translating specialized humanitarian security skills into civilian employment. I took a job as a driver for a local startup company in Kitchener, a position that paid the bills but left me feeling disconnected from the work that had given my life meaning for over a decade.

* * *

An Unexpected Call

In early December 2018, my phone rang with a number I didn't recognize. The voice on the other end identified himself as a programme executive with the World Council of Churches (WCC). The call came completely out of the blue; I'm still not sure how they obtained my contact information, but it felt like a lifeline thrown to someone who had been treading water in civilian mediocrity.

The World Council of Churches operates one of the most significant ecumenical programs in the Holy Land through their Ecumenical Accompaniment Programme in Palestine and Israel (EAPPI). Founded in 2002 in response to a call from the Heads of Churches in Jerusalem, this program brings international volunteers from over 20 countries to serve as "Ecumenical Accompaniers" for three-month terms throughout the West Bank, including East Jerusalem. The WCC's mission in the region centres on witnessing life under occupation, engaging with local Palestinians and Israelis, pursuing just peace, and working to change the international community's involvement in the conflict. Their work involves monitoring human rights violations, providing protective presence at checkpoints and areas of friction, and supporting local peace initiatives while maintaining a continuous presence of 25-30 accompaniers on the ground.

The opportunity was short but intriguing: a three-week deployment to Jerusalem to assist with setting up security protocols for the WCC's regional operations. The work would also involve supporting these ecumenical volunteers based throughout the West Bank, many of whom worked in volatile areas with minimal security support. Since 2002, over 1,500 international volunteers had served in this capacity, and the program had grown to become the WCC's flagship project in addressing the Israeli-Palestinian conflict. After months of driving delivery routes through Kitchener's suburban streets, the prospect of returning to meaningful fieldwork that would directly support people engaged in peace-building and human rights monitoring felt like oxygen to someone who had been holding their breath.

I was honoured to receive the call and decided to take three weeks of vacation from my mundane driving job to get back in the field and do what I loved. In early January 2019, I arrived in Jerusalem eager to start fieldwork once again, knowing that I would be contributing to a program that had been providing protective presence and advocacy for justice in one of the world's most complex conflict zones for nearly two decades.

* * *

Immediate Immersion

I met with the field security officer for WCC, and we immediately began developing security plans and comprehensive security risk assessments for the Jerusalem office. The work was familiar yet challenging, creating protocols that could protect international staff and local volunteers operating in one of the world's most politically complex environments.

During those three weeks, I was able to visit several field locations, including Nablus, Jericho, and Hebron. Each location presented unique security challenges, from navigating checkpoint protocols to understanding the complicated relationship between different communities living in close proximity under tense circumstances.

222

Hebron was the most challenging location we visited. It was deeply saddening to witness firsthand the effects of settlers taking over Palestinian properties and the daily confrontations that resulted. Watching families being accosted in their own neighbourhoods, seeing children walking to school under military escort, and observing the systematic erosion of normal community life was profoundly disturbing. This trip definitely had an eye-opening effect on me and fundamentally changed my perspective on the Israeli-Palestinian conflict.

During this assignment, I also assisted with developing a comprehensive security training package for new volunteers coming into the country. The WCC brought volunteers in cohorts throughout the year, and each group needed orientation not just to the political and cultural context but also to the specific security protocols that would keep them safe while serving in such a volatile environment. Drawing on my years of training development with World Vision and other organizations, I was able to create modules that balanced practical security awareness with cultural sensitivity.

I also had the honour of taking part in a volunteer transition ceremony, which united outgoing volunteers who had completed their service with newly arriving cohorts. These ceremonies were deeply meaningful, representing both the continuity of the WCC's mission and the personal transformations that occurred when people chose to serve in such challenging circumstances.

* * *

Moments of Historical Reflection

During one of my few free days, which were rare given the intensive nature of the deployment, the Executive Director took me to visit the historic site of Masada. Having watched the movie "Masada" in the 1970s, I was captivated by the story of Jewish resistance against Roman occupation, making this a truly unforgettable experience. Unfortunately, the cable car lift wasn't operational that day, which meant we had to make the arduous climb up the serpentine path on the eastern side of the mountain fortress, the same route ancient defenders would have used. The physical challenge of ascending the steep, rocky trail in the desert heat only intensified the connection I felt to this historic site.

Massada, Israel

Standing on those ancient ramparts, looking out over the Dead Sea, I found it surreal to see the massive earthen siege ramp the Romans had constructed on the western side of the mountain, still clearly visible after nearly two thousand years. The engineering feat was staggering; hundreds of thousands of tons of earth and stone methodically built up the mountain-side to breach the seemingly impregnable fortress. Equally haunting were the clearly defined rectangular outlines below, marking where the Roman legions had established their siege camps, systematically surrounding Masada to prevent any possibility of escape. The tactical precision of the Roman siege, preserved in the landscape itself, provided a chilling demonstration of military strategy that transcended time.

The Roman ramp at Massada, Israel

This moment of historical perspective contextualized the modern struggles I was witnessing throughout the West Bank in ways I hadn't anticipated. The patterns of occupation, resistance, and the human cost of conflict seemed to echo across millennia, written into the very geography of this ancient land.

* * *

The Reality of Barriers

The West Bank's landscape is etched with concrete barriers, checkpoints, and restricted crossings, each a reminder of decades of tension and negotiations that rarely translate into real security for ordinary people. Security here wasn't just about protocols and risk assessments; it was personal and relational. My experience with trauma and institutional skepticism, as detailed in "A Soldier's Cry," became invaluable in understanding how fear and mistrust shape daily life for communities on all sides of the conflict.

Walking through the ancient cobblestone streets of Jerusalem's Old City, and even when taking public buses through the newer sections of the city, I found it deeply unsettling to witness the normalization of weaponization in daily civilian life. Israeli parents routinely carried assault rifles while walking their children to school, shopping at markets, or attending community events. Since the occupation prohibits Palestinian civilians from carrying arms, it felt profoundly abnormal and tragic to see one side of a

226

civilian population heavily armed while going about ordinary family activities. The sight of a mother adjusting her child's backpack with an M16 slung across her shoulder, or fathers discussing homework while rifles hung casually from their shoulders, illustrated how conflict had transformed even the most mundane parental responsibilities into militarized acts. This asymmetry of access to weapons, where one community moved through daily life armed while another was systematically disarmed, revealed the deeper structural inequalities that no security protocol could adequately address.

The "peace walls" aren't merely political symbols; they define daily existence for thousands of people. Teachers guide class-rooms of children through the psychological impacts of grow-ing up near barriers. Community activists must navigate ever-changing permit systems that dictate family movements, medical emergencies, and job access. The real challenge was working alongside local leaders to translate international best practices into culturally appropriate approaches for a landscape shaped by decades of mistrust and pain, where the very concept of security had different meanings for different communities separated by walls, checkpoints, and fundamentally different relationships to state power.

* * *

Professional Transition

Following my three-week deployment, I returned to Canada, where I started working for Canada Post as a supervisor, another civilian job that provided income but lacked the sense of purpose I found in humanitarian work. However, shortly after my return in late January 2019, I received another call that would change my trajectory: the World University Service of Canada (WUSC) had received my application and was interested in starting the recruitment process.

The West Bank deployment, brief as it was, had reminded me why I had chosen humanitarian security as more than just a career; it was a calling. Working in one of the world's most intractable conflicts had reinforced lessons I'd learned from my own trauma journey: that protection isn't just about physical security but about creating spaces where dignity and hope can survive even amid the highest barriers.

The experience also highlighted how my personal history of institutional betrayal and psychological fragmentation, rather than being professional liabilities, had become assets for understanding and serving communities whose trust had been repeatedly broken. In the West Bank, where every day presents new risks and disappointments, the ability to listen authentically, validate unseen wounds, and model resilience became perhaps the most vital service I could offer.

Beyond the professional aspects of the deployment, this trip was truly a blessing. Being able to visit the holy city of Jerusalem and walk through such a treasured and precious

228

location was profoundly moving. As a Roman Catholic, the opportunity to visit the Church of the Holy Sepulchre held immense significance for me. I took time to pray directly at this most sacred site, finding the peace and perspective that only comes from connecting with something greater than oneself.

The Church of the Holy Sceptre, Jerusalem

Throughout my life, and particularly during all my deployments, I have turned toward God in moments of uncertainty and stress. Taking time to pray has always provided comfort and strength, especially when dealing with my disability and the ongoing effects of trauma. In Jerusalem, surrounded by centuries of faith and pilgrimage, those moments of prayer

229

felt especially powerful and restorative.

23

A Global Role: WUSC Years

The recruitment process with the World University Service of Canada (WUSC) was long and thorough; it took six months to finally secure my role as their security advisor. They invited me to Ottawa for a formal in-person interview in June 2019, at which point they made the offer. On July 2, I began my work with WUSC and relocated from Kitchener to Ottawa. I found a home to rent just outside the capital in Kanata and moved my family to join me.

When I joined WUSC, I immediately noticed there was significant work ahead to improve the organization's security posture, which suited me perfectly. I had returned to my true calling. The main challenge was integrating a humanitarian security perspective into a development organization with extensive volunteer coordination programs. This required adapting my crisis-zone experience to contexts where the threats were different but the need for systematic risk management was equally critical.

I met daily with my boss, the Chief Human Resources Officer, who was wonderful to work with and understood the value of bringing professional security management to WUSC's global operations. It wasn't long before I was given my first field opportunity: a special assignment to Sri Lanka for what was initially planned as a one-week deployment.

While in Sri Lanka, I was asked to extend my stay to a full month to serve as acting country director, ensuring operations could continue while we recruited a permanent replacement. This role enabled me to utilize my extensive experience as a response security advisor, showcasing my versatility in adapting to changing circumstances. It was a tremendous honour and proved to the organization that I was a capable asset who could step beyond traditional security responsibilities when needed.

* * *

COVID-19 and Organizational Development

Not long after this assignment, in December 2019, the reality of the COVID-19 pandemic began appearing on our radar. Early in the new year, we started assessing the severity of this emerging global crisis and began planning to evacuate our international volunteers back to their home countries. Through creative logistics and innovative thinking, we successfully evacuated all international personnel in March 2020, drawing on my experience with emergency evacuations in conflict zones.

232

On March 21, 2020, the world went into lockdown that lasted just over a year. During this unprecedented pause, I discovered a positive aspect: the chance to develop templates and designs that would serve as the foundation of WUSC's comprehensive security risk management framework. Working closely with the Chief Human Resources Officer, we developed a comprehensive intranet site designed specifically for security resources, training materials, and operational protocols.

In a sense, the pandemic was a blessing that allowed us to enhance WUSC's security infrastructure in ways that would have been very difficult during normal operations. With the world working remotely, I took the opportunity to discuss with my boss the possibility of moving back to Kitchener, where we wanted to buy a home. I was given permission to relocate and continue working remotely, an arrangement that proved both personally satisfying and professionally effective.

* * *

Return to Field Operations

It was a long year, but once vaccines were introduced globally, things slowly began opening up. In June 2021, WUSC began a new program in Mali, requiring personnel deployment to the country. WUSC became the first Canadian International Non-Governmental Organization (INGO) to return to field activities, following all international COVID protocols, a pioneering move that required careful planning and risk assessment.

I was sent in first to assess the situation, with a small team scheduled to arrive a week after me. Prior to the trip, I was able to recruit a logistics/administration/security assistant who would help pave the way for the following team. This recruitment proved invaluable because it was based on a recommendation from a former colleague with whom I had worked during my Haiti deployment, highlighting how the humanitarian community's informal networks often provide the most reliable pathways to trustworthy local expertise. The professional relationships forged during crisis deployments frequently became the foundation for successful operations in new contexts, where personal recommendations carried more weight than formal credentials.

Return to the field post COVID, Bamako, Mali

It was surprising when I arrived in Bamako to discover that, apart from providing vaccination certificates at the airport, life was completely normal in the country. There was no masking or social distancing required anywhere, a stark contrast to the restrictions still in place across much of the world.

When the Director of Operations arrived, we already had a makeshift office established, a vehicle with a driver arranged, and much of the other logistics completed. We conducted one field visit to Segou, where we would be implementing our program, before I returned to Canada, having successfully established WUSC's operational footprint in post-COVID Mali.

* * *

Professional Partnerships and Innovation

Shortly after my return from Mali, the Director of Security for MEDA, located in Kitchener, reached out to discuss developing a localized version of Hostile Environment Awareness Training (HEAT). He and I worked in partnership for several months and finally developed our SCORE (Security in Complex Operational and Remote Environments) course, which I mentioned in The Trainers Arena.

I genuinely enjoyed this collaboration, as we successfully completed five training sessions before he moved to a new position, which unfortunately ended the SCORE program. The partnership demonstrated how individual expertise could be leveraged across organizational boundaries to benefit the broader humanitarian community, a principle I'd learned during my years with World Vision but could now apply as a more senior professional.

$$* * *$$

Guyana: Field Adventures and Complex Regional Operations

Among my most challenging assignments was the October 2024 deployment to Guyana and Suriname for the ENGAGE and SAC projects. Unlike many of my previous deployments that were centered around office setups and urban security assessments, this mission exemplified the kind of hands-on fieldwork I had always thrived on, spending most of my time in remote locations rather than behind a desk.

The adventure began immediately with our first deployment to Region 1, where we travelled in a small Cessna Caravan aircraft to reach areas that were otherwise completely inaccessible by road. Our second field mission took us from our base operations; we took jet boats up the mighty Essequibo River from Bartica, navigating the chocolate-coloured waters past the 365 islands that dot this historic waterway. These jet boat runs became our primary mode of transportation as we visited remote indigenous communities scattered along the river system, each requiring careful security assessment and protocol development.

Essequibo River Jet Boat, Guyana

The real adventure intensified when we reached Itabec, where our mission took on an almost expeditionary character. Here, our mode of transportation shifted to ATVs, which we used to traverse rugged terrain and cross rivers on makeshift ferries. The most memorable moment came when we crossed the border into Brazil on one of these improvised ferries, a fascinating example of how remote communities create their own transportation solutions.

However, what should have been a straightforward border crossing quickly became a diplomatic challenge when we encountered Brazilian military personnel stationed at the frontier. Given the heightened tensions between Venezuela and Guyana over the Essequibo territory, Brazil had significantly reinforced its military presence along this border region. The soldiers, part of the enhanced security measures following the territorial disputes, were understandably cautious about our cross-border movement.

Brazil/Guyana Border crossing on pontoon boat, Itabec, Guyana

Understandably, the soldiers only spoke Portuguese, while our team only spoke English, creating an immediate communication barrier. Just as the situation was becoming potentially problematic for our mission timeline, I discovered that one of the soldiers stationed there spoke Spanish. Drawing on my language skills, I was able to explain our mission in Guyana, reassuring them that we were simply conducting a small security assessment in the area and wanted to have lunch in the small village of Uiramutã. The soldiers, once they understood our humanitarian purpose and limited scope, were friendly and professional, ultimately allowing us to proceed to the village.

On the Brazilian side, we enjoyed a leisurely lunch in Uiramutã, the northernmost municipality in Brazil and a community located entirely within the Raposa Serra do Sol Indian Reservation. This provided a welcome respite from the

intense security assessment work while giving me a chance
to observe cross-border dynamics that would be crucial for
understanding regional threat patterns. The experience also
demonstrated how geopolitical tensions, in this case, the
Venezuela-Guyana Essequibo dispute, create ripple effects
that impact development operations even in seemingly remote locations.

On our return journey, we encountered the same Brazilian
soldiers, who now recognized us and gave friendly waves as
we crossed back into Guyana, completing what had turned
into both a diplomatic and operational success. The entire
experience reinforced an important lesson about field security
work: flexibility and communication skills can be just as
important as formal protocols when navigating complex
border regions during times of regional tension.

From Lethem, our southward journey to Aishalton took us
deep into the Rupununi savanna. This remote community
of indigenous peoples had recently been connected to the
world through satellite internet, representing the kind of
technological leapfrogging that was creating new opportunities and new vulnerabilities in these isolated regions. The
drive to Aishalton itself was an adventure, taking us through
landscapes that seemed untouched by modern development,
where our security protocols had to account for everything
from vehicle breakdowns to medical emergencies hours away
from any assistance.

But perhaps the most spectacular part of the mission came
on our drive north from Lethem to Fairview, where we

encountered some of nature's most breathtaking waterfalls along the Essequibo River system. The stunning backdrop for conducting security assessments was the Kumu Falls area, located about 30 miles from Lethem at the foot of the Kanuku Mountains. These weren't just scenic stops; each location required evaluation for staff safety, emergency evacuation routes, and communication capabilities. The waterfalls along this route, with their thundering cascades and pristine natural beauty, reminded me why this work was so important: we were helping to ensure that development programs could safely reach some of the world's most beautiful and marginalized communities.

Waterfalls near Fairview, Guyana

What struck me most about this field-intensive deployment was how it demonstrated the evolution of modern development work. The ENGAGE project's focus on empowering Indigenous youth, particularly young women, in regions that required security frameworks that could protect staff while respecting traditional ways of life. Every ATV ride, every jet boat journey, and every river crossing was simultaneously an operational necessity and a security assessment opportunity. I was documenting not just current threats but also anticipating how development activities might change risk profiles in communities that had operated in isolation for generations.

The sixteen-day mission combined the physical adventure I had always loved about humanitarian work with the strategic thinking I had developed over years of security management. Whether navigating makeshift ferries between Guyana and Brazil or developing evacuation procedures for communities accessible only by small aircraft, this deployment reminded me that effective security work often occurs far from offices and conference rooms. It occurs in the field, where real people face real challenges, and where the solutions we develop can make the difference between programs that transform lives and programs that never get off the ground due to preventable security incidents.

Six Years of Global Impact

I have now been with WUSC for six years and absolutely love how my position within the organization continues to evolve and expand. I have been deployed to numerous locations, including South Sudan, Mali, Guyana, Iraq, Jordan, Uganda, Kenya, Sri Lanka, Côte d'Ivoire, and Ghana. Many of these deployments involved new office startups, a specialty I've developed that combines security assessment with operational planning and local relationship building.

Each deployment has reinforced lessons learned over my entire humanitarian career: that effective security management requires cultural sensitivity, local partnerships, and the ability to adapt protocols to specific contexts while maintaining core protective principles. The hypervigilance and threat assessment skills born from my military sexual trauma, refined through years of crisis response, have found their most mature application in helping WUSC establish safe, effective operations in challenging environments worldwide.

Most recently, I completed another deployment to South Sudan, assisting in paving the way for security protocols that would enable a successful program launch. The country that had tested me so severely in 2014 during my World Vision deployment now represented an opportunity to apply everything I'd learned about balancing operational access with duty of care, proof that professional growth can transform even the most traumatic professional experiences into sources of expertise and confidence.

The WUSC years have represented not just career stability, but the opportunity to build something lasting: institutional security capacity that will protect staff and volunteers long after my own deployment days are finished. It's the kind of legacy that makes sense of everything that came before, the trauma that taught me vigilance, the crises that taught me resilience, and the setbacks that taught me perseverance.

24

Absent, Yet Present

Humanitarian work demands immersion in crises half a world away, yet it also requires an emotional presence that transcends distance. This paradox of being "absent, yet present" has defined my life since 2008, when I first traded the Ottawa routine for Khartoum's embassy corridors.

* * *

The Personal Cost of Service

Every deployment meant missing birthdays, graduations, and ordinary evenings at home. My sons grew up with a father whose body was often absent but whose heart was fully committed to protecting vulnerable communities. Bedtime stories gave way to video calls from grim field offices, and emergency security briefings took the place of a father's hug. My family learned to celebrate milestones by webcam, silently bearing the weight of my departures and returns.

Nevertheless, despite the miles, I strove to remain emotion-ally present. I cultivated traditions, late-night phone calls from crisis zones, daily check-ins when security allowed, and sharing field photos so my sons could glimpse the landscapes that called me away. Each message was a reminder: though I served abroad, my love and concern remained rooted at home.

* * *

Mental Deployments at Home

Even in civilian life, my mind maintained a constant state of alertness. I became accustomed to conducting meticulous risk assessments, which included scanning parking lots at grocery stores, identifying exit routes in restaurants, and anticipating potential crises before they occurred. Family vacations often felt like covert field operations: identifying safe rooms, exit plans, and medical resources. My hypervigilance, born of CPTSD and honed through deployments, kept me mentally "deployed" even when I was physically present.

These habits sometimes created tension. Loved ones asked me to relax, to "leave work at work." But switching off the protective instincts that had saved lives in Haiti and Syria wasn't simple. Over time, I learned to communicate these challenges, explaining that my alertness was both a survival skill and a part of my identity. Gradually, my family and friends gradually began to understand that my presence, even at home, carried the imprint of every crisis I'd managed.

245

* * *

Technology as Bridge and Barrier

Modern communication presented both advantages and disadvantages. WhatsApp messages from Gaziantep sparked hope on quiet Kitchener evenings, yet the ping of an urgent field update could abruptly sever family dinner conversation. Email chains from Beirut arrived alongside school report cards in my inbox, blending professional urgency with personal normalcy.

I set boundaries, designating family-only times with phones off and scheduling predictable "deployment-free" weekends, but emergencies rarely adhered to calendars. My loved ones learned that sometimes security demands took precedence. Yet they also discovered the value of my work, as local volunteers and field staff sent their gratitude directly to my personal number, reinforcing the significance of my remote presence.

* * *

Lessons in Legacy

As my sons matured, they saw that service carries sacrifice and that protecting others sometimes means being unable to protect those closest to you from emotional absence. They learned resilience, too: adapting to a father who returned

246

home changed by violence he'd witnessed and challenges he'd navigated.

In turn, my family became my anchor. Their unwavering support grounded me after every crisis, reminding me that the most important missions begin at home. Teaching my sons about empathy, responsibility, and courage felt as vital as any security training I delivered abroad. I realized that my legacy wouldn't be measured solely by protocols written or evacuations led, but by the lessons I modelled for those I loved most.

* * *

Integrating Two Worlds

Eventually, I found my role with WUSC allowed a measure of balance, a stable base from which to deploy selectively, ensuring that my family's needs were as carefully planned as any security operation. Working remotely from Kitchener after the pandemic provided rare proximity to home, even as I continued to serve global programs.

The distance between crisis zones and my front door narrowed when I recognized that presence isn't only physical. It's emotional availability, honest communication about trauma's burdens, and deliberate efforts to connect despite competing demands.

In living the paradox of being "absent, yet present," I discovered that true protection encompasses both professional responsibility and personal commitment. My expertise in security ensured the safety of others in perilous situations, while my commitment to emotional presence helped my family weather the inevitable challenges of humanitarian work.

In the end, service and sacrifice are inseparable, and the most resilient communities, whether in conflict zones or at home, are those bound by trust, presence, and the conviction that no distance can sever the ties that truly matter.

25

Between Deployments: Forging Resilience in the Lulls

Even when the world's most urgent crises fade from the headlines, the crucible of trauma continues to shape those who serve on the front lines. The spaces between deployments are not "time off" but vital chapters in the alchemy that transforms raw fear into the tools needed to protect others and to sustain one's own purpose and well-being.

Teaching and Learning in Unlikely Arenas

Drawing on trauma-forged skills, I stepped into classrooms far from conflict zones, becoming both guest instructor and eager student of global extremes.

- **Phuket, Thailand (Nov. 2011).** Amid tropical humidity, I assisted with some of the World Vision's HEAT modules before guiding participants along the Andaman coast through hostile-environment exercises. Monsoon winds and hidden coves tested our lessons as fiercely as any checkpoint in Khartoum or Port-au-Prince.

- **Nairobi, Kenya (Aug. 2011).** Assistant facilitator of HEAT under the equatorial sun, we simulated ambushes and hostage scenarios. Afterwards, a getaway to Amboseli's savanna revealed how apex predators, like humanitarians, must continually adapt when "terrain shifts beneath them."
- **Cape Town, South Africa (May 2011).** At the GRRT annual meeting, strategy sessions gave way to a moving visit to Robben Island, Nelson Mandela's prison, followed by scooter runs along Chapman's Peak Drive. These respites proved that brief escapes can sharpen resolve for challenges ahead.

Global Security Advising: Geography as Teacher

Between crisis deployments, I immersed myself in diverse operational landscapes, each site a unique lesson in the interplay of terrain, culture, and risk.

- **Colombia (June 2011).** From Cali's urban sprawl to Bucaramanga's high plateaus, Santa Marta's coastal settlements, and the salt flats outside Bogotá, I helped build risk-management systems that accounted for everything from cartel-controlled neighbourhoods to commercial corridor vulnerabilities.
- **Nepal (March 2011).** My first Himalayan trek was a simulated earthquake drill. Cycling borrowed bicycles along terraced rice fields, I discovered how altitude and thin air test both body and mind and how local ingenuity shapes security solutions.

Two Wheels, One Compass: The Harley Years

Between 2011 and 2015, my Harley-Davidson became a refuge and compass for reflection:

- Riding from Managua's colonial streets to the coffee farms of Estelí, from Granada's volcanic shores to Tegucigalpa's winding mountain passes, each mile honed my ability to read terrain and anticipate risk.
- Weekend runs with the Costa Rica Harley Owners Group forged community bonds and provided meditative clarity, a necessary counterbalance to the chaos of deployment.

R&R and Renewal

Brief respites overseas fueled both camaraderie and growth:

- **Oxford, U.K. (Mid-2012).** A GRRT psych debrief introduced vulnerability as a strength.
- **Cyprus and Dakar Training Seminars.** Exposure to new security and trauma-care approaches broadened my own recovery horizon.
- **Spain and France (2012–2015).** Wandering olive groves and Loire Valley vineyards with my wife grounded my spirit, while chapel services in San José anchored me spiritually.

Integrating Calm with Crisis Response

The paradox of thriving in chaos yet struggling with calm underscores the necessity of deliberate integration:

- **Quiet Rituals:** "Deployment-free" weekends (phones off, maps put away) retrain neural pathways toward stillness.
- **Mindfulness and Movement:** Breathwork counteracts hyperarousal; long bike rides harness restless energy.
- **Local Purpose:** Teaching community first aid and mentoring veterans to translate frontline skills into everyday leadership.

Between deployments are not pauses but vital interludes where trauma's lessons crystallize into wisdom. Each classroom I've entered, each foreign highway I've ridden, and each political divide I've navigated has added strands to the neural architecture of survival. The vigilance once needed to spot danger on a Syrian checkpoint, the compartmentalization that kept me functioning under Phuket's palm fronds, and the emotional regulation that steadied me on Bogotá's salt flats, all these responses, once unbidden reflexes, have been intentionally refined into competencies I now teach to others standing at the thresholds of danger.

In these interludes, we learn that **resilience** is not simply the ability to survive new crises but the capacity to integrate trauma into meaningful purpose long after the emergency alert fades. The alchemy of wounds to wisdom continues, between deployments, across continents, and into every quiet moment that demands courage to heal and the will to protect.

26

Thriving in Chaos, Struggling with Calm

The Adrenaline Architecture

For years, my nervous system learned to flourish under fire. I became laser-focused in the face of danger, whether dodging IEDs on Syrian highways, coordinating evacuation routes in South Sudan, or guiding humanitarian teams through the immediate aftermath of Haiti's earthquake. In those moments, hypervigilance honed by trauma was no longer a burden but an invaluable tool. My mind processed threats with clarity; my body moved with purpose. Dissociative moments, which once felt like losing touch with reality, transformed into protective compartments, enabling me to function when those around me were on the brink. Chaos was, paradoxically, my realm of comfort.

Yet when I returned home, that same heightened state transformed everyday life into a minefield. A late-night text message sounded like an imminent threat. The restaurant patio transformed into a memorized network of escape routes. Peaceful weekends felt unbearably tense; my mind searched for danger in quiet streets where none existed. My restlessness showed itself in the smallest ways: pacing in grocery store aisles, reheating evacuation routes before family dinners, and scanning the ceiling for potential entry points at home. Stillness triggered the same biological alarm as incoming mortar fire; calm felt like a harbinger of chaos.

Over time, I realized that surviving war zones and navigating humanitarian crises had deepened my reliance on that fight-or-flight architecture. I thrived on urgent missions where every second mattered. In civilian life, however, my trauma-wired instincts worked against me, creating stress where there should have been none. I longed for the next crisis just to feel a sense of purpose and clarity I couldn't attain in everyday calm.

Learning to live fully in both worlds, alert to danger but open to peace, has become my most important task. I began by intentionally carving out "deployment-free" weekends: devices turned off, no security briefings to read, and no evacuation maps to review. At first, the silence felt unbearable, but I discovered it offered a different kind of focus, an opportunity to practice presence instead of vigilance. I developed new rituals to ground myself: mindful breathing exercises, long bike rides to channel restless energy, and volunteer work locally that reminded me how to be useful without the urgency of crisis.

Slowly, I integrated the skills I'd honed under fire into my daily life. Threat assessment became situational awareness: noting unfamiliar faces in a crowd, yes, but also appreciating the shapes of tree shadows on a summer afternoon. Compartmentalization evolved into healthy boundaries: I learned to set aside work worries during family dinners and stored evacuation plans in a folder I only opened when necessary. The dissociation that had allowed me to survive now served as a reminder to check in with my emotions rather than run from them.

This journey taught me that true resilience isn't about avoiding danger or calming the mind permanently; it's about expanding the contexts in which I can thrive. Crisis and calm are not opposites to be chosen over one another but parts of a spectrum I've learned to navigate. I still respond sharply to sudden noises and still map escape routes in my mind, but now I can also lean into stillness, knowing it won't last forever and that my skills remain ready when they're needed most.

My service in conflict zones taught me how to save others; learning to embrace calm is teaching me how to save myself. By mastering both, I'm finally honouring all the parts of my story, the soldier who needs urgency to feel alive and the survivor who deserves peace to heal.

* * *

The Unbearable Weight of Peace

Yet back home, in the absence of crisis, those same abilities became psychological prisons. The grocery store checkout line triggered the same fight-or-flight response as Syrian checkpoints. Dinner conversations felt unbearably loud when my mind expected the tactical silence that preceded raids. Restaurant patios became threat landscapes to be mapped and monitored rather than spaces for relaxation and connection.

An approaching car in an empty parking lot, a cup spilling in the kitchen, and the phone's ring echoing like an air raid siren triggered the adrenaline that once saved lives. My nervous system, calibrated for constant danger, interpreted peaceful environments as ominously wrong. Calm felt like the glare of a storm, a fleeting respite before the impending violence.

Family gatherings became endurance tests. While others relaxed into conversations about weekend plans or local news, I found myself cataloguing exit routes, assessing potential threats, and struggling to engage with concerns that felt trivial after witnessing starvation, displacement, and systematic violence. Small talk about traffic or weather felt like speaking a foreign language after months of coordinating evacuations and managing life-or-death logistics.

Sleep became elusive in civilian beds, which felt too soft, too quiet, and too distant from the radio communications that had provided reassurance during deployment nights. The silence that others found restorative felt oppressive, leaving space for memories to resurface: the smell of death in Malakal, the sound of incoming mortars, and the weight of decisions that had determined whether colleagues lived or died.

* * *

The Identity Trap

Between deployments, I wrestled with a profound emptiness that civilian life couldn't fill. The structure of emergencies, where every second mattered and every action served a clear purpose, gave way to the formless anxiety of ordinary time. Nine-to-five predictability felt like imprisonment; social obligations felt like performance art. I longed for the next mission even as my body begged for respite, caught between exhaustion and addiction to the meaning that only crisis could provide.

Family trips and home renovations triggered restlessness that bordered on panic. While others saw vacation and stability, I saw stagnation and vulnerability. My heart pounded for the next deployment alert, the next opportunity to feel useful, competent, and alive. The skills that made me valuable in humanitarian emergencies, rapid decision-making, threat assessment, and emotional compartmentalization, had no application in suburban tranquilly.

These experiences created a devastating paradox: the work that had given my life meaning was slowly destroying my ability to find meaning anywhere else. I was becoming

257

addicted to crisis, dependent on chaos for a sense of purpose
that peaceful environments couldn't provide. The trauma
responses that enabled my professional effectiveness were
sabotaging my personal healing.

* * *

Learning to Embrace Stillness

Integration became my newest front line, more challenging
than any conflict zone I'd navigated. I learned to channel
hypervigilance into mindful awareness, transforming threat
scanning into meditative attention to present-moment details: the texture of coffee cup handles, the pattern of shadows
on walls, and the rhythm of my own breathing. Therapy
sessions became mission briefings for the work of healing,
each appointment a deployment into the dangerous territory
of my own psyche.

I scheduled "deployment-free" weekends and honoured
them as sacred, treating rest as rigorously as I once treated
security protocols. I practiced patience in traffic jams with the
same dedication I'd once applied to checkpoint negotiations.
I rehearsed my presence at home, like rehearsing emergency
procedures and making deliberate efforts to engage with
conversations about ordinary concerns without mentally
retreating to more "important" priorities.

Local volunteering provided a bridge between crisis work
and civilian life, offering opportunities to use protective

instincts in non-emergency contexts. Teaching security awareness to community organizations, mentoring young people interested in humanitarian careers, and supporting veteran transition programs created purposeful connections without requiring deployment travel.

Physical exercise became essential for managing the physio-logical arousal that had no outlet in peaceful environments. Long walks with my dog, Zeus, channelled the restless energy that once powered me through crisis zones. Weight training provided controlled stress that satisfied my nervous system's need for challenge without requiring actual danger.

* * *

The Ongoing Journey

Through trial and error, I discovered that true resilience isn't about always running toward crisis but about embracing calm as fiercely as chaos. Each peaceful morning became a mission: grounding breath by breath, noticing sunlight streaming through windows, reminding myself that safety could feel safe rather than threatening. I reframed my identity, not just as a protector in conflict zones, but as a guardian of peace in ordinary life.

The work of integration never ends. I still feel the magnetic pull of distant emergencies, still struggle with the pace of civilian healing, and still find grocery stores more challenging than Syrian checkpoints. But I've learned to honour both sides of my psychological landscape, recognizing that my ability to thrive in chaos and my struggle with calm are two faces of the same resilience coin, a resilience born in military sexual trauma, refined through humanitarian service, and tested anew every time I choose presence over performance and stillness over stimulation.

The paradox endures, but it no longer defines me. I am learning to be as brave in peace as I've been in war, as skilled at rest as I've been in response, and as committed to healing as I've been to helping. The boy broken by institutional betrayal has become a man who understands that the greatest protection sometimes means protecting yourself from the very skills that once saved your life.

In learning to struggle productively with calm, I've discovered that recovery isn't about eliminating trauma responses but about expanding the contexts in which I can thrive. Home is no longer exile from purpose; it's another kind of mission field, where the work is gentler but no less essential and where the victories are quieter but no less meaningful.

* * *

End of Part III Summary

The Ripple Effects and New Purpose (2016–Present)

The collapse of my World Vision career had stripped away institutional identity, but it couldn't erase the expertise forged in trauma and refined through global service. These years revealed that true resilience isn't about avoiding institutional betrayal; it's about learning to rise each time with more profound wisdom and stronger boundaries.

From the IRC's broken promises to CARE's meaningful partnerships, from the West Bank's complex peace walls to WUSC's stable embrace, I discovered that my greatest contribution wasn't just managing security in crisis zones; it was modelling how to transform wounds into wisdom, how to carry trauma without being consumed by it, and how to serve others while protecting themselves, which institutions had repeatedly failed to safeguard.

The paradox of thriving in chaos while struggling with calm became not a problem to solve but a reality to integrate. My hypervigilance, dissociation, and emotional compartmentali zation, once symptoms of a "damaged" soldier, had become specialized tools for protecting the innocent and vulnerable. But they also required careful management, deliberate rest, and the ongoing work of learning to be as brave in peace as I had been in war.

The absent father learning presence, the crisis specialist learning calm, and the institutional survivor learning trust, each challenge revealed new facets of a journey that began with military sexual trauma but had expanded into something larger: a mission to protect others from the abandonment I had experienced, to teach the resilience I had been forced to develop, and to prove that broken things could indeed be rebuilt stronger than before.

The ripple effects of trauma had spread across continents and decades, touching lives in ways I was only beginning to understand. But the new purpose was clear: not just survival, but transformation of self, of systems, and of the silence that had once protected predators and abandoned survivors.

IV

Integration, Advocacy and Legacy

In the final stretch, the lessons forged from trauma and honed in global crises converge. Integration is no longer just survival, it's finding wholeness after fragmentation, drawing strength from every chapter before. Advocacy becomes purpose: using my story to champion change for those still silenced or imperilled. Legacy is the measure, not of accolades, but of compassion and courage, what endures when the missions are over, and by what we leave behind for the next generation of protectors.

27

Lessons from Military Wounds

Thirty-six years have passed since the military sexual trauma that ended my career and shattered my trust in institutions. Three decades of distance, humanitarian service, and global perspective have transformed those wounds from sources of shame into wellsprings of wisdom, not just for my own healing, but for the systemic changes our military desperately needs.

The Universal Pattern of Institutional Failure

My humanitarian career revealed a sobering truth: the military's response to my assault wasn't an aberration; it was part of a universal pattern of institutional self-preservation that transcends organizations, cultures, and contexts. From humanitarian agencies dismissing staff PTSD to development organizations ignoring sexual harassment, I witnessed the same denial, victim-blaming, and protective silence that had greeted my reports in 1989.

In Syria, I worked alongside aid workers whose organizations responded to their trauma with skepticism rather than support. In South Sudan, I saw how institutions prioritized operational continuity over individual welfare. In Nigeria, I observed the familiar dynamic: survivors blamed for "not following protocol" while systemic failures remained unaddressed. The script was always the same: protect the institution's reputation, minimize liability, and hope the problem quietly disappears.

This pattern recognition became one of my most valuable professional assets. Having experienced institutional betrayal firsthand, I could detect early warning signs that others missed: the subtle shift when leadership viewed staff trauma as inconvenient rather than tragic, the defensive responses when protocols failed to prevent harm, and the tendency to treat survivors as problems rather than people deserving support.

The Bitter Transformation of Symptoms into Strengths

Military sexual trauma rewired my nervous system in ways that would prove prophetic. The hypervigilance that made civilian life exhausting became the sixth sense that detected threats before violence erupted. The emotional numbing that damaged relationships enabled clear thinking during mass casualty events. The dissociation that once felt like weakness became the ability to compartmentalize effectively during crisis response.

The institution that broke me had inadvertently created

266

exactly the skills needed to protect others from institutional failure. Every trauma response that military psychiatrists had pathologized, the persistent scanning for danger, the inability to trust authority, and the compulsive need to plan for worst-case scenarios, became professional competencies that kept humanitarian teams alive in the world's most dangerous places.

This irony wasn't lost on me: the military had discarded me as "damaged goods," yet humanitarian organizations sought my expertise precisely because of how that damage had shaped my capabilities. The wounds they refused to acknowledge had become wisdom they desperately needed.

What Distance Taught About Justice

Time and professional success provided perspective on my military experience that the immediate aftermath couldn't offer. I learned to distinguish between personal healing and institutional accountability, understanding that I could rebuild my life while still demanding systemic change. My recovery didn't depend on military admission of guilt, but military reform required survivors willing to speak truth about institutional failure.

Working with trauma survivors worldwide taught me that healing isn't linear and justice isn't singular. Some survivors found peace through forgiveness, others through advocacy, and many through service to prevent similar harm. My path involved transforming personal trauma into professional purpose, using the skills that abuse had taught me to protect others from experiencing similar abandonment.

The humanitarian sector's evolving approach to trauma-informed practice showed what progressive institutions could look like. Organizations that acknowledged the psychological costs of difficult work, provided immediate support for staff experiencing trauma, and created cultures where vulnerability was met with care rather than suspicion. These weren't perfect institutions, but they demonstrated that change was possible when leadership chose courage over convenience.

Blueprint for Military Reform

Three decades of institutional experience across multiple sectors revealed what military reform could look like if leadership found the courage to prioritize people over politics:

Immediate Response Protocols: When sexual assault is reported, the first response must be belief, support, and protection, not investigation of the survivor's credibility or motives. Military leaders must understand that institutional loyalty means protecting the vulnerable, not silencing the inconvenient.

Trauma-Informed Culture: Military training must include comprehensive education about sexual trauma's neurological impact, the psychology of disclosure, and the long-term effects of institutional betrayal. Leaders need skills to recognize trauma responses, provide appropriate support, and distinguish between symptoms and character defects.

Survivor-Centred Justice: Military justice systems must prioritize survivor welfare over institutional reputation. This means believing survivors, providing immediate support services, ensuring fair investigations, and creating consequences for both perpetrators and leaders who enable abuse through negligence or cover-up.

Peer Support Networks: The military must formalize peer support programs led by survivors who understand both trauma's impact and institutional dynamics. Survivors supporting one another offer a level of credibility and understanding that even the most well-trained professional counsellors cannot provide.

Accountability Without Retaliation: Military culture must evolve to view reporting an assault as an act of courage rather than as disloyalty, and to see the protection of unit integrity as a commitment rather than a betrayal of institutional solidarity. This requires leaders to model appropriate behaviour, enforce policies, and transform the culture to celebrate truth-telling instead of maintaining silence.

Breaking the Silence, Building the Future

Writing "A Soldier's Cry" wasn't just personal catharsis; it was an institutional challenge. Every survivor who speaks truth challenges the silence that shields predators and abandons survivors. My humanitarian credibility gave weight to survivor testimony, proving that military sexual trauma survivors could rebuild successful careers and contribute meaningfully to society if institutions chose support over abandonment.

The lessons from military wounds extend beyond individual healing to systemic transformation. My hypervigilance became a humanitarian asset, not despite institutional failure, but because of it. My emotional numbing became a crisis management skill, not in spite of trauma, but because trauma taught compartmentalization that peaceful environments couldn't provide.

The boy broken by military sexual trauma became a man whose mission was ensuring others wouldn't experience similar institutional abandonment. Every humanitarian worker I trained, every security protocol I developed, and every crisis I managed carried forward the determination that institutional failure wouldn't define the institutional future.

The Continuing Mission

Military wounds taught me that healing and advocacy are inseparable, that personal recovery and systemic change must advance together. My CPTSD and DID aren't obstacles to overcome but realities to integrate, sources of insight rather than sources of shame. The fragments of identity that trauma created, survivor, protector, analyst, teacher, work together now in service of a mission larger than personal healing.

The military that betrayed me in 1989 exists within systems that can be changed by courage, persistent advocacy, and the refusal to let institutional convenience triumph over individual dignity. Every survivor who speaks, every leader who listens, and every policy that prioritizes people over politics moves us closer to institutions worthy of the service they demand.

The lessons from military wounds are written in scar tissue and validated through decades of service: broken things can be rebuilt stronger, trauma can become wisdom, and the most effective protectors are often those who know intimately what it means to need protection.

28

The Trainer's Arena

Following my training event in Afghanistan with Armadillo at Large, the training bug bit me. The experience of teaching BBC journalists how to navigate hostile environments had revealed something I hadn't expected: the same skills that trauma had forced me to develop could be systematically taught to others. The hypervigilance that had once been a burden could become a curriculum; the threat assessment abilities born from military sexual trauma could protect people I would never meet in places I might never visit.

When I returned to Haiti as World Vision's Response Security Manager, I seized the opportunity to organize a Kidnap and Ransom (K&R) course, inviting the World Vision Office of Corporate Security (OCS) training team to Haiti to conduct this specialized three-day program. This marked my first encounter with the OCS training team: professionals to the maximum and very well respected within the humanitarian security community.

The Director of the WVOCS training team brought an impressive presence and was exceptionally well-versed in all aspects of security training. Observing the team's work was akin to witnessing experts in their field: they were able to simplify complex security concepts for humanitarian workers who had never considered personal protection protocols, hostage survival techniques, or family emergency planning. The K&R course was very successful, and observing the team in action intensified my desire to become a trainer myself.

However, my current role as Response Security Manager didn't permit that kind of involvement. The position required constant focus on immediate operational security rather than the strategic thinking that training development demanded. It wasn't until I joined the Global Rapid Response Team that I would have more influence and opportunity to move into training roles.

I took my own Hostile Environment Awareness Training (HEAT) course in 2010 as a participant while serving as security manager in Haiti. The experience was quite intense: five days of simulated kidnappings, hostile checkpoint negotiations, vehicle ambush scenarios, and psychological pressure designed to test decision-making under extreme stress. However, the course imparted valuable knowledge and equipped me with numerous practical tools that proved indispensable in my subsequent deployments.

The course revealed something important about my own professional development: while I had survived real hostile environments and developed effective coping mechanisms,

I had never received formal training in the systematic approaches that could make those skills transferable to others.
The HEAT course provided frameworks for understanding
threat assessment, risk management, and crisis response that
organized my instinctive knowledge into teachable methodologies.

* * *

Building Relationships with the Training Team

The GRRT provided me with the opportunity to regularly
assist the OCS training team. This demand grew as I gained
more field experience and demonstrated competency in articulating the practical applications of security protocols. My
relationship with the team was growing, but not without some
bumps. Training requires different skills than operational
security management: the ability to create safe learning
environments for people processing difficult material, patience with participants who learn at different speeds, and
the emotional intelligence to recognize when someone is
struggling with content that might trigger their own trauma
responses.

The OCS training team conducted three to four HEAT courses
per year in various global locations, and I began participating
as a guest trainer at most of these events, with my primary
focus in Nairobi. The Kenya location was strategic for several reasons: it served World Vision operations across East
Africa, provided a relatively stable environment for intensive

training, and offered participants exposure to the security challenges they might face in nearby high-risk countries without actually putting them at risk.

Working as a guest trainer allowed me to contribute the field experience that complemented the team's instructional expertise. While they provided systematic frameworks and institutional knowledge, I could offer deployment stories, practical examples, and the kind of situational awareness that only comes from actually living through the scenarios we were teaching. The combination proved powerful for participants who needed both theoretical understanding and practical intuition.

* * *

Trauma as Teaching Tool

What I didn't fully understand at first was how my Complex PTSD and Dissociative Identity Disorder actually enhanced my effectiveness as a trainer in unexpected ways. The hyper-vigilance that made civilian life exhausting became an asset in interpreting training room dynamics; I was able to detect when participants were struggling with challenging material, when someone was triggered by scenarios that resonated too deeply, or when the group energy was shifting in ways that necessitated intervention.

The dissociative episodes that had once been sources of shame became teaching moments about stress responses and psychological first aid. I could recognize the signs of someone beginning to dissociate during intense simulations and help them ground themselves before the experience became overwhelming. My own journey through trauma gave me credibility when discussing the psychological impact of humanitarian work that academic training manuals couldn't provide.

The newly acquired trauma from my years as a response security advisor and the accumulated weight of Bangui hotel firefights, Malakal bunkers, Syrian checkpoint negotiations, and South Sudan evacuations provided a reservoir of authentic examples that made abstract security concepts tangible for participants. Unlike trainers who taught from textbooks, I could describe the actual sound of incoming mortars, the specific feeling of negotiating with armed groups, and the precise decision-making process required when evacuation plans activate.

But perhaps most importantly, my experience with institutional betrayal and the long journey back to purpose gave me unique insight into how to create psychologically safe learning environments. I understood viscerally how it felt to have your trust violated by the very system meant to protect you, which made me especially attuned to ensuring that training participants felt supported rather than judged and empowered rather than frightened.

Reading the Room

The heightened situational awareness that CPTSD had embedded in my nervous system translated directly into training facilitation skills. I could detect subtle shifts in participant engagement, identify who was processing difficult material versus who was simply bored, and recognize when someone needed individual attention without public attention. The same threat assessment skills I used in conflict zones helped me navigate the interpersonal dynamics of diverse groups learning high-stress material together.

My dissociative episodes, once a source of professional liability, became windows into understanding how stress affects cognitive processing. I could explain to participants why their minds might "go blank" during crisis scenarios, validate their experiences of feeling disconnected during intense simulations, and provide practical grounding techniques that I'd developed through years of managing my own psychological responses.

The training environment became a place where my fragmented sense of self actually served a purpose. Different aspects of my identity, the survivor, the analyst, the protector, and the teacher, could emerge as needed to meet participants wherever they were in their learning journey. The psychological splitting that had once been a symptom became a resource for connecting with people experiencing their own stress responses to difficult material.

Authentic Authority

Training participants could sense the authenticity of lived experience versus theoretical knowledge. When I described the physical sensations of being in a hostile environment, the adrenaline surge of checkpoint negotiations, the exhaustion of constant hypervigilance, and the psychological toll of repeated exposure to human suffering, participants recognized that this wasn't academic instruction but hard-won wisdom.

The newly layered trauma from my years as a security advisor added depth and complexity to my teaching that wouldn't have existed if I'd remained in safer roles. Each deployment had added new layers of understanding about how stress affects decision-making, how cultural contexts shape threat perception, and how the cumulative impact of repeated exposure to violence changes a person's psychological baseline.

This accumulation of operational trauma, paradoxically, made me a more effective trainer because I could speak to the full spectrum of humanitarian experiences, from the exhilaration of successful operations to the soul-deep exhaustion of constant vigilance, and from the pride of protecting others to the guilt of surviving when others didn't. Participants could see in my presentation of material that I understood not just the technical aspects of security work but also its profound personal costs and unexpected rewards.

The integration of my psychological reality with my professional expertise created a training approach that was both technically competent and emotionally intelligent. I

278

wasn't just teaching security protocols; I was modelling how someone could carry trauma and still function effectively, how wounds could become wisdom, and how the most broken people often become the best protectors of others.

* * *

Developing Local Capacity

In 2012, the OCS training team developed the Security Awareness in National Theatres (SAINT) course specifically designed for local nationals. This represented a significant evolution in humanitarian security training, recognizing that national staff often faced different and sometimes greater risks than international personnel but had historically received less comprehensive security preparation.

The SAINT course was offered in many countries; however, my main focus became assisting with SAINT delivery in LACRO (Latin America and Caribbean Regional Office). Living in Costa Rica made it logical for me to assist when I wasn't deployed to emergency responses. The region presented unique training challenges: countries with different threat profiles, from natural disasters in Haiti to criminal violence in Honduras, political instability in various contexts, and the complex dynamics of working in communities where World Vision had long-term development programs rather than emergency responses.

I worked with a seasoned team of security managers through-

279

out the region, conducting courses in locations such as Honduras, Panama, and Ecuador. Each context required adaptation of the core SAINT curriculum to local realities. In Honduras, we emphasized urban security and gang-related threats. In Panama, the focus was on balancing development programming with security protocols in remote indigenous communities. In Ecuador, we addressed the intersection of natural disaster preparedness with ongoing political tensions.

The SAINT courses revealed something important about humanitarian security: the most effective protection often comes from local knowledge and community relationships rather than international protocols. National staff understood cultural dynamics, political sensitivities, and emerging threats in ways that international security advisors never could. Our role as trainers was to provide frameworks and tools that enhanced their existing knowledge rather than replacing it.

* * *

Expanding Training Beyond World Vision

Following my tenure with World Vision in 2016, I was able to take this training experience to other organizations and contexts. The skills I'd developed in curriculum design, adult learning principles, and security-specific pedagogy proved transferable across the humanitarian sector.

During my assignment with the International Rescue Committee (IRC) in Nigeria, I provided a two-day security course for my team in Maiduguri that was well received. The Maiduguri context presented particularly acute challenges: operating at the epicentre of the Boko Haram insurgency, managing security for programming in areas where the threat landscape changed daily, ensuring staff safety, and maintaining operational access for communities in desperate need of humanitarian assistance. The training had to tackle the challenges of operating in a city under siege, where suicide bombings and armed attacks posed constant threats and where the boundaries between safe and dangerous areas could fluctuate abruptly.

When I joined Food for the Hungry on a contract position in early 2017, I was able to provide a security management session for their Haiti team. Returning to Haiti as a trainer rather than an emergency responder provided a different perspective on the country's security challenges and my own professional development. The training emphasized security for long-term development programming instead of the crisis response protocols that I had previously focused on.

* * *

Innovation in Conflict Settings

While working with CARE International on the Syria response from 2017 to 2018, I took training to a different level by working directly with Syrian partners based inside the country. This presented unprecedented challenges: how do you provide security training to people operating in active conflict zones when normal training environments aren't available? How do you address the psychological impact of providing security education to people who are already living through the scenarios you're teaching them to survive?

I was able to successfully deliver a security management course for all partners working with multiple International Non-Governmental Organizations (INGOs), creating a universal framework for security risk management that could be applied across different organizational mandates and operational approaches. The training had to account for the complex realities of cross-border programming, the unpredictable nature of shifting conflict lines, and the emotional toll on local staff who were serving their own communities while those communities were under attack.

The Syria training experience taught me that security education in active conflict zones requires different approaches than traditional HEAT or SAINT methodologies. Participants weren't learning hypothetical scenarios; they were processing real experiences while developing skills for tomorrow's threats. The training had to serve as both skill development and trauma processing, requiring integration of psychological support with practical security education.

* * *

The SCORE Partnership

In my current role with the World University Service of Canada (WUSC), I was able to work with a colleague from another organization to partner in the development and delivery of a new training program. This colleague brought extensive experience from different humanitarian contexts, and the fact that we lived in the same city (Kitchener) enabled regular collaboration on curriculum development.

Together, we built what we called Security in Complex Operational and Remote Environments (SCORE). The course represented an evolution of traditional HEAT and SAINT methodologies. We incorporated lessons learned from years of delivering security training in various contexts and adapted to the emerging threats and operational realities that humanitarian workers faced in the 2020s.

The growing complexity of threat situations includes the unexpected mixing of traditional categories such as conflict, crime, and politics; the mental health effects resulting from constant exposure to security risks; the connection between physical and digital security along with information management; and the unique challenges faced by organizations in remote or complicated areas where regular security support is unavailable.

However, my experiences, both personal and professional, had taught me that realistic security training simulations could inadvertently retraumatize participants who carried their own histories of violence, assault, or psychological

283

trauma. From my mentors at World Vision, I had learned the critical importance of psychosocial support during field simulations and the necessity of preparing participants for the psychological impact of intensive training scenarios.

I was adamant that SCORE include comprehensive trauma-informed protocols. Before any simulation exercises, we implemented mandatory briefings about the psychological effects of realistic training scenarios. We established clear opt-out procedures, provided onsite psychosocial support throughout the training, and created safe spaces for participants to process difficult emotions that might arise during exercises. I made it clear to my training partner: without these safeguards, I would not participate in the program.

This wasn't just about best practices; it was about ensuring that our training strengthened humanitarian workers without causing additional harm. Too many security training programs focused solely on tactical skills while ignoring the psychological readiness and resilience required for field-work. SCORE was designed to build both physical and mental preparedness while respecting the diverse backgrounds and experiences participants brought to the training.

We successfully built and delivered a total of five SCORE courses, one in Kitchener and four in Ottawa. The program attracted participants from across the Canadian humanitarian sector, including staff from WUSC, MEDA, Oxfam, Food for the Hungry, and other smaller organizations that couldn't afford to send staff to international training programs. The trauma-informed approach we pioneered became a model that other training programs began to adopt, recognizing that effective security training must account for the whole person, not just their tactical skills.

* * *

The evolution of my training, from participant to guest trainer to curriculum developer, reflected my own professional journey from survivor to specialist to educator. Each role built on previous experiences while requiring new skills and perspectives. The trauma that had once isolated me from normal human interaction had become a teaching tool that could help others develop the awareness and resilience needed to serve in dangerous environments while protecting their own mental health and personal relationships.

The trainer's arena became the space where personal wounds transformed most clearly into professional purpose, where the painful lessons of institutional betrayal and trauma survival became curricula that could protect others from similar harm. In teaching others to assess threats and manage risks, I was also teaching them to trust their instincts, maintain situational awareness, and preserve their humanity in environments designed to erode it.

* * *

Acknowledgment of Mentors

The evolution from trauma survivor to security trainer would not have been possible without the guidance and support of exceptional professionals who saw potential where others might have seen only scars.

I would like to make a special honourable mention to the World Vision Office's Corporate Security Training team for helping me become a sound trainer. I have much respect for this team, not only for their technical expertise and professional standards, but also for their willingness to invest in someone whose path to training was unconventional. They recognized that lived experience, when properly channelled and systematically developed, could enhance traditional security education in ways that pure academic preparation could not.

The OCS team taught me that effective training requires more than just knowledge of subject matter; it demands understanding of adult learning principles, cultural sensitivity, psychological awareness, and the ability to create environments where people can process difficult material safely. They showed me how to transform war stories into learning objectives, how to structure scenarios that challenged participants without traumatizing them, and how to measure training effectiveness beyond simple knowledge retention.

I would also like to thank my colleague who partnered with me in developing the SCORE course. His willingness to collaborate across organizational boundaries, to experiment with new approaches to security training, and to invest countless hours in curriculum development demonstrated the kind of professional generosity that advances the entire humanitarian sector. Our partnership proved that innovation often emerges from the intersection of different experiences and perspectives and that the best training programs are built through collaboration rather than competition.

The transformation from someone who survived institutional betrayal to someone who could help others navigate hostile environments safely required more than personal resilience; it required mentors who believed in redemption, colleagues who valued authenticity, and institutions willing to invest in unconventional expertise. The trainer's arena became the space where trauma found its most constructive expression, where the lessons learned through pain could be systematically shared to prevent others from experiencing similar harm.

In teaching others to protect themselves, I had finally learned to protect something essential in myself: the belief that broken things could be rebuilt stronger, that wounds could become wisdom, and that the most effective guardians are often those who know intimately what it means to need protection.

29

Restorative Engagement

The online group fell silent as I finished sharing my story with the Restorative Engagement circle. On my monitor, three defence representatives, an Air Force Colonel (female), an Air Force Major (female), and a Navy Captain (male), sat with expressions that reflected something I hadn't expected to see: genuine understanding, acknowledgment, and what appeared to be a commitment to change. They were all in their home offices during these two-day video sessions, not in uniform, which somehow made the setting feel more personal and less institutional.

It had taken me nearly three years since the class action settlement to finally participate in the RE process. The decision didn't come from external pressure or a phone call seeking help; it emerged from my own journey toward stability in therapy and a growing sense that my silence was no longer serving me or others who might benefit from my experience.

The Path to Engagement

The invitation to participate in Restorative Engagement had been sitting in my email for weeks. As part of the CAF-DND Sexual Misconduct Class Action Settlement, the program offered class members like me the opportunity to share our experiences directly with defence representatives, contributing to institutional cultural change and potentially finding personal healing through the process.

For years, I had convinced myself that I wasn't ready, that my trauma was too complex, and that speaking about it would only reopen wounds that I was finally learning to manage. But as my therapy sessions became more consistent and effective, I began to recognize that my reluctance wasn't just about protecting myself; it was about questioning whether my voice could actually contribute to meaningful change.

The breakthrough occurred during a particularly challenging therapy session through my Employee Assistance Program (EAP) at work, where we addressed my diagnosis and its effects on my prior work at World Vision. My therapist had asked me a simple question: "What would it mean to you if another veteran, struggling with similar experiences, never had to go through what you went through?"

That question lingered with me for some time. As a global security advisor, I spent my career identifying risks and developing strategies to protect others. Yet here was a risk, the ongoing impact of institutional sexual misconduct, that I had the knowledge and experience to help address, and I was choosing silence.

Preparing for Vulnerability

The RE representatives worked with us over several sessions leading up to the formal engagement, helping to create the narrative that would be followed. This collaborative approach felt genuine because we were part of the process, not just subjects being processed. They understood that my experience as a male survivor carried specific challenges: the additional stigma, the way military culture had taught me that victimization was incompatible with strength, and the isolation that came from being part of a statistic that many people didn't even know existed. Over 40 percent of the class action claims had been filed by men, yet the narrative around military sexual trauma still often focused exclusively on women's experiences.

Before the session, I had extensive internal conversations, both with my different parts and with my support system, preparing ourselves to be aware of any triggers or sensitivities that might arise. My wife was tremendous support during the entire process, understanding that this wasn't just about revisiting past trauma but about potentially contributing to institutional change. My therapist helped us prepare by working through potential triggers and ensuring we had grounding techniques ready if dissociation or other PTSD symptoms emerged.

In a sense, I, the host, was not always present when delivering my case to the defence representatives. My DID system activated during particularly intense moments, with different parts of my identity stepping forward as needed. But we managed to show our true self during this engagement, the integrated survivor who had learned to function despite institutional betrayal, who had rebuilt a meaningful career, and who understood both the personal cost of trauma and its potential for transformation into wisdom.

Through multiple preparatory sessions, I learned to articulate not just what had happened to me between 1985 and 1989, but how it had shaped my subsequent decades of service, my transition to civilian life, my relationships with family and colleagues, and my approach to the humanitarian work that had become my second career.

Most importantly, I learned to frame my experience not as a personal failure or weakness, but as an institutional failure that had systemic solutions. The trauma I carried wasn't just mine; it belonged to a system that had failed to protect me and thousands of others, and that system had a responsibility to change.

The Power of Institutional Acknowledgment

The day of my formal engagement session, I shared details I had never voiced outside of therapy, describing impacts that had rippled through every aspect of my life. Without going into the exact details, I provided the information that I share in "A Soldier's Cry," the multiple assaults during basic training and trade training, the institutional responses that compounded the trauma, and the decades of struggling to

291

rebuild trust in authority and purpose in service.

These officers had received our briefs ahead of time to gain
a basic understanding of our traumas, which I appreciated.
It meant we didn't have to start from scratch in explaining
context, and they came prepared to listen rather than simply
react. All three were very attentive to the stories we three
survivors relayed to them, asking thoughtful questions and
responding with what felt like genuine empathy rather than
bureaucratic distance.

I was relieved when these officers showed genuine feelings
from our experiences, mine in particular. The Air Force
colonel's eyes reflected understanding when I described
the impact on my family relationships. The major asked
thoughtful questions about how my military sexual trauma
had affected my transition to civilian work. The Navy captain nodded with what appeared to be recognition when I
explained how institutional betrayal had shaped my approach
to leadership in humanitarian contexts. He was also surprised
by my acknowledgment that MST starts as early as the cadet
system and has never been addressed.

When I finished speaking, sharing details I had carried in
silence for nearly four decades, the response wasn't uncomfortable silence. It was respectful, processing, and ultimately
transformative.

The Senior Defence Representative responded with words
I had never expected to hear from the institution I had
served: "We failed you. The system failed you, and we take

responsibility for that failure. Your experience matters, your voice matters, and we are committed to ensuring this doesn't happen to others."

It wasn't absolution; nothing could return the decades I had lost to my mental health condition, relationship difficulties, and professional challenges rooted in unaddressed trauma. But it was acknowledgment, and that acknowledgment created space for something I hadn't felt in years: a sense that my experience could contribute to something larger than my own healing.

The Limits of Resolution

However, I am still not sure how far the military will take this acknowledgment or whether meaningful systemic change will result. This uncertainty is part of why I am writing these two books, to ensure that survivor voices remain heard and accountability continues, regardless of how institutional responses evolve.

The 900-million-dollar settlement, while acknowledging other survivors and not diminishing their experiences, was not nearly enough to address the scope of harm that had been done. The DVA pension was also inadequate, as it failed to take into account the depth of the various trauma experiences. In my case, eight assaults during basic training and two during trade training created complex trauma that affected every aspect of my subsequent life, yet the compensation framework couldn't adequately account for such accumulated harm.

There was no closure for me in the traditional sense, but participating in the RE process did reopen some old wounds while also providing a path toward something resembling acknowledgment. It forced me to revisit traumatic memories in detail, which triggered PTSD symptoms and dissociative episodes that took weeks to fully process. However, it also provided me with the chance to directly confront institutional representatives who appeared genuinely dedicated to learning and transformation.

I don't know how the military has changed since the 1980s. The officers I spoke with seemed earnest in their commitment to reform, but institutions are complex systems that resist change even when individual leaders are well-intentioned. The cultural transformation required to prevent future harm will take decades and sustained commitment from multiple generations of leadership.

Looking Toward Leadership Engagement

I believe this initial step was worth it, and I am looking forward to the next step, "The Executive Leadership" circle, if selected. The opportunity to share survivor perspectives with senior military leadership could contribute to policy changes and cultural shifts that prevent others from experiencing what I endured.

Yet I approach this possibility with cautious optimism rather than naive hope. I've learned through decades of institutional experience that acknowledgment is only valuable if it translates into sustained action. The RE process created space for difficult conversations, but lasting change will require continued pressure, ongoing survivor advocacy, and institutional commitment that extends beyond individual leaders' terms of service.

Integration and Ongoing Healing

I am nowhere near healed, but I am learning how to manage my DID when PTSD symptoms arise. The RE process taught me that healing doesn't require any particular timeline or institutional validation. My dissociative identity disorder isn't something to overcome but rather a reality to integrate, a survival mechanism that enabled me to endure trauma and rebuild a meaningful life in its aftermath.

I am grateful to the Operational Stress Injury (OSI) network and the work we are doing together. The peer support opportunities, trauma-informed therapeutic approaches, and survivor advocacy initiatives provide frameworks for continued growth while contributing to institutional accountability.

The RE experience continues to inform my conversation with myself about formal peer support. Having shared my story with institutional representatives and witnessed their genuine response, I feel more prepared to engage with other survivors in structured support settings. The vulnerability needed for the RE process served as practice for the ongoing vulnerability required in peer support relationships.

The Continuing Mission

What remains clear is that healing doesn't require any particular approach or timeline. The RE process taught me that my voice has value, that institutional acknowledgment is possible, and that survivor experiences can contribute to meaningful change when institutions are willing to listen and learn.

Therapy continues to provide stability and growth. Whether peer support becomes part of my journey will depend on my continued assessment of what serves both my healing and my ability to contribute meaningfully to the healing of others.

The conversation continues, informed by growing stability, expanding understanding, and the ongoing recognition that service can take many forms, including the service of sharing our stories, challenging institutional failures, and supporting others in finding their own paths to healing and purpose.

For now, I remain committed to the mission of transformation, personal healing that contributes to institutional change, individual recovery that serves collective accountability, and survivor advocacy that ensures the voices of those harmed by military sexual misconduct continue to be heard and honoured.

The RE process was one step in a longer journey toward justice and healing. The books I'm writing represent another step. The ongoing work of institutional reform and survivor support represents the mission that will continue long after my own healing journey reaches whatever completion is possible for someone carrying the wounds and wisdom that military sexual trauma creates.

In participating in the RE process, I learned that institutions can begin to change when they're presented with survivor truth and genuine commitment to doing better. Whether they will sustain that commitment remains to be seen. But survivors will continue to speak, continue to advocate, and continue to transform their wounds into wisdom that serves both their own healing and the protection of others who serve.

30

Peer Support and Survivor Advocacy

The online group fell silent as I finished sharing my story with the Restorative Engagement circle. On my monitor, the defence representatives, a mix of senior officers, sat with expressions that reflected something I hadn't expected to see: genuine understanding, acknowledgment, and what appeared to be a commitment to change.

It had taken me nearly three years since the class action settlement to finally participate in the RE process. The decision didn't come from external pressure or a phone call seeking help; it emerged from my own journey toward stability in therapy and a growing sense that my silence was no longer serving me or others who might benefit from my experience.

The Path to Engagement

The invitation to participate in Restorative Engagement had been sitting in my email for a few weeks. As part of the CAF-DND Sexual Misconduct Class Action Settlement, the program offered class members like me the opportunity to share our experiences directly with defence representatives, contributing to institutional culture change while potentially finding personal healing through the process.

For years, I had convinced myself that I wasn't ready, that my trauma was too complex, and that speaking about it would only reopen wounds that I was finally learning to manage. But as my therapy sessions became more consistent and effective, I began to recognize that my reluctance wasn't just about protecting myself; it was about questioning whether my voice could actually contribute to meaningful change.

The breakthrough occurred during a particularly challenging therapy session through my Employee Assistance Program (EAP) at work, where we addressed my diagnosis and its effects on my prior work at World Vision. My therapist had asked me a simple question: "What would it mean to you if another veteran, struggling with similar experiences, never had to go through what you went through?"

That question lingered with me for some time. As a global security advisor, I spent my career identifying risks and developing strategies to protect others. Yet here was a risk, the ongoing impact of institutional sexual misconduct, that I had the knowledge and experience to help address, and I was choosing silence.

Finding My Voice in the RE Process

The Restorative Engagement process itself was unlike anything I had experienced in traditional therapy or military
settings. Working with trauma-informed restorative practitioners from the Sexual Misconduct Support and Resource
Centre, I was able to co-design my participation in a way that
felt safe and empowering.

The practitioners understood that my experience as a male
survivor carried specific challenges: the additional stigma,
the way military culture had taught me that victimization was
incompatible with strength, and the isolation that came from
being part of a statistic that many people didn't even know
existed. Over 40 percent of the class action claims had been
filed by men, yet the narrative around military sexual trauma
still often focused exclusively on women's experiences.

Through multiple preparatory sessions, I learned to articulate
not just what had happened to me between 1985 and 1989,
but how it had shaped my subsequent decades of service, my
transition to civilian life, my relationships with family and
colleagues, and my approach to the humanitarian work that
had become my second career.

Most importantly, I learned to frame my experience not as a
personal failure or weakness, but as an institutional failure
that had systemic solutions. The trauma I carried wasn't just
mine; it belonged to a system that had failed to protect me

300

and thousands of others, and that system had a responsibility to change.

The Power of Institutional Acknowledgment

The day of my formal engagement session, I entered the room carrying nearly four decades of silence. When I finished speaking, sharing details I had never voiced outside of therapy, and describing impacts that had rippled through every aspect of my life, the silence that followed wasn't uncomfortable. It was respectful, processing, and ultimately transformative.

The Senior Defence Representative, a Brigadier-General whose own military bearing suggested she understood service from the inside, responded with words I had never expected to hear from the institution I had served: "We failed you. The system failed you, and we take responsibility for that failure. Your experience matters, your voice matters, and we are committed to ensuring this doesn't happen to others."

It wasn't absolution; nothing could return the decades I had lost to my mental health condition, relationship difficulties, and professional challenges rooted in unaddressed trauma. But it was acknowledgment, and that acknowledgment created space for something I hadn't felt in years: a sense that my experience could contribute to something larger than my own healing.

The Question of Peer Support

The time following my RE session brought unexpected clarity about some things but profound uncertainty about others. The process had connected me with other survivors, some through the formal program, others through the broader network of class action members who were finding their voices. What struck me was how many of us had navigated our healing journeys in isolation, each reinventing approaches to therapy, developing personal strategies for managing triggers, and learning to integrate our military experience with civilian life without the benefit of peer understanding.

I learned about the CAF-DND Peer Support Program as I completed my RE process. The program offered something that traditional therapy, while valuable, couldn't provide: connection with others who shared not just the experience of military sexual trauma, but the specific cultural context in which it occurred.

My therapist is instrumental in helping me achieve stability in therapy, but there are certain aspects of my experience, the way military culture had shaped my response to trauma, the specific challenges of transitioning from warrior identity to humanitarian work, and the intersection of service pride and victimization, were areas where peer understanding could offer unique insights.

But knowing that peer support might be valuable and being ready to engage with it were two very different things.

Wrestling with Vulnerability

The RE process had required me to be vulnerable in a structured, time-limited way with people whose role was to listen and respond institutionally. Peer support would require ongoing vulnerability with people who shared similar wounds, a prospect that felt both appealing and terrifying.

Part of my hesitation stemmed from learned patterns of isolation. For nearly four decades, I had managed my trauma largely alone. I had developed coping strategies, built a successful civilian career, and maintained my commitment to humanitarian work. There was something both comforting and limiting about the independence this isolation had created.

But as I reflected on this resistance to vulnerability, I realized I was already deep in a process of exposure that I had chosen for myself. Writing these two books, "A Soldier's Cry" and "Resilience Redeployed," had required a level of vulnerability that surpassed anything I had experienced in therapy or even in the RE process.

Every chapter I wrote meant revisiting trauma, examining failures, and exposing thoughts and experiences I had kept private for decades. The act of putting my story into words, of organizing my experiences into narratives that others might read, had been its own form of peer support preparation. I was already practicing the vulnerability that formal peer support would require, just in a different medium.

The writing process had taught me that vulnerability could be managed, that I could choose how much to reveal and when, and that sharing difficult experiences, even with future, unknown readers, could be healing rather than retraumatizing. Each chapter completed was evidence that I could be vulnerable and remain whole, that my story could serve purposes beyond just my own processing.

Yet writing was still a solitary act, mediated by the page and the future reader. Peer support would require real-time vulnerability with people whose own wounds might interact with mine in unpredictable ways. The control I maintained through writing, the ability to revise, to choose my words carefully, and to protect certain details would be much harder to maintain in live conversation with other survivors.

I also wrestled with questions about readiness. Was I stable enough in my own healing to be helpful to others? Was I healed enough to avoid being retraumatized by hearing others' stories? Could I engage in peer support without losing the professional boundaries that had been crucial to my work at WUSC?

My therapists and I spent several sessions exploring these questions. They helped me recognize that the desire to be "perfect" before helping others was itself a trauma response, the same perfectionism that had kept me functional but isolated for decades. She also pointed out that my questions about readiness, combined with my willingness to write about my experiences, suggested exactly the kind of self-awareness that could make me effective in peer support roles.

The Professional Intersection

My roles in the NGO world provide a unique perspective on the potential value of peer support. As one of the few employees with military experience, I notice that other veterans occasionally seek me out for informal conversations about transition challenges, work stress, and the sometimes difficult process of integrating military identity with civilian purpose.

These conversations aren't therapy or formal support; they are simply moments when someone who had served found value in speaking with someone else who understood military culture from the inside. I started to understand that formal peer support programs could potentially facilitate and enhance these informal connections.

Through my network of humanitarian security professionals, I had also connected with other veterans who had found their way into NGO work. Many carried experiences of trauma, transition challenges, and the ongoing work of integrating military identity with civilian purpose. Some had found peer support valuable; others, like me, were still considering whether and how to engage with it.

Observing from the Margins

Rather than diving immediately into peer support participation, I find myself studying the landscape of available options. The CAF-DND Peer Support Program offers multiple formats, individual peer matching, formal group sessions, and informal discussion platforms, allowing participants to engage in ways that feel safe and appropriate for their healing stage.

I read research about peer support effectiveness, particularly for veterans dealing with military sexual trauma. The evidence was compelling: peer support could provide validation, reduce isolation, offer practical coping strategies, and create community in ways that complemented but didn't replace professional therapy.

I also learned about the challenges. Peer support groups could be retraumatizing if poorly facilitated. Individual peer matching required careful screening and ongoing support. The very vulnerability that made peer connection powerful also made it potentially risky.

Questions About Contribution

As my own healing progressed through continued therapy, I found myself increasingly drawn to questions about contribution rather than just recovery. The RE process had shown me that sharing my experience could contribute to institutional change. But could it also contribute to individual healing for others struggling with similar challenges?

I began to see potential parallels between peer support and other aspects of my humanitarian work. Risk assessment required understanding context, building trust, and sharing information that could protect others from harm. Peer support seemed to involve similar skills applied to different challenges, using personal experience to help others navigate risks I had already encountered.

At the same time, I recognized important differences. My professional work maintains clear boundaries between my personal experience and my advisory role. Peer support would require integrating personal experience directly into the helping relationship. This integration feels both potentially powerful and personally challenging.

The Question Remains Open

As I write this chapter, the question of peer support partic-ipation remains unresolved. The CAF-DND Peer Support Program continues to evolve, and I continue to learn more about how it might fit with my ongoing healing journey. I am no longer questioning whether I need continued support; therapy has taught me that healing is an ongoing process rather than a destination. The question is whether peer support represents a next step in that process for me.

Some days, the prospect of connecting with other survivors feels exactly like what I need: community, understanding, and the opportunity to contribute to healing beyond my own. Other days, it feels overwhelming, a vulnerability I'm not yet ready to embrace.

My therapist reminds me that this ambivalence is valuable information worth honouring. I can apply the same careful assessment I use in security work to make decisions about my own healing journey. Peer support will be available when and if I decide I'm ready for it.

Looking Forward

What I know for certain is that the RE process has changed my understanding of my own story and my potential role in supporting institutional change. Whether or not I choose to participate in formal peer support programs, I have moved from silence to a willingness to speak about my experience in ways that might benefit others.

My work at WUSC has become more informed by my understanding of trauma and resilience. I am more attuned to signs of distress in colleagues, more skilled at creating psychologically safe spaces for difficult conversations, and more aware of how personal experiences can inform professional contributions without overwhelming them.

The informal conversations with other veterans continue. Occasionally these feel like peer support, even without formal structure or training. Perhaps these organic connections are preparing me for more structured engagement, or perhaps they represent their own valuable form of mutual support.

What remains clear is that healing doesn't require any particular approach or timeline. The RE process taught me that my voice has value. Therapy continues to provide stability and growth. Whether peer support becomes part of my journey will depend on my continued assessment of what serves both my healing and my ability to contribute meaningfully to the healing of others.

The conversation with myself about peer support continues, informed by growing stability, expanding understanding, and the ongoing recognition that service can take many forms, including the service of sharing our stories and supporting others in finding their own paths to healing and purpose.

For now, the question remains open, and I'm learning to be comfortable with that uncertainty while remaining open to the possibilities it might hold.

31

The Institutional Mirror

Sitting in my home office watching my monitor, preparing for my Restorative Engagement session with CAF representatives, I experienced a moment of uncomfortable clarity. The nervous energy in my stomach, the hypervigilance scanning the room for exits, and the careful rehearsal of what I would and wouldn't share, all of it felt hauntingly familiar. I had felt exactly the same way thirty-five years earlier, preparing to report my assault to military authorities.

The only difference was that this time, I understood what was happening. Decades of humanitarian work had taught me to recognize institutional patterns, to see beyond individual failures to systemic problems that repeated across organizations, cultures, and contexts. The military, which had betrayed me in 1989, was not unique in its failures; it was merely adhering to a script that I would repeatedly encounter in the humanitarian sector.

The Parallel Patterns

My first glimpse of this pattern came during my deployment to South Sudan in 2014, when I watched aid workers struggling with trauma responses that their organizations couldn't or wouldn't acknowledge. A colleague who had witnessed mass atrocities was told to "take a few days off and get back out there." Another staff member, experiencing panic attacks after a security incident, was quietly moved to a "less stressful" position, code for professional sidetracking.

The language was different from what I had heard in military contexts, but the underlying message was identical: your trauma is inconvenient, your symptoms are disruptive, and your value to the organization depends on your ability to function despite what you've experienced. Whether the institution wore military fatigues or humanitarian logos, the response to individual vulnerability followed the same defensive playbook.

This recognition became a lens through which I could analyze both sectors with uncomfortable clarity. The military had taught me what institutional betrayal looked like; the humanitarian sector showed me that such betrayal wasn't an aberration but a predictable pattern that emerged whenever organizational self-preservation conflicted with member protection.

* * *

Comparative Analysis: Two Sectors, Same Script

Denial and Minimization

In military culture, I never reported the sexual assaults because my perpetrator made explicit threats against my life if I spoke out. During a security briefing in Port-au-Prince, a colleague confided that flashbacks to the 2010 earthquake had begun paralyzing her in street checkpoints. When she asked her manager for time to process, she was told, 'Stress is part of the job, just get back to work.' The underlying message was clear: my silence was the price of survival, and the institution's unspoken complicity enabled this terror to flourish unchallenged. The meticulously upheld myth that military units consisted of unflappable warriors capable of overcoming any obstacle necessitated the concealment of my victimization. My trauma didn't fit the narrative, so the system created conditions where reporting seemed impossible rather than having to confront the implications of acknowledging such violations existed within their ranks.

The humanitarian sector employs slightly different language but follows the same logic. When staff experience trauma, the default response is often "mission continuity over staff welfare." Organizations acknowledge that the work is difficult but resist recognizing that difficulty can cause lasting harm requiring systematic support. Humanitarian organizations struggle to admit that their noble missions can harm the people who carry them out, just as the military couldn't acknowledge that soldiers could be victimized by their own system.

312

During my time with World Vision, I witnessed this pattern repeatedly. The organization encouraged staff who developed PTSD symptoms after witnessing atrocities to view their responses as temporary stress rather than legitimate trauma. When I disclosed my pre-existing PTSD stemming from military sexual trauma, the organization either dismissed these reports outright or made it clear they did not want to hear about conditions that predated my humanitarian service. The organization had extensive protocols for protecting beneficiaries but minimal frameworks for acknowledging that protectors themselves might need protection, particularly those who arrived already carrying invisible wounds from previous institutional failures.

Survivor Blaming and Scapegoating

The military's response to my declining performance and obvious struggles was dismissive and incurious. Rather than investigate why a previously competent soldier was deteriorating, they focused on surface-level behavioural issues. Why wasn't I following procedures as sharply? Why was my performance declining? Why couldn't I maintain the standards I had previously met? The institution showed no interest in understanding the root causes of my struggles, preferring to treat symptoms rather than examine what might have gone wrong under their watch.

Humanitarian organizations employ remarkably similar tactics when staff experience trauma or security incidents. "You should have known the risks" becomes the default response, as if understanding them intellectually could prevent psychological damage from witnessing human suffering. Staff who develop addiction issues are treated as disciplinary problems rather than trauma survivors seeking relief from symptoms their organizations helped create.

My own termination from World Vision exemplified this pattern. Despite seven years of exemplary service in some of the world's most dangerous environments, my struggle with pornography addiction, a common but rarely discussed coping mechanism for trauma survivors, was treated as a character flaw rather than as a symptom of accumulated trauma that the organization had a responsibility to address. The focus was on my failure to maintain appropriate boundaries rather than on the institutional failure to provide adequate support for someone managing complex PTSD in high-stress environments.

Institutional Self-Protection

Both sectors prioritize institutional reputation over individual welfare when these interests conflict. The military protected the chain of command by silencing survivors who might expose leadership failures. Humanitarian organizations protect donor relationships and operational access by downplaying the true cost of their missions on staff well-being.

This self-protection manifests in carefully managed information flows. Military incident reports sanitize traumatic events to protect operational security and institutional image. Humanitarian organizations' internal communications acknowledge staff trauma privately while presenting sanitized versions to donors and the public that emphasize resilience and impact rather than human cost.

The result in both cases is institutional learning that occurs slowly, if at all, because accurate information about systemic problems never reaches decision-makers with the authority to implement meaningful change.

Inadequate Support Systems

Perhaps the most damaging parallel is how both sectors have developed support systems that appear comprehensive on paper but fail catastrophically when confronted with complex trauma cases. Military support systems in the 1980s were designed around the assumption that soldiers were fundamentally strong individuals who might need temporary assistance rather than people who could develop chronic conditions requiring long-term, specialized care.

Humanitarian organizations today make similar assumptions through Employee Assistance Programs that focus on short-term, crisis-intervention models. These systems work adequately for staff experiencing temporary stress but fail completely when confronted with military sexual trauma survivors, individuals with pre-existing PTSD, or staff who develop complex trauma responses through accumulated exposure to human suffering.

My experience with World Vision's EAP services illustrated this limitation perfectly. The Headington Institute provided valuable support for many staff members, but their model couldn't accommodate someone whose trauma preceded their humanitarian service and was being exacerbated by deployment environments. The system was designed to address humanitarian trauma, not to support staff who brought military trauma into humanitarian contexts.

The Common Root: Organizational Culture Over Individual Welfare

The deeper I examined both sectors, the more I recognized a fundamental cultural similarity: both prioritize institutional survival over member protection when these goals conflict. This priority shapes everything from resource allocation to crisis response to leadership development.

In military culture, this manifests as the expectation that individual soldiers will sacrifice everything, including their psychological wellbeing, for mission success. The institutional motto, "service before self" becomes a justification for abandoning service members when they need institutional support most.

Humanitarian culture employs different language but follows similar logic. The emphasis on serving "the most vulnerable" creates implicit pressure on staff to minimize their own needs and to view personal trauma responses as selfish indulgences that detract from the organizational mission.

Both cultures create environments where asking for help is interpreted as weakness, where trauma responses are considered professional liabilities rather than natural consequences of difficult work, and where institutional loyalty is measured by willingness to suffer in silence.

How Personal Experience Informed Vision for Change

Living inside both systems provided insights that external observers might miss. The hypervigilance that made me unemployable in civilian settings became a professional asset in humanitarian security work, but only because I learned to channel trauma responses productively rather than eliminating them. This experience taught me that effective institutional change required understanding trauma as a complex phenomenon that could be both a liability and an asset depending on organizational response.

My dissociative episodes, once sources of shame and professional vulnerability, became windows into understanding how stress affects cognitive processing under extreme conditions. Rather than pathologizing these responses, effective organizations could learn to accommodate and even utilize the unique perspectives that trauma survivors bring to high-stress environments.

Most importantly, my experience taught me that institutional betrayal creates specific kinds of wisdom that can inform institutional reform. Survivors understand viscerally how organizations fail, what early warning signs look like, and what systemic changes could prevent similar harm. But this wisdom only becomes useful when institutions create space for survivor voices and demonstrate genuine commitment to

317

learning from past failures.

Specific Recommendations for Military Reform

Based on my experience in both sectors, military reform requires changes that go beyond policy adjustments to fundamental cultural transformation:

Trauma-Informed Leadership Training: Military leaders need comprehensive education about trauma's neurological impact, the psychology of disclosure, and the long-term effects of institutional betrayal. This training should emphasize that supporting trauma survivors strengthens rather than weakens unit effectiveness and that institutional loyalty means protecting the vulnerable rather than silencing the inconvenient.

Survivor-Centred Justice Processes: Military justice systems must be redesigned to prioritize survivor welfare over institutional convenience. This means believing survivors from the outset, providing immediate support services regardless of investigation outcomes, ensuring fair and transparent investigations, and creating meaningful consequences for both perpetrators and leaders who enable abuse through negligence or cover-up.

Cultural Transformation Beyond Policy: Policy changes alone cannot eliminate military sexual trauma; they must be accompanied by cultural shifts that celebrate courage in reporting assault, create psychological safety for vulnerability, and redefine strength to include seeking help when needed.

This transformation requires sustained commitment from senior leadership and the consistent modelling of trauma-informed values.

Accountability Without Retaliation: The military must develop systems that distinguish between institutional accountability and individual persecution. Survivors who report assault must be protected from both formal retaliation and informal ostracism, while the institution must be held accountable for systemic failures that enable abuse.

Specific Recommendations for Humanitarian Sector Reform

The humanitarian sector's reform needs are different but equally urgent:

Beyond Traditional EAP Models: Humanitarian organizations need mental health support systems designed around the reality that trauma exposure is occupational rather than exceptional. This means providing long-term therapeutic relationships, specialized trauma treatment, and addiction support that understands the connection between trauma and substance use. Support systems must accommodate pre-existing trauma conditions rather than assuming all staff arrive psychologically intact.

Veteran-Inclusive Organizational Practices: Organizations must develop hiring, onboarding, and management practices that leverage rather than marginalize military experience. This includes training hiring managers to understand military culture, creating interview processes that allow veterans to translate skills effectively, and establishing support systems that can address pre-existing trauma rather than waiting for crises.

Long-Term Mental Health Support Integration: Rather than treating mental health as a separate, personal issue, organizations must integrate psychological support into professional development frameworks. This means recognizing that managing mental health conditions can enhance rather than diminish professional capacity and creating career pathways that accommodate ongoing therapeutic needs.

Addiction as Trauma Symptom Recognition: Organizations must develop a sophisticated understanding of addiction, which frequently represents attempts to manage untreated trauma rather than simply moral failures. This requires addiction policies that emphasize treatment over termination and recognition that supporting recovery serves both individual and organizational interests.

Universal Principles for Institutional Change

Both sectors could benefit from adopting universal principles for trauma-informed institutional change:

Leadership Courage Over Convenience: Effective reform requires leaders willing to prioritize member welfare over institutional convenience, even when this creates short-term complications. This courage must be modelled consistently and rewarded systematically to become embedded in organizational culture.

Survivor Voices as Essential to Reform: Institutional change cannot occur without meaningful participation from those who have experienced institutional failure. Survivors possess unique insights into how systems fail and what changes could prevent similar harm, but these insights only become useful when institutions create safe, meaningful opportunities for survivor participation in reform processes.

Culture Change as Strategic Imperative: Both sectors must recognize that trauma-informed practices aren't just moral obligations but strategic necessities. Organizations that cannot support their members through difficult experiences will lose talent, fail to achieve missions, and perpetuate cycles of harm that ultimately undermine their effectiveness.

Measuring Success Through Member Wellbeing: Reform efforts must establish metrics that prioritize member wellbeing alongside traditional performance indicators. Success should be measured not just through mission accomplishment but through retention rates, advancement opportunities, workplace satisfaction, and recovery outcomes for members experiencing trauma or addiction.

The Mirror's Reflection: What Both Sectors Can Learn

The most powerful insight from comparing both sectors is recognizing opportunities for cross-sector learning and collaboration:

Cross-Sector Knowledge Transfer: The military's evolving approach to sexual misconduct, while imperfect, demonstrates that even highly traditional institutions can develop trauma-informed practices when they commit to change. Humanitarian organizations could adapt military innovations in survivor support while avoiding military mistakes in justice processes.

Similarly, the humanitarian sector's emphasis on cultural sensitivity and community-based approaches could inform military efforts to create more inclusive, supportive cultures for trauma survivors.

Shared Accountability Frameworks: Both sectors could benefit from developing shared standards for trauma-informed practices, creating accountability mechanisms that transcend individual organizations, and establishing cross-sector communities of practice focused on institutional reform.

Joint Advocacy for Trauma-Informed Practices: Rather than working in isolation, reform advocates in both sectors could coordinate efforts to promote trauma-informed practices across institutions. Military sexual trauma survivors and humanitarian workers experiencing organizational betrayal face similar challenges and could strengthen advocacy efforts through collaboration.

Breaking the Cycle

The institutional mirror reflects uncomfortable truths about how organizations respond to member vulnerability, but it also reveals opportunities for transformation. My journey from military betrayal through humanitarian service to advocacy work demonstrates that survivors can become catalysts for institutional change rather than just survivors of institutional failure.

This transformation requires survivors willing to risk additional vulnerability by speaking truth about institutional harm, institutions willing to examine their own failures honestly, and leaders courageous enough to prioritize member welfare over organizational convenience. The cycle of institutional betrayal can be broken, but only through sustained commitment to placing human dignity above institutional self-preservation.

This comparative analysis has strengthened my belief that institutional change is both feasible and essential. The military that betrayed me in 1989 is slowly developing more trauma-informed approaches to sexual misconduct. The humanitarian sector that dismissed me in 2016 is gradually recognizing the need for better mental health support. These changes occur slowly and imperfectly, but they demonstrate that institutions can learn and grow.

The responsibility for breaking cycles of institutional betrayal belongs to all of us: survivors who find courage to speak, institutions that choose growth over defensiveness, and com-

munities that demand accountability from the organizations
they support. The mirror shows us not just where we've failed,
but where we can choose to do better.

The boy broken by military sexual trauma became a man committed to ensuring that institutions live up to their highest
aspirations rather than their lowest common denominators.
This work continues because the need for it continues, and
because every survivor who speaks truth creates possibilities
for others to find their own paths from betrayal to purpose,
from silence to advocacy, and from institutional failure to
institutional transformation.

32

Diagnosing Institutional Failures

The email arrived on a Thursday morning while I was preparing for a security briefing about our upcoming deployment to South Sudan. The sender was a former Marine who had read "A Soldier's Cry" and had been struggling to establish his place in the civilian workforce since his medical discharge three years earlier. His message was both heartbreaking and familiar: "I thought humanitarian work would be a good fit for someone like me, but I can't seem to navigate past the interviews. They see my military experience as either a liability, or they romanticize it in ways that make me uncomfortable. Do you have any advice?"

That email crystalized something I had been thinking about for months as I watched talented veterans struggle to find meaningful civilian employment while humanitarian organizations complained about skills shortages in areas where veterans excelled: crisis management, cross-cultural communication, security assessment, and leadership under pressure. There was a fundamental disconnect between what veterans

could offer and what the humanitarian sector was prepared
to receive.

The Current State: Missed Opportunities

The humanitarian sector today operates with an unfortunate
paradox. We work in some of the world's most challenging
environments, dealing with crisis, trauma, and complex
security situations, yet our organizational cultures often lack
the frameworks to effectively support staff who bring direct
experience with these realities.

Veterans who transition to humanitarian work often find
themselves caught between two worlds. Either we dismiss
their military experience as irrelevant to "peace-building"
work, or we exoticize it in ways that reduce complex professional skills to simple stereotypes. Meanwhile, the unique
support needs that come with military service, understanding
of trauma, recognition of hypervigilance as both an asset and
a challenge, and appreciation for the way military culture
shapes communication and decision-making are rarely acknowledged in civilian workplaces.

Such neglect represents a massive waste of human potential.
Research consistently shows that veterans bring valuable
skills to civilian organizations: adaptability, crisis management, leadership, cross-cultural competence, and resilience.
The humanitarian sector, which desperately needs these
skills, is failing to create conditions where veterans can thrive
while contributing their expertise.

The EAP Limitation: A Case Study in Institutional Blindness

My own experience at World Vision illustrates a critical gap in how even well-intentioned humanitarian organizations approach veteran support. World Vision, like many larger NGOs, contracted with the Headington Institute for Employee Assistance Program services. The Headington Institute has built an impressive reputation for supporting humanitarian workers facing stress and trauma, developing frameworks that many organizations have adopted.

But here's what these systems often miss: they're designed to address trauma acquired during humanitarian work, not trauma that veterans bring with them from military service.

During my time at World Vision, I struggled with PTSD and DID stemming from my military sexual assault, which affected my work performance and led to trauma-related addiction as a coping mechanism. Despite having access to EAP services through the Headington Institute, the support system was not equipped to understand or address pre-existing military trauma that was being triggered by humanitarian work environments.

The result was predictable: my trauma-related challenges were interpreted as performance issues rather than as symptoms of untreated military sexual trauma that required specialized, informed support.

This isn't a failure of the Headington Institute specifically;

their work with humanitarian organizations is valuable and necessary. Rather, it illustrates a systemic limitation in how EAPs are typically structured. Most EAPs are designed around short-term, crisis-intervention models that assume employees are fundamentally healthy individuals facing temporary difficulties. They're not designed to support employees who are managing ongoing mental health conditions that require long-term, specialized understanding.

My PTSD and DID were dismissed, and I was subsequently terminated due to addiction-related performance issues, which reflects a failure of institutional understanding. World Vision's systems were sophisticated enough to recognize that humanitarian work creates trauma, but they were not sophisticated enough to recognize that some employees arrive already carrying trauma that humanitarian environments can exacerbate.

The situation was further complicated by the workplace dynamics when I informed a colleague and the Security Operations Director about the disclosure of my pre-existing mental health conditions. While some colleagues and supervisors express superficial support for mental health awareness, the reality is that many do not want the responsibility that comes with actually knowing about an employee's PTSD diagnosis. There's an unspoken preference for plausible deniability; they would rather attribute performance issues to character flaws or lack of commitment than acknowledge that they're witnessing trauma symptoms that require accommodation and specialized understanding. This creates a catch-22 for trauma survivors: suffer in silence and risk being labelled as unreliable, or disclose your condition and risk being considered a liability. The institutional message is clear: we support mental health in theory, but in practice, we prefer employees whose trauma doesn't interfere with productivity or require us to adapt our management approaches.

Learning from Military Sexual Trauma Advocacy

My experience participating in the CAF Restorative Engagement process taught me something crucial about institutional change: organizations can transform their cultures when they commit to understanding and addressing the experiences of their most vulnerable members. The military's evolving approach to sexual misconduct, while far from perfect, demonstrates that even highly traditional institutions can develop trauma-informed practices when they recognize the cost of maintaining harmful cultures.

The humanitarian sector could learn from this example. Just as the military is slowly recognizing that sexual trauma affects readiness and mission effectiveness, humanitarian organizations need to understand that failing to support veteran employees affects both individual well-being and organizational capacity.

The principles emerging from military sexual trauma advocacy, survivor-centred approaches, trauma-informed practices, and institutional accountability could be adapted for broader application in humanitarian organizations. Instead of expecting veterans to conform to civilian workplace cultures that don't understand their experiences, organizations

could develop veteran-inclusive practices that benefit everyone.

33

Prescription for Change

Beyond Traditional EAPs: A Trauma-Informed Approach

The vision begins with recognition that the humanitarian sector is inherently trauma-exposed. Staff work with populations affected by conflict, disaster, and displacement. They witness suffering, navigate dangerous environments, and bear the burden of addressing overwhelming needs with limited resources. Veterans joining this work often bring their own trauma histories while also being particularly skilled at operating in trauma-affected environments.

Traditional EAPs, with their focus on short-term intervention and crisis management, are insufficient for this reality. What's needed is a fundamental shift toward trauma-informed organizational cultures that recognize trauma as a normal response to abnormal situations, whether it was acquired in military service or humanitarian work.

A trauma-informed humanitarian sector would acknowledge these realities systematically rather than individually. Organizations would:

Implement universal trauma-informed practices that benefit all staff while specifically supporting those with military trauma histories. This means creating psychologically safe workplaces, providing ongoing mental health support, and developing policies that recognize trauma's impact on work performance and professional development. Crucially, the change includes understanding that addiction can be a symptom of trauma rather than simply a performance issue.

Ensure the development of veteran-inclusive hiring and onboarding processes that surpass the mere act of marking the veteran box for diversity metrics. This includes training hiring managers to understand military experience, creating interview processes that allow veterans to effectively translate their skills, developing onboarding programs that help veterans navigate civilian organizational cultures, and establishing support systems that can address pre-existing trauma rather than waiting for a crisis.

Establish comprehensive mental health support that goes beyond EAP models to include long-term therapeutic relationships, specialized trauma treatment, and addiction support that understands the connection between trauma and substance use. This isn't about lowering standards; it's about creating conditions where talented individuals can contribute effectively while managing health challenges.

Organizational Culture Transformation

The cultural changes required go beyond policies and programs. They require fundamental shifts in how humanitarian organizations understand competence, resilience, and professional development.

Redefining Strength and Vulnerability: Military culture often equates asking for help with weakness, while humanitarian culture sometimes romanticizes self-sacrifice and burnout as dedication. A veteran-inclusive humanitarian sector would model different approaches to both, recognizing that seeking support is professional competence and that sustainable impact requires sustainable practices. My experience at World Vision taught me that organizations that can't hold space for employee vulnerability ultimately lose valuable talent and institutional knowledge.

Integrating Security and Safety Mindsets: Veterans often bring sophisticated understanding of risk assessment and crisis management. Rather than seeing this as militarization of humanitarian space, organizations could recognize these skills as essential for staff safety and program effectiveness. The hypervigilance that can be challenging in civilian social situations becomes an asset in security assessment and emergency response.

Leveraging Cross-Cultural Competence: Military service often involves extensive cross-cultural training and experience. Veterans who have served in international deployments bring cultural competencies that are directly relevant to humanitarian work. Organizations need frameworks for recognizing and utilizing this experience rather than assuming it's irrelevant to "development" contexts.

Understanding Trauma as Professional Experience: Rather than seeing PTSD, anxiety, or other trauma responses as disqualifying conditions, veteran-inclusive organizations would recognize that lived experience with trauma can enhance rather than diminish capacity for trauma-informed practice. This doesn't mean ignoring symptoms or avoiding treatment, but rather integrating healing and professional contribution in ways that serve both individual and organizational needs.

Professional Development and Career Pathways

A veteran-inclusive humanitarian sector would create clear pathways for professional growth that recognize military experience as valuable preparation rather than irrelevant background. This means:

The sector should develop mentorship programs that pair veterans with experienced humanitarian professionals who understand both military culture and civilian organizational dynamics. These mentorships would focus on skill translation, cultural navigation, and career development rather than simply "fixing" veterans to fit civilian moulds.

Creating specialized roles that specifically leverage veteran experience, security focal points, emergency response coordinators, and training specialists for high-risk environments. These roles would be integrated into organizational structures rather than marginalized as "military" positions.

We are committed to providing ongoing professional development that enables veterans to continue their growth while honouring their background. This includes trauma-informed leadership training, advanced security management, and specialized skills development in areas where military experience provides a foundation for humanitarian expertise.

Supporting ongoing mental health needs as part of professional development rather than as separate "personal" issues. Organizations that recognize mental health as integral to professional capacity create environments where employees can excel while managing health challenges sustainably.

Systemic Change Through Partnership

Individual organizations can implement veteran-inclusive practices, but sector-wide transformation requires coordinated effort. This means building partnerships between humanitarian organizations, veteran service organizations, and government agencies focused on veteran employment.

Research and Evidence Building: We need better data about veteran employment in the humanitarian sector, what works, what doesn't, and what barriers exist. This research should be conducted with veterans rather than about us, centering our voices in understanding our own experiences. This includes an honest assessment of how current EAP models serve or fail veteran employees.

Policy Advocacy: Government funding for humanitarian organizations could include requirements or incentives for veteran-inclusive practices. This isn't about quotas but about creating systematic support for organizations that want to do better. It also means advocating for mental health approaches that understand addiction as a symptom of trauma rather than simply a disciplinary issue.

Professional Networks: Creating communities of practice that connect veterans working across different humanitarian organizations, sharing best practices and providing mutual support. These networks could also include civilian colleagues committed to veteran inclusion.

Personal Integration with Professional Vision

My own journey from military service through crisis and isolation to meaningful humanitarian work has taught me that healing and contribution are not sequential processes but interrelated ones. The stability I've found in therapy, the insights from the RE process, and the ongoing work of integration have all been enhanced by having meaningful work that utilizes my experience while serving larger purposes.

Writing "A Soldier's Cry" forced me to examine how my military sexual trauma had shaped my civilian transition. That examination revealed not just personal healing needs but also structural barriers that affect many veterans attempting similar transitions. The silence I maintained for decades wasn't just about personal shame; it was also about professional environments that couldn't hold space for the complexity of veteran experience.

My dismissal from World Vision, while painful at the time, ultimately taught me that organizations that can't support their employees through health challenges lose valuable talent and miss opportunities for institutional learning. A more trauma-informed approach might have recognized my addiction as a symptom requiring treatment rather than as a performance issue requiring termination.

The humanitarian sector I envision would eliminate the need for such either/or choices. Veterans could speak about our experiences, including trauma, without fear of professional consequences. We could leverage our skills while receiving the support we need to do so sustainably. We could contribute to organizational missions while managing health conditions that, properly supported, can enhance rather than diminish our professional capacity.

Implementation Strategies

This vision requires practical steps that organizations can begin implementing immediately:

Assessment and Planning: Organizations should conduct veteran-inclusive workplace assessments, identifying current barriers and opportunities. This assessment should include input from veteran staff and consultation with veteran service organizations. Critically, the process includes honest evaluation of whether current EAP models adequately serve veteran employees with complex trauma histories.

Training and Development: All staff, particularly managers and HR professionals, need training on veteran culture, trauma-informed practices, and inclusive leadership. This training should address both practical skills and unconscious biases. It should also include understanding of how trauma can manifest as performance issues and how addiction often represents attempts to manage untreated trauma.

Policy Development: Organizations need policies that specifically address veteran needs while benefiting all staff, flexible work arrangements, mental health support, career development pathways, and conflict resolution processes that understand military communication styles. This includes policies that recognize addiction as a health condition requiring treatment rather than simply a disciplinary matter.

Partnership Building: Humanitarian organizations should develop formal partnerships with veteran service organizations, creating pipelines for veteran recruitment while ensuring ongoing support. These partnerships should be reciprocal, with humanitarian organizations contributing to the veteran community while veteran organizations help the humanitarian sector understand veteran experiences.

Measuring Success

A veteran-inclusive humanitarian sector would measure success not just through employment numbers but through retention, advancement, and well-being metrics. Success indicators would include:

- **Veteran retention rates** that match or exceed general employee retention
- **Career advancement** for veteran employees at rates proportional to their representation in the workforce
- **Workplace satisfaction** measures that show veterans feel valued and supported
- **Organizational outcomes** that demonstrate how veteran inclusion enhances mission effectiveness
- **Recovery and reintegration** rates for veterans dealing with trauma or addiction-related challenges rather than simply termination rates

Most importantly, success would be measured by the elimination of stories like mine at World Vision, about talented veterans being dismissed for trauma-related challenges that could have been addressed through proper support and acknowledgement of pre-existing PTSD challenges when informed.

The Ripple Effect

The changes required to create veteran-inclusive humanitarian organizations would benefit everyone. Trauma-informed practices support all staff dealing with difficult work. Flexible approaches to mental health support help all employees navigate health challenges. Crisis management skills and security awareness benefit entire teams working in challenging environments.

Furthermore, veteran-inclusive humanitarian organizations would be better positioned to work effectively in conflict and post-conflict settings where understanding of military culture and security dynamics enhances program effectiveness. Organizations that successfully integrate veterans would have competitive advantages in recruitment, retention, and service delivery in complex emergencies.

Organizations that can support employees through health challenges rather than simply terminating them would also build more resilient, committed workforces while contributing to broader societal goals of veteran reintegration and mental health recovery.

Looking Forward

The vision I'm describing isn't utopian; it's practical and necessary. The humanitarian sector faces increasing complexity, growing security challenges, and mounting pressure to demonstrate effectiveness. Veterans represent an underutilized resource for addressing these challenges while bringing lived experience of resilience, adaptation, and service under pressure.

The question isn't whether the humanitarian sector can afford to become more veteran-inclusive; it's whether it can afford not to.

My personal experience indicates that veterans who secure meaningful civilian employment that acknowledges their service and meets their support needs can significantly contribute to organizational missions. We bring not just skills but dedication, understanding of sacrifice, and commitment to service that aligns closely with humanitarian values. We also bring lived experience with trauma and recovery that can inform more effective trauma-informed practices for entire organizations.

The Marine who emailed me eventually found his place in humanitarian work, but only after months of struggle that could have been avoided with better organizational practices. Every veteran who gives up on finding meaningful civilian work, or who is dismissed for trauma-related challenges, represents not just individual tragedy but also collective loss of potential contribution.

The vision for a better sector is ultimately about creating conditions where service continues in new forms, where military experience becomes a foundation for civilian contribution, and where the skills developed in uniform enhance rather than complicate civilian missions. It's about building a humanitarian sector worthy of the veterans who choose to serve it, capable of maximizing their contributions to global well-being, and sophisticated enough to support the complex needs that come with complex experience.

This transformation won't happen automatically, but it will happen if enough organizations commit to making it happen. The vision begins with recognition that current approaches are insufficient, develops through commitment to doing better, and succeeds through sustained action by individuals and institutions willing to do the difficult work of cultural change.

In writing both "A Soldier's Cry" and this book, I've learned that healing and contribution are not mutually exclusive; they can be mutually reinforcing when organizations create conditions that support both. The humanitarian sector has an opportunity to lead in demonstrating how trauma-informed approaches can enhance rather than diminish organizational effectiveness while serving both individual and collective goals of healing and service.

V

Transformation and Teaching

The collapse of my career at World Vision did not mark an end, but a transformation. Stripped of institutional identity yet armed with hard-earned experience, I discovered that true resilience does not lie in avoiding falls, but in how we rise again. These years brought new organizations, a deeper understanding of the persistence of trauma, and a gradual recognition that my greatest contribution might not be to protect others in crisis zones but to teach them to protect themselves while honouring their own wounds.

34

The Alchemy of Wounds to Wisdom

In the crucible of extreme adversity, where violence, chaos, and profound loss converge, trauma imprints itself on the nervous system, forging neural pathways that underpin hypervigilance, dissociation, and emotional compartment alization. What once were survival symptoms can, with conscious cultivation, be transmuted into professional strengths: heightened threat detection, rapid decision-making under pressure, and the capacity to function with clarity when others falter. This chapter examines the neurological and real-world metamorphosis of trauma responses into humanitarian security expertise.

Hypervigilance as a Life-Saving Sensorium

- Neural Basis: Trauma-induced amygdala sensitization lowers the threshold for detecting threat cues, while strengthened connections to the prefrontal cortex enable faster appraisal and response.
- Field Example: In Nyal, South Sudan (2014), I noticed an

anomalous pattern of movement among civilians near our distribution site, too synchronized to be ordinary traffic and too jittery to be unarmed buyers. Recognizing the subtle rise in tension, I halted the NFI moments before armed elements attempted to intercept the supplies. The preemptive adjustment averted a violent ambush and protected both aid workers and beneficiaries.

- Lesson: Hypervigilance, when refined by training, becomes an early-warning system, detecting micro-expressions, irregular group patterns, or environmental anomalies well before overt threats materialize.

Dissociation as Compartmentalized Command

- Neural Basis: Repeated trauma can strengthen the brain's ability to "shut off" the limbic system and route processing through more analytical, detached networks, enabling a person to function in extreme duress at the expense of full emotional engagement.
- Field Example: During the 2010 Haiti earthquake response, an aftershock toppled a precarious wall near my team's makeshift office. I felt the impact shift my balance, yet, in the compartmentalized state, 1 instructed colleagues on evacuation routes, coordinated radio updates, and verified team headcounts before acknowledging the pounding in my chest. Once the crisis stabilized, the delayed emotional reaction arrived as a controlled tremor rather than paralysis.
- Lesson: Strategic dissociation allows crisis managers to maintain operational coherence amid sensory and emotional overwhelm, preserving the capacity for direction

and protection until danger has truly passed.

Emotional Numbing as Crisis Focus

- Neural Basis: Down-regulation of the anterior cingulate cortex and reduced activation of the insula can blunt emotional pain and anxiety, allowing individuals to maintain focus on immediate tasks despite surroundings of destruction or human suffering.
- Field Example: In Gaziantep (2013) during Syria's civil war, I coordinated daily multi-agency security briefings while screening dozens of images from shell-shattered villages. Rather than being immobilized by the scale of civilian devastation, the numbing response enabled me to synthesize reports, negotiate checkpoint protocols, and draft evacuation contingencies, tasks requiring calm objectivity in a heartbreak-laden context.
- Lesson: While long-term emotional numbing is unhealthy, its acute application can shield humanitarian leaders from burnout during rapid assessments and planning, ensuring that systems and people remain protected when empathy alone cannot carry the load.

Transforming Neural Pathways Through Training

- Reinforcement: Intentional training, simulations, scenario-based exercises, and trauma-informed facilitation reinforce adaptive uses of hypervigilance, dissociation, and numbing, converting spontaneously developed survival mechanisms into reliable professional competencies.

- Neuroplasticity: By repeatedly activating the prefrontal circuits that govern threat analysis, decision-making, and emotional regulation in controlled environments, specialists solidify these pathways, reducing the risk of uncontrolled triggers and ensuring responsiveness remains calibrated to actual threats.
- Ongoing Calibration: Regular after-action reviews and psychological check-ins help maintain the balance between operational capacity and mental health, preventing over-reinforcement of survival circuits that could impair reintegration into less extreme contexts.

Conclusion

The neural alchemy from wound to wisdom lies in recognizing that the very responses that trauma implants, once pathologized, can become the most powerful assets in environments where human lives depend on split-second awareness and unflinching clarity. With proper training, thoughtful reflection, and support that understands trauma, humanitarian security professionals can use hypervigilance, compartmentalization, and emotional regulation not as heavy weights to carry but as skills to develop, showing resilience that comes from not just surviving but also from meaningful change.

35

Teaching What Trauma Taught

The morning light streams through the windows of the training room in downtown Ottawa as I watch twelve humanitarian workers from various organizations settle into their chairs. Coffee cups steam, notebooks open, and there's that familiar mixture of anticipation and apprehension that marks the beginning of a Security in Complex Operational and Remote Environments (SCORE) course. What they don't yet know is that everything I'm about to teach them about threat assessment, crisis management, and survival in hostile environments was first learned not in any classroom, but in the wreckage of institutional betrayal and the long journey back to purpose.

The Paradox of Trauma-Informed Teaching

Standing before this group, I carry an unusual credential: my complex PTSD and dissociative identity disorder aren't obstacles to overcome in my teaching; they are the very tools that make me effective. The hypervigilance that once made

grocery shopping exhausting now allows me to read a training
room with surgical precision, detecting when participants are
triggered, disengaging, or processing difficult material in
ways that require intervention.

"Before we begin," I tell the group, "I want you to understand
that everything we're going to learn about staying safe in
dangerous places comes from people who have learned these
lessons the difficult way. Security isn't theoretical. It's
written in the experiences of those who've needed protection
and sometimes didn't receive it."

The statement lingers in the air, fostering vulnerability and
establishing credibility. I don't explicitly state that the
individual who experienced these lessons firsthand, shaped
by institutional betrayal, now stands before them, their
nervous system acting as an expert at detecting threats.

Reading the Room: Hypervigilance as Teaching Asset

As I begin the first module on situational awareness, my
own hypervigilance scans the room with the same intensity I
once brought to Syrian checkpoints or South Sudan security
assessments. The participant in the front row whose leg
is bouncing suggests anxiety; the woman by the window
who keeps checking her phone might be dealing with an
emergency at home; the man whose arms are crossed and
whose jaw is tight could be resistant to the material or
triggered by discussions of vulnerability.

These observations aren't distractions from teaching; they

350

are integral to it. Research confirms that trauma survivors often develop enhanced threat detection abilities. What was once a symptom of hyperarousal became a professional asset when channelled appropriately. I can detect subtle shifts in group dynamics that might indicate someone is struggling with the content, which allows me to adjust my approach before a participant becomes overwhelmed.

"I notice some tension in the room," I say, pausing the technical presentation about risk matrices. "Learning about threats and vulnerabilities can bring up uncomfortable feelings. That's normal and actually valuable. Your body's wisdom is part of your security toolkit."

The acknowledgment creates space for participants to breathe. Several people visibly relax. This is trauma-informed pedagogy in action: recognizing that security training inherently involves discussing scenarios that can trigger stress responses and normalizing those responses rather than pushing through them.

Dissociation as Educational Tool

Living with Dissociative Identity Disorder means that different aspects of my identity can emerge during training, each bringing unique perspectives and capabilities. What was once experienced as fragmenting symptoms has evolved into a teaching resource that enhances rather than undermines my effectiveness.

During scenario-based exercises, when participants practice

checkpoint negotiations or hostage survival techniques, I can step outside my emotional responses to observe and coach with clinical detachment. The same dissociative capacity that once felt like losing myself now enables me to remain present and supportive while participants process challenging material.

"In high-stress situations," I explain to the group as we prepare for a kidnapping simulation, "your mind might feel like it's separating from your body. This isn't weakness; it's actually a survival mechanism. Some of you might experience such feelings during our exercise. If that happens, it's information, not pathology."

The normalization of dissociative responses serves multiple purposes. It validates participants who might experience these reactions during training or real deployments, reducing shame and self-judgment. It also provides practical information about stress responses that could save lives in actual crisis situations.

The Authority of Lived Experience

When I teach about the psychological impact of captivity, my voice carries a weight that no academic textbook could provide. The participants don't know the specific details of my military sexual trauma, but they can sense the authenticity of lived experience with institutional failure, betrayal, and the long journey back to trust.

"When people ask me how to prepare psychologically for

deployment to high-risk environments," I tell the group during a module on stress management, "I tell them that resilience isn't about avoiding psychological injury. It's about learning to function with whatever wounds you carry while maintaining your ability to protect others."

This perspective, born from decades of managing complex trauma while maintaining professional competence, offers participants a framework that goes beyond traditional resilience training. Instead of promoting the myth of invulnerability, I model integration: acknowledging wounds while demonstrating their transformation into wisdom.

Teaching Institutional Awareness

Perhaps the most unique element of my training approach is the integration of institutional literacy. Having experienced betrayal by both military and humanitarian organizations, I bring a perspective on institutional dynamics that protects participants from naive trust while maintaining their ability to work within systems.

"Every organization you work for has written policies about supporting staff through traumatic events," I explain during a session on managing relationships with headquarters. "What they don't tell you is how those policies work in practice, what happens when organizational interests conflict with individual welfare, and how to protect yourself while remaining professional."

This isn't cynicism; it's preparation. Research shows that

institutional betrayal significantly increases the psychological impact of trauma. By teaching participants to maintain appropriate boundaries with organizations while fully committing to their humanitarian mission, I help them avoid the institutional betrayal that devastated my own early career.

Participants Who Benefited: A Case Study in Connection

During a SCORE course in 2023, I noticed that Sarah, a logistics coordinator preparing for her first deployment to Somalia, was struggling with the kidnapping simulation. Her breathing had become shallow, and she was dissociating in ways that suggested the exercise was triggering trauma responses rather than building capacity.

Instead of pushing through the exercise, I approached her during a break. "This material can bring up difficult feelings," I said quietly. "Would it be beneficial to step outside for a moment?"

What followed was a conversation that exemplified trauma-informed training. One participant disclosed that she was a survivor of sexual assault, and the powerlessness inherent in kidnapping scenarios was triggering shame and freeze responses. Rather than treating the issue as a training problem, I reframed it as valuable information.

"Your body is giving you important data about stress responses," I explained. "In a real kidnapping situation, understanding how trauma affects your nervous system could be life-saving information. Let's talk about how to work with these responses rather than against them."

Over the next two days, she participated in modified exercises that honoured her trauma history while building practical skills. Months later, she emailed from a conflict zone: "The training probably saved my life. When our convoy was attacked, I didn't freeze because I understood what my body was doing and had tools to work with it."

This is the power of trauma-informed training: instead of requiring participants to overcome their trauma responses to learn security skills, it teaches them to integrate those responses into their professional competence.

The Neuroscience of Trauma-Informed Teaching

What makes my teaching approach effective isn't just personal experience; it's the integration of that experience with evidence-based understanding of how trauma affects learning and performance. Research demonstrates that trauma survivors often develop enhanced pattern recognition, threat assessment capabilities, and stress tolerance that can be significant assets in high-risk environments.

During training modules on threat assessment, I explain how hypervigilance operates: "Your nervous system is constantly scanning for potential threats. In peaceful environments, this can be exhausting. But in genuinely dangerous places, it becomes a survival skill. Understanding when to increase and decrease stress levels is crucial.

This neuroeducational approach helps participants understand their own stress responses while providing practical
frameworks for managing them. Instead of pathologizing
trauma responses, I teach participants to recognize them as
adaptive capabilities that require skillful management.

Building Psychological Safety in Security Training

Creating psychologically safe learning environments for security training requires a different approach than traditional
adult education. Participants are learning about scenarios
designed to trigger stress responses: kidnapping, assault,
institutional abandonment, and moral injury. Without careful
attention to psychological safety, such training can retraumatize rather than empower.

"This room is a laboratory for learning about stress and
resilience," I tell participants at the beginning of each course.
"We're going to practice scenarios that are designed to activate your nervous system. That's the point. But we're also
going to practice managing those activations in ways that
serve your mission rather than overwhelming you."

The emphasis on choice and control reflects core trauma-
informed principles. Participants can modify exercises, take
breaks when needed, or engage with material at their own
pace. This isn't accommodation for weakness; it's recognition that true security competence requires self-awareness
and self-regulation.

The Integration of Multiple Perspectives

Living with DID means that different aspects of my identity contribute to teaching in ways that enhance rather than complicate the experience. The analyst in me can break down complex security concepts into manageable components. The protector can model calm authority under pressure. The survivor can speak authentically about recovery and resilience. The teacher can weave these perspectives together into coherent learning experiences.

"In crisis situations," I explain during a module on decision-making under pressure, "different aspects of your personality might emerge to handle different challenges. The part of you that's good at analysis might step forward during planning phases. The part that's good at relationships might take over during negotiations. This isn't losing control; it's adaptive flexibility."

This perspective, informed by my own experience of identity integration, helps participants understand their own stress responses and psychological resources in more nuanced ways.

Training Outcomes: Measuring Success

The effectiveness of trauma-informed security training extends beyond traditional metrics of knowledge retention or skill demonstration. Success includes participants' ability to maintain psychological wellness while performing high-stress work, their capacity to recognize and respond to trauma in others, and their skill in creating psychologically safe team environments.

Follow-up surveys consistently show that participants in
trauma-informed security courses report higher confidence
in managing stress, better team cohesion in challenging
deployments, and more effective support for colleagues
experiencing difficulties. As one participant wrote months
after training: "I learned that being strong doesn't mean not
being affected by difficult experiences. It means knowing how
to function effectively with whatever you're carrying."

The Philosophy of Teaching What Trauma Taught

The deepest lesson from my teaching experience is that
trauma, when properly integrated, becomes a source of
wisdom rather than simply a wound to overcome. The hypervigilance that once isolated me from normal social interaction
now enables me to create safer learning environments. The
dissociation that once felt like losing myself now allows me
to remain present for others when they're struggling. The
institutional skepticism born from betrayal now protects my
students from naive trust while maintaining their ability to
serve.

"Trauma doesn't disqualify you from security work," I tell
each group as we conclude our time together. "Properly understood and integrated, it can make you better at protecting
others. The question isn't whether you've been wounded.
The question is whether you've learned to transform those
wounds into wisdom."

This is the essence of trauma-informed security training: not the elimination of trauma responses, but their integration into professional competence. This approach does not deny institutional fallibility but rather prepares individuals to navigate systems within appropriate boundaries. The development of resilience honours both strength and vulnerability, rather than promising invulnerability.

As participants leave our training courses, they carry more than technical knowledge about threat assessment and crisis management. They carry a framework for understanding their own psychological responses as professional assets, tools for creating supportive team environments, and the recognition that the most effective protectors are often those who understand most intimately what it means to need protection.

The boy broken by military sexual trauma has become a teacher whose greatest qualification isn't the absence of wounds, but their transformation into wisdom that can protect others. Every hypervigilant scan of a training room, every dissociative moment channelled into clear instruction, and every institutional insight born from betrayal becomes a gift offered to the next generation of protectors.

This is what trauma taught: that broken things can be rebuilt stronger, that wounds can become wisdom, and that the most powerful teaching often emerges from the deepest healing. In teaching others to navigate dangerous environments while protecting their psychological welfare, I complete a circle that began with my own survival and continues with their preparation to serve in a world that desperately needs protectors who understand both strength and vulnerability.

36

The Ripple Network

Even the smallest pebble creates widening circles when dropped in water. Over two decades of security training and mentorship have cast countless pebbles into the humanitarian world, and this chapter traces the ripples that followed, highlighting individuals I've guided, programs shaped by my influence, and lives spared by skills I helped impart.

Reaching across Organizations

2012 Hostile Environment Awareness Training (HEAT) - Nairobi

In collaboration with the World Vision Office of Corporate Security (OCS) team, I served as a guest trainer and conducted a five-day HEAT program for international staff. The Director of Security Training personally expressed relief and enthusiasm that I could not only participate but also co-facilitate, citing the value of firsthand field experience combined with instructional skill.

2013 Security Awareness in National Theatres (SAINT) – Honduras

I assisted the Regional Security Director for LACRO World Vision's inaugural SAINT course for national staff in Zamorano Pan, Honduras, which marked the program's first regional delivery. Developed context-specific modules on urban gang dynamics and checkpoint negotiations, empowering local teams with structured security protocols tailored to Honduras's particular risks.

2018 "Train-the-Trainer" Program – Gaziantep

Co-facilitated an intensive training-of-trainers course for Syrian national NGO personnel engaged in cross-border humanitarian operations. Over five days, participants were equipped with advanced adult-learning techniques, scenario-based facilitation skills, and modular curriculum templates, enabling them to deliver HEAT and SAINT content within Syria's northern governorates.

2022 SCORE Course Debut – Kanata (Ottawa Region)

- Designed and delivered the second Security in Complex Operational and Remote Environments (SCORE) pilot course to a mixed cohort of participants from Canadian NGOs and academic institutions. The five-day program combined lessons from HEAT and SAINT, emphasizing how to assess risks, understand basic digital security, and manage stress for working in remote areas.

Building a Second-Generation Network

Many of the train-the-trainers who have attended or participated in our many courses have gone on to become peer instructors themselves, expanding the network of security-aware humanitarian workers by another layer.

Each story represents a life protected, a mission preserved, and a lesson passed forward. The ripple network I helped build now spans from Ottawa to Juba, from Gaziantep to Kathmandu, and from Port-au-Prince to Jerusalem. Though my own journey began in trauma and exile, the ripples of my training have seeded resilience in others, ensuring that the next generation of aid workers is better prepared, more supported, and more effective.

And so the circle continues, each new instructor, each new life saved, sending ripples outward, proof that one person's experience, transformed through purpose, can become a network of protection and hope that spans the world.

37

Legacy in Motion

As this account draws toward its horizon, the story of trauma, resilience, and service remains unfinished, an echo that transforms into action. The work of healing and protection is ever-evolving, and the legacy we build depends on how we carry today's insights into tomorrow's challenges.

From Personal Survival to Collective Stewardship

The journey from military sexual trauma to humanitarian security specialist taught that survival alone cannot define a life; purpose does. Legacy isn't what one accomplishes in isolation but what one enables in others. Every security protocol refined, every training curriculum delivered, and every policy reformed becomes a step toward equipping the next generation of humanitarians to enter crisis zones with competence, compassion, and courage.

A Vision for Trauma-Informed Humanitarianism

Emerging professionals will inherit complex conflicts shaped by climate disasters, protracted violence, and mass displacement. They'll need more than logistics expertise; they will require:

- *Trauma-Informed Mindsets*: Recognizing that both aid recipients and aid providers carry wounds; integrating psychological first aid and self-care as core operational skills.
- *Cross-Sector Fluency*: Bridging military precision and humanitarian ethics, learning from each sector's strengths to enhance collective impact.
- *Adaptive Leadership*: Navigating ambiguity with humility, fostering inclusive decision-making that values local voices and lived experience.

Cultivating the Next Generation

Legacy in motion means creating pathways for veterans and civilian specialists alike to co-learn. This requires:

1. **Mentorship Networks** that pair seasoned veterans with entry-level humanitarians to translate combat-honed skills into crisis management frameworks.
2. **Integrated Training Hubs** where NGO staff, military personnel, and first responders exchange best practices in security, trauma care, and operational ethics.
3. **Policy Advocacy Coalitions** to ensure institutional cultures, from defence ministries to humanitarian agencies,

adopt survivor-centred, trauma-informed practices as standards rather than exceptions.

The Bridge We Remain

My ongoing role is not merely as a trainer or advisor, but as a bridge, connecting the precision and discipline of military training with the empathy and principles of humanitarian action. By sharing my lived experience, championing peer support, and helping institutions reckon with past failures, I aim to keep that bridge strong for those who follow.

Moving Forward Together

Legacy is not just a final chapter; it represents a continual commitment. Each emerging aid worker, security specialist, or veteran-turned-humanitarian carries forward the lessons of resilience, transformation, and service. As we encounter new crises, be they technological, environmental, or geopolitical, our collective wisdom expands.

May this story serve as both map and compass for all who seek to transform wounds into wisdom, isolation into solidarity, and survival into enduring service. In doing so, we ensure that every life intersecting with ours benefits from a world strengthened by shared vulnerability, courageous healing, and legacy in motion.

38

Full Circle: A New Kind of Service

The morning light filters through my office window as I review the security briefing notes for our upcoming deployment to South Sudan. On my desk sits a copy of "A Soldier's Cry," now published and reaching readers who share similar struggles, alongside the manuscript pages of this book, "Resilience Redeployed," which tells the continuing story of how trauma can be transformed into purpose.

Forty-one years after joining the Canadian Armed Forces, after the assaults that changed everything, and nearly two decades into my humanitarian career, I'm finally beginning to understand what service means to me now.

From Soldier to Survivor to Servant

The journey hasn't been linear. There was no clean transition from military service to civilian purpose, no clear moment when I stopped being a soldier and became something else. Instead, there has been a gradual integration, a slow recognition that the person I was, the person I became through trauma, and the person I'm becoming through healing and service are all part of the same story.

In "A Soldier's Cry," I wrote about the young man who joined the military with idealistic notions of service and country. That soldier believed that service meant following orders, protecting others through strength, and putting mission before self. The multiple assaults shattered that understanding, leaving me to reconstruct my identity around survival rather than service.

For decades, survival was service enough. Getting through each day without breaking completely, maintaining professional competence despite internal chaos, and finding ways to function in civilian workplaces that felt foreign and unwelcoming, these became my missions. I didn't realize it at the time, but learning to survive with dignity was its own form of service, both to myself and to the family and colleagues who needed me to be present and functional.

The transition to humanitarian work wasn't planned as a return to service; it was planned as an escape from the corporate environment that felt meaningless after military experience. But gradually, I began to recognize familiar elements: the mission focus, the commitment to something larger than individual gain, and the willingness to work in difficult conditions for important purposes.

What I didn't anticipate was how my trauma history would become an asset rather than a liability in humanitarian work.

Building Bridges Between Past and Present

Writing this book, "Resilience Redeployed," has helped me understand how all the pieces fit together. The hypervigilance that made civilian social situations exhausting proved invaluable in security assessment work. The ability to compartmentalize emotions that had isolated me from family became essential for functioning in crisis environments. The hard-won understanding of how institutions can fail vulnerable people informed my approach to now protecting WUSC volunteers and staff in challenging deployments.

The peer support networks I've been exploring, the trauma-informed practices I've been advocating for, and the veteran-inclusive organizational changes I've been promoting, all of these emerged from recognizing that my personal struggles reflected broader systemic challenges that could be addressed. Each chapter of this book has been both an act of self-examination and an exploration of how individual experience can inform collective solutions.

The relationship with my mother, which I explored in depth in Chapter 8, taught me that healing family bonds requires acknowledging past harm while building toward future connection. This same principle applies to my relationship with institutions, the military that failed to protect me, the humanitarian organizations that could do better at supporting veterans, and the systems that could be transformed through committed effort.

Trauma as Teacher

Writing about my experience with DID in Chapter 10 forced me
to confront how deeply the multiple assaults had fragmented
my sense of self. But therapy helped me work through that
fragmentation while I built competence in humanitarian
work, teaching me that integration is possible, not just
psychological integration, but also professional and personal
integration that honours all aspects of experience.

The hypervigilance that I described in Chapter 11 isn't something I've overcome; it's something I've learned to channel
productively. In security assessment work, the ability to
notice small details, sense potential threats, and maintain situational awareness becomes professional competence rather
than a personal burden.

The chapter I wrote about moral injury helped me understand
that the guilt and shame I carried weren't just about personal
trauma but about institutional failures that affected many
others. This recognition transformed my understanding of
service itself. Service wasn't just about protecting others from
harm; it could also be about transforming harm into wisdom,
isolation into connection, and survival into contribution.

Integration Rather Than Replacement

The question that haunted my early civilian transition was
whether I could still be a soldier without being in the military.
I believed I had to choose between honouring my military
experience and creating a fulfilling civilian life. The humani-

tarian sector has taught me that this was a false choice.

Chapter 22, where I explored finding my footing at WUSC, marked a turning point in this understanding. The leadership skills I developed as an NCO translate directly to crisis management in humanitarian settings. The cross-cultural competence gained through international deployments enhances my ability to work with diverse teams and communities. The deep understanding of institutional dynamics, how organizations work, how they fail, and how they can be changed, serves both my security advisory role and my advocacy work.

Most importantly, the military values that shaped my character, service before self, integrity, and excellence, align perfectly with humanitarian principles. The difference isn't in the values but in their application. Instead of serving my country through military action, I serve humanity through development work. Instead of protecting fellow soldiers, I protect humanitarian workers. Instead of following orders, I provide advice that helps others make informed decisions.

Integration happened gradually, through small recognitions that civilian service could honour military service rather than replace it. Each successful security assessment, each colleague supported through crisis, and each volunteer safely deployed and returned became evidence that my military experience had prepared me for civilian contribution rather than disqualified me from it.

The Power of Vulnerability

Perhaps the most unexpected transformation has been learning to lead through vulnerability rather than strength. Military leadership culture taught me to project confidence, hide uncertainty, and never show weakness. Humanitarian leadership has taught me that authenticity, openness about challenges, and willingness to admit mistakes often create more trust and effectiveness than traditional command presence.

Chapter 20, where I examined the intersection of faith and trauma, explored how my relationship with God had been complicated by institutional betrayal but ultimately strengthened through personal healing. This spiritual dimension of recovery has informed my approach to humanitarian work, recognizing that we serve not just human needs but human dignity and the divine spark in every person we encounter.

The writing process for both books has been an exercise in professional vulnerability. Sharing details about military sexual trauma, addiction struggles, and mental health challenges carries professional risks in any sector. But it has also created opportunities for connection and impact that would have been impossible through traditional professional relationships.

Chapter 23, where I explored the ongoing work of rebuilding family relationships, taught me that vulnerability can be a form of strength, not the absence of boundaries but the conscious choice to lower barriers that no longer serve protective purposes.

Colleagues at WUSC have shared their own struggles after learning about my journey. Veterans considering humanitarian work have reached out after reading "A Soldier's Cry." My willingness to be vulnerable about my challenges has created space for others to be vulnerable about theirs, building the kind of authentic professional community that enhances both individual well-being and organizational effectiveness.

The Restorative Journey

Chapter 28, where I explored my participation in the CAF Restorative Engagement process, marked another crucial turning point. Speaking truth about institutional harm to the very institution that had caused it was both terrifying and liberating. The acknowledgment I received didn't erase decades of pain, but it created space for transformation, both personal and institutional.

The RE process taught me that institutions can change when they're presented with evidence of harm and clear pathways for improvement. My participation wasn't just about personal healing, it was about contributing to cultural change that could prevent others from experiencing institutional betrayal.

This experience informed the vision I outlined in Chapter 26 for a more veteran-inclusive humanitarian sector. The same principles that made the RE process effective, survivor-centred approaches, institutional accountability, and trauma-informed practices, could be applied to create organizational cultures that better support all employees while maximizing their contributions.

Institutional Change Through Personal Action

The individual journey has always been connected to broader systemic questions. My experience with military sexual trauma highlighted institutional failures that affected thousands of others. My struggles with civilian transition reflected barriers that challenge many veterans seeking meaningful post-military careers.

The books I'm writing, the advocacy work I'm engaged in, and the organizational changes I'm promoting are all attempts to transform personal experience into institutional improvement.

Chapter 22, where I explored thriving amid chaos, helped me understand that the skills developed through trauma recovery, adaptability, resilience, and crisis management are exactly the skills needed for effective humanitarian work. Rather than seeing my trauma history as something to overcome in order to serve, I began to see it as preparation for the kind of service the world needs.

The vision for veteran-inclusive humanitarian organizations isn't an abstract policy recommendation; it's a practical application of lessons learned through lived experience. Every barrier I have encountered, every valuable support I received, and every missed opportunity for better integration provides data that can be used to build more effective systems.

The Ripple Effect

Service, I've learned, is often indirect. The security assessments I write protect people I'll never meet. Colleagues who join WUSC after my departure will benefit from the organizational policies I help develop. "A Soldier's Cry" has already reached veterans struggling with challenges I've faced, and this book, "Resilience Redeployed," represents my attempt to share not just the problems but the possibilities for transformation.

Each act of service creates possibilities for further service. The veteran who finds meaningful humanitarian work through networks I've helped build might go on to mentor other veterans. The organizational changes we implement at WUSC might be adopted by other NGOs. The willingness to speak publicly about military sexual trauma and successful civilian transition might encourage others to break their own silence while pursuing their own paths to meaningful contribution.

This ripple effect represents a form of service that my younger military self never could have imagined. Instead of protecting through strength and weapons, I'm protecting through vulnerability and truth. Instead of following orders toward predetermined objectives, I'm creating space for others to discover their own missions.

Full Circle, Not Closed Circle

The "full circle" in this chapter's title doesn't mean returning
to where I started. The young soldier who joined the CAF in
1983 was idealistic but naive, committed but unprepared for
the complexities of institutional service. The humanitarian
practitioner I've become carries that same commitment to
service but with a more profound understanding of both
human vulnerability and human resilience.

Writing about the intersection of military experience and
humanitarian work in Chapters 7-22 helped me understand
that this isn't about replacing one identity with another but
about expanding identity to include new possibilities. I'm still
a soldier in the sense that matters most, someone committed
to serving others and protecting the vulnerable. But I'm also
a survivor, a healer, an advocate, and a bridge-builder.

The work continues because the need continues. Chapter
24, where I explored the ongoing questions about peer support, reminds me that healing is never finished; it's always
evolving, always opening new possibilities for growth and
contribution.

My participation in the RE process was meaningful, but it
was one conversation in a larger ongoing dialogue about
institutional change. My work at WUSC is fulfilling, but it's
one organization in a sector that could better serve both its
mission and its people. My books are published or nearly
published, but they're contributions to conversations that
will continue long after I'm gone.

Legacy and Continuation

What I hope to leave behind isn't a perfect model but a lived example that transformation is possible. That military sexual trauma, while devastating, doesn't have to define or limit a life. The civilian transition, while challenging, can lead to meaningful second careers that honour military service while serving new purposes. That healing and service can reinforce rather than compete with each other.

The vision for veteran-inclusive humanitarian organizations that I outlined in Chapter 26 will require many voices and many years of sustained effort to realize. But it begins with individual stories like mine, veterans willing to share both struggles and successes, organizations willing to learn and adapt, and communities committed to supporting both healing and contribution.

"A Soldier's Cry" told the story of harm and survival. "Resilience Redeployed" tells the story of recovery and contribution. Together, they represent one example of how broken pieces can be reassembled into something both beautiful and useful.

The morning light that filters through my home office window illuminates both books on my desk, the published story of where I've been and the nearly complete story of where I'm going. But these aren't endings; they're foundations for whatever form of service comes next.

Service continues, but its forms evolve. The commitment to

something larger than myself that drew me to military service now expresses itself through humanitarian work, advocacy, writing, and creating space for others to find their own paths to healing and purpose.

This is the full circle, not a return to innocence but an integration of experience, not the replacement of military identity but its expansion into new forms of service that honour the past while building toward a future where trauma can be transformed into wisdom, isolation into connection, and survival into contribution to the greater good.

Forty-one years after that idealistic young man first put on a uniform, I'm still learning what it means to serve. But now I know that service takes many forms and that the most profound service sometimes emerges from our deepest wounds, transformed through healing into gifts we can offer to a world that desperately needs both our strength and our vulnerability.

The story continues because service continues, because the need for healing and hope and human connection continues. And I am grateful for the journey, for the opportunity to serve, and for the recognition that even our most difficult experiences can become sources of light for others navigating similar darkness.

Epilogue: Continuing the Mission

As sunlight filters into my office, I reflect on forty years of service, survival, and transformation. The journey from military sexual trauma to global security specialist has been characterized by profound wounds and hard-won wisdom. Three enduring insights guide my path forward:

Service Reimagined

Service is not defined by uniforms or battlefields alone but by using one's unique experiences to protect and empower others. Channelling the hypervigilance, compartmentalizati on, and resilience forged through trauma into humanitarian security, training, and advocacy becomes a professional strength. Service evolves from following orders to pioneering new ways to keep people, both beneficiaries and staff, safe.

Institutional Accountability

True organizational change requires more than just poli- cies; it demands survivor-centered cultures that prioritize human dignity over reputation. Acknowledgement of past failures, whether military sexual misconduct or untreated team trauma, is essential for reform. Institutions must embed trauma-informed practices, transparent justice processes,

and support systems that treat PTSD and addiction as professional competencies needing care rather than character flaws
warranting dismissal.

Thriving in Dual Worlds

The skills that enable us to function under fire, acute threat
assessment, rapid decision-making, and emotional regulation can feel disorienting in peaceful settings. Learning
to balance presence in calm with readiness for crisis transforms professional hypervigilance into mindful awareness
and lifelong adaptability. Cultivating "deployment-free"
time, integrating therapeutic practices, and building local
community ties ensure that we honour both our warrior and
our healer identities.

As the world confronts escalating natural and human-made
crises, these lessons, service reimagined, institutional accountability, and thriving across contexts, offer a blueprint
for resilience. May the wounds we carry continue to shape our
ability to protect, to heal, and to inspire the next generation
of guardians in the unending quest for human dignity.

* * *

A Final Message to Readers

To every veteran who has suffered in silence and every humanitarian worker carrying invisible wounds: your survival
is a testament to grace under pressure, and your experience

380

is a gift to any organization willing to listen. The very traits that trauma instilled in you, hypervigilance, adaptability, and unwavering commitment, can become your greatest assets when reframed and supported.

To leaders and colleagues in humanitarian and military institutions: honour the courage it takes to speak up. Recognize that vulnerability is not weakness; it is the pathway to resilience, innovation, and genuine protection for everyone under your care. Invest in trauma-informed cultures, veteran-inclusive policies, and peer support that sustains rather than discards those who have given so much.

My mission endures not because danger is ending, but because people will always need protection, physical, psychological, and systemic. I carry forward the lessons of every crisis, every betrayal, and every breakthrough: broken things can be refashioned into strengths that serve the most vulnerable. May our collective efforts ensure that no soldier, no aid worker, and no survivor ever stands alone in the darkness again.

Advocacy Summary: Resilience Redeployed

🖉 Resilience Redeployed – Advocacy Summary
Transforming Military Trauma into Humanitarian Leadership
Laurence M. Baird | Based in Kitchener, Ontario, Canada
Contact: lbaird81@gmail.com
Speaking Engagements | Media Inquiries | Academic Access

🔎 What This Book Covers

Resilience Redeployed is the first memoir to chronicle the complete journey from military sexual trauma survivor to international humanitarian security specialist, demonstrating how institutions can transform survivors into their most effective protectors.

It draws from my lived experiences: military sexual trauma in the Canadian Armed Forces (1985-1989), two decades of civilian struggle and recovery, diplomatic security work in Sudan, humanitarian deployments across Haiti, Syria, South Sudan, and beyond, and the development of trauma-informed security management practices.

This book includes:

- A trauma-to-leadership transformation narrative based on Post-Traumatic Growth Theory
- Field accounts from the world's most dangerous humanitarian crises (2009-2018)
- A blueprint for trauma-informed security management in crisis environments
- Evidence that hypervigilance and threat assessment are professional assets, not disabilities
- A call to action for military, humanitarian, and security sector reform

🧠 Key Findings

1. Trauma Survivors Make Superior Security Specialists

- Hypervigilance becomes professional-grade threat assessment capability
- Experience with vulnerability creates expertise in protection
- Crisis management skills developed through survival translate directly to emergency response

2. Institutional Abandonment Wastes Human Capital

- Military discharge processes discard trauma survivors as "damaged goods."
- Humanitarian organizations fail to recognize trauma recovery as professional qualification
- Society loses protection expertise when survivors are

marginalized rather than developed

3. The Wounded Healer Paradigm Works

- Those who have needed protection understand protection better than those who haven't
- Proximity to pain develops empathy and effectiveness in crisis response
- Survivor leadership creates psychologically safe environments for vulnerable populations

4. Current Security Training Misses Critical Elements

- Traditional security protocols focus on external threats while ignoring internal trauma dynamics
- Cultural sensitivity training lacks trauma-informed perspectives
- Local staff protection protocols consistently favour international over national personnel

5. Humanitarian Security Requires Systemic Reform

- Acceptance strategies in conflict zones depend on authentic relationship-building, not just technical protocols
- Evacuation planning must include trauma-informed psychological preparation
- Career pathways for trauma survivors in security roles remain largely unexplored

✎ Policy & Program Recommendations

Military & Veterans Affairs:

✓ Create trauma survivor career rehabilitation programs within CAF

✓ Reform service record review processes to account for trauma context

✓ Establish trauma-informed leadership training for all command levels

✓ Develop "second chance" pathways for institutional re-engagement

✓ Recognize hypervigilance and crisis management as transferable professional skills

Humanitarian Sector:

✓ Implement trauma-informed security management as industry standard

✓ Create specialized recruitment pathways for trauma survivors in security roles

✓ Establish equal protection protocols for international and local staff

✓ Fund survivor-led security training programs and peer mentorship networks

✓ Integrate psychological resilience building into all emergency response training

Policy & Social Reform:

✓ Recognize military sexual trauma as service-connected for all benefits and opportunities

✓ Fund research on trauma-to-leadership transformation pathways

✓ Create tax incentives for organizations that demonstrate trauma-informed hiring practices

✔ Establish survivor protection policies with real enforcement mechanisms

🎙 Speaking Topics & Media Angles

- From Broken to Bulletproof: How Military Trauma Created a Humanitarian Security Expert
- The Wounded Healer Model: Why Our Best Protectors Carry Invisible Scars
- Hypervigilance as Asset: Reframing Trauma Symptoms as Professional Advantages
- Security in Syria: Managing Protection in the World's Most Dangerous Humanitarian Environment
- Local Staff, Global Impact: Trauma-Informed Approaches to International Security
- The Cost of Abandonment: What Organizations Lose When They Discard Trauma Survivors
- From Victim to Specialist: The Professional Development Path for Trauma Recovery

🏛 Academic & Training Uses

🎖 Military & Security Studies Programs

- Case studies in trauma-informed leadership and command
- Professional development for security sector reform
- Post-conflict transition and veteran integration strategies

🎖 Humanitarian Studies & International Development

386

- Security management in complex emergencies
- Cultural competency and acceptance strategies in conflict zones
- Local staff protection and career development frameworks

🌑 Psychology & Trauma Studies

- Post-Traumatic Growth and professional identity reconstruction
- Complex PTSD and functional adaptation in high-stress careers
- Institutional betrayal recovery and organizational trust rebuilding

🌑 Business & Organizational Development

- Trauma-informed hiring practices and workplace accommodation
- Crisis leadership and decision-making under extreme stress
- Transforming organizational failures into learning opportunities

🌍 International Applications

- Crisis Response Organizations: UN, MSF, IRC, World Vision, CARE
- Military & Defense: NATO, peace-keeping forces, veteran transition programs
- Security Contractors: Private security firms, diplomatic

protection services

- Academic Institutions: Conflict resolution, humanitarian studies, trauma psychology
- Government Agencies: Foreign affairs, emergency management, veteran services

♿ Download & Contact Info

- Media & Interview Requests: lbaird81@gmail.com
- Speaking Engagements: lbaird81@gmail.com
- Academic Permissions: lbaird81@gmail.com
- A print-ready PDF version of this sheet available upon request
- Based in Kitchener, Ontario | International travel available
- Available for: panels, media interviews, organizational training, policy consultations

↯ Core Message

This is not a story about overcoming trauma; it's about transforming trauma into professional expertise. Every organization has the choice: abandon those who challenge your comfort zone, or learn from their survival wisdom. The question is not whether trauma survivors can contribute; it's whether institutions are brave enough to receive what they offer.

Copyright & Usage

For academic, organizational training, or policy development purposes, you may excerpt content from this book with attribution. Contact me regarding bulk orders for training programs or institutional development initiatives.

"The soldier's scream became the protector's wisdom. Now it's time for institutions to listen."

Laurence M. Baird

Acknowledgements

To my family, who paid the highest price for my service:

I am deeply grateful to my wife, whose unwavering love and patience supported me during the most challenging periods of trauma and extended periods away from humanitarian work. You believed in the man I could become when I could not, and you stood by me as I learned to transform pain into purpose.

I am deeply grateful to my sons, whose resilience, understanding, and pride in their work gave meaning to every sacrifice. You grew up with a father often absent in body but never in heart, and your support remains my greatest motivation to build a better world.

To my mother, whose absence became its own form of presence in my life. The complexity of our relationship taught me that understanding doesn't always require proximity and that sometimes the most important lessons come from learning to love despite the distance. That you only recently learned of the trauma that has defined so much of my story reminds me that we are all carrying invisible burdens, even from those closest to us.

I extend my deepest gratitude to those who have faith in rebuilding broken things:

I am deeply grateful to the Canadian Corps of Commissionaires for giving a damaged veteran a second chance and demonstrating that military experience can be an asset rather than a liability.

I am deeply grateful to my colleagues at World Vision's Global Rapid Response Team, particularly my supervisors and teams I deployed with, who recognized my potential as a trauma survivor and trusted me to safeguard lives in high-risk areas. Your faith enabled me to discover that my wounds could become wisdom.

I am deeply grateful to CARE International's Global Security Director in Amman and Director of Global Security, whose invitation to lead partner security assessments in Syria rekindled my sense of purpose, and to the local teams in Jordan and Beirut, who taught me the power of partnership.

To the World Council of Churches programme executive in Jerusalem, whose unexpected call reminded me that service can renew the spirit, even after years of civilian mediocrity.

I am grateful to the leadership of World University Service of Canada, who embraced my unconventional journey and supported my remote work from Kitchener, enabling me to build lasting security capacity across WUSC's global programs.

391

I want to express my gratitude to my fellow survivors
and the helpers:

To every military sexual trauma survivor who has walked
this path in silence, your courage in speaking truth to power
lights the way for others. We are not broken; we are boundary-
breakers.

To the local staff, translators, drivers, and national colleagues
who kept me safe in Khartoum, Port-au-Prince, Malakal,
Gaziantep, Bangui, Kathmandu, Maiduguri, and beyond. Your
knowledge, courage, and dedication saved countless lives.
The real heroes of humanitarian work are those who stay
when internationals go home.

I am grateful to the little boy in Bangui, whose silent hand in
mine taught me the true purpose of protection. Although I
may never see you again, the quiet trust you showed changed
everything.

To the institutions that shaped me:

I am deeply grateful to Harvard University's Humanitarian
Initiative, whose Humanitarian Response Intensive Course
seamlessly combined field experience and academic insight,
demonstrating the perpetual nature of learning.

I am deeply grateful to the Office of Corporate Security training team at World Vision, whose expertise and mentorship
taught me how to transform my trauma responses into
professional teaching tools.

I am grateful to the experienced team at the International Rescue Committee, who welcomed me into their peer programs in Nigeria, demonstrating the mutual learning potential between seasoned veterans and humanitarian professionals.

I am deeply grateful to MEDA's Director of Security, whose collaboration on the SCORE course demonstrated the power of cross-organizational innovation.

To all the NGOs and local partners, from Sudan to Sri Lanka, who opened their doors and trusted a veteran-turned-trainer to guide their teams toward safer futures.

To those who didn't live to see this story:

To every aid worker who paid the ultimate price while serving others, your sacrifice demands that we do better.

Special recognition:

To Abousfian Abdelrazik, whose dignity in exile reminded me that sometimes the most dangerous thing you can do is simply be human within an inhumane system.

To my psychiatrists, counsellors, and EAP therapists, who taught me that trauma does not define us; how we carry it forward does.

To my editors and early readers, whose insights and encouragement shaped these pages into a story that might help others find their way from darkness to light.

To the Canadian Armed Forces: despite everything, the values of service, sacrifice, and protecting others became the foundation for all that followed, even when the institution failed me.

Finally:

To every reader who carries invisible wounds from service to others, whether in military, humanitarian, medical, or any field where protecting others extracts a personal cost, your struggles matter, your service counts, and your story deserves to be told.

This book exists because countless people refused to let a broken veteran stay broken. It belongs to all of you.

"We are not what happened to us. We are what we choose to become."

Glossary

Complex PTSD (C-PTSD)

A form of post-traumatic stress disorder that arises from prolonged, repeated trauma, often including difficulty regulating emotions, altered self-perception, and trouble with relationships.

Dissociative Identity Disorder (DID)

A complex psychological condition characterized by two or more distinct identity states (or "parts") and gaps in memory for everyday events, often arising after extreme trauma.

Hypervigilance

A heightened state of sensory sensitivity accompanied by an exaggerated intensity of behaviours whose purpose is to detect threats.

Hostile Environment Awareness Training (HEAT)

A five-day security course designed to prepare personnel for working in high-threat areas, covering threat assessment, kidnapping survival, crisis communication, and personal protective measures.

Security Awareness in National Theatres (SAINT)

A localized security training model for national staff operating in contexts where humanitarian crises intersect with cultural, political, or conflict dynamics.

Restorative Engagement (RE)

Restorative Engagement (RE) is a survivor-centred process that involves individuals who have experienced institutional harm meeting with organizational representatives to share their experiences and contribute to institutional learning and cultural change.

Institutional Betrayal

Institutional Betrayal occurs when an institution, such as a military or humanitarian organization, reacts to an individual's trauma or reported harm by refuting, disregarding, or concealing it, thereby exacerbating the initial harm.

Trauma-Informed Practice

An approach that recognizes the widespread impact of trauma, actively seeks to avoid re-traumatization, and incorporates understanding into policies, procedures, and practices.

About the Author

Laurence Baird is a Canadian humanitarian security specialist, military sexual trauma survivor, and advocate whose career spans over two decades in high-risk environments across the globe. Born in 1965, he enlisted in the Canadian Armed Forces in 1984 but was discharged in 1989 following military sexual trauma that would shape both his personal journey and professional mission.

After years of struggling with complex PTSD and institutional betrayal, Baird rebuilt his life through service to others, discovering that his trauma-informed skills were invaluable in protecting vulnerable populations worldwide. His human-itarian career began in 2008 with a deployment to Sudan, where he served as mission security manager for the Canadian

Embassy during the Abousfian Abdelrazik crisis.

Baird went on to serve with World Vision's Global Rapid Response Team from 2010 to 2016, deploying to crisis zones including Haiti after the 2010 earthquake, Kenya during the 2011 Horn of Africa famine, Syria, South Sudan, Nepal following the 2015 earthquake, and the Central African Republic. He developed comprehensive security protocols and instructed in Hostile Environment Awareness Training programs that protected hundreds of aid workers serving the world's most vulnerable populations.

His expertise extends across multiple organizations and contexts. He has worked with CARE International, the International Rescue Committee, the World Council of Churches, and other major humanitarian agencies. Since 2018, he has served as Global Security Advisor for the World University Service of Canada (WUSC), where he provides technical support and security training across over 25 countries.

Baird holds a Certificate in Humanitarian Response from Harvard University and has played a key role in developing the Security in Complex and Operationally Remote Environments (SCORE) training course. As a certified peer supporter and multilingual professional, he has served in over 65 countries throughout his career.

Beyond his operational work, Baird has become a leading advocate for military sexual trauma survivors and trauma-informed practices within both military and humanitarian sectors. He works to break the silence surrounding military sexual misconduct and demonstrates how survivors can transform their experiences into tools for protecting others.

Resilience Redeployed is his second book, a raw, unflinching memoir that chronicles his journey from institutional betrayal to becoming a specialist in protecting others who serve in the world's most dangerous places. Through his story, Baird offers hope to other survivors while challenging institutions to build systems worthy of trust.

Baird continues his humanitarian security work globally while advocating for survivors of institutional trauma and developing more effective, trauma-informed approaches to crisis response and protection.

You can connect with me on:
- https://www.linkedin.com/in/labhrainnbaird
- https://www.facebook.com/DvlDog

Also by Laurence Baird

As a military sexual trauma advocate, Baird was among the first Canadians to participate in the Armed Forces' Restorative Engagement process and continues to push for institutional reforms that transform survivors from abandoned victims into valuable assets. His work bridges the gap between personal trauma recovery and professional security expertise, demonstrating that those who have needed protection often become the most effective protectors of others.

Baird holds certifications in humanitarian security management and crisis response and speaks internationally on trauma-informed leadership, institutional betrayal recovery, and the transformation of military experience into humanitarian service. He lives in Kitchener, Ontario, and continues to deploy globally for humanitarian emergencies while advocating for military sexual trauma survivors and organizational reform.

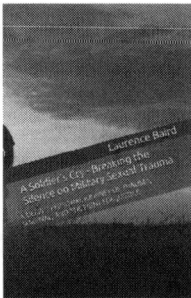

A Soldier's Cry: Breaking the Silence on Military Sexual Trauma
Laurence Baird's powerful debut memoir unveils the hidden wounds of a Canadian veteran betrayed by his own military. From institutional denial and the aftermath of assault to a journey of healing and advocacy, this unflinching account gives voice to survivors of military sexual trauma and challenges institutions to honour their duty of care.

Manufactured by Amazon.ca
Bolton, ON

51163860R00236